Helping Skills Training for Nonprofessional Counselors

Helping Skills Training for Nonprofessional Counselors provides comprehensive training in mental health first aid.

Through a trusted approach, grounded in evidence-based psychological research and counseling theory, this training manual provides step-by-step instruction in helping skills written exclusively for nonprofessionals. Focusing on the basics of nonprofessional counseling, the author has written an easy-to-read text that pinpoints strategies, action steps, and investigation procedures to be used by nonprofessionals to effectively aid those in distress. The LifeRAFT model integrates multi-theoretical bases, microskills training, evidence-based techniques, and instruction on ethical appropriateness. It also includes case studies, session transcripts, and practice exercises.

With undergraduate students in applied psychology and nonprofessional counselors being the primary beneficiaries of this text, it is also ideal for anyone seeking training to effectively respond to mental health crises encountered in their everyday lives.

Elizabeth L. Campbell, PhD, LP, LMFT, CCC, is an associate professor of psychology at Whitworth University with over a decade of experience in counseling, researching, and teaching about the helping professions. She is an approved therapist supervisor and certified career counselor, and she provides therapy and supervises associate clinicians in private practice. Dr. Campbell has authored 16 peer-reviewed journal articles and book chapters.

Helping Skills Training for Nonprofessional Counselors

The LifeRAFT Model—Providing Relief through Actions, Feelings, and Thoughts

Elizabeth L. Campbell

Routledge
Taylor & Francis Group
NEW YORK AND LONDON

First published 2020
by Routledge
52 Vanderbilt Avenue, New York, NY 10017

and by Routledge
2 Park Square, Milton Park, Abingdon, Oxon, OX14 4RN

Routledge is an imprint of the Taylor & Francis Group, an informa business

Library of Congress Cataloging-in-Publication Data
Names: Campbell, Elizabeth L. (Psychologist), author.
Title: Helping skills training for nonprofessional counselors : the lifeRAFT model—providing relief through actions, feelings, and thoughts / Elizabeth L. Campbell.
Description: New York, NY : Routledge, 2020. | Includes bibliographical references and index.
Identifiers: LCCN 2019050155 (print) | LCCN 2019050156 (ebook) | ISBN 9780367143428 (hardcover) | ISBN 9780367143435 (paperback) | ISBN 9780429031380 (ebook)
Subjects: LCSH: Counseling psychology. | Counselors—Training of. | Mental health.
Classification: LCC BF636.6 .C3626 2020 (print) | LCC BF636.6 (ebook) | DDC 158.3068/3—dc23
LC record available at https://lccn.loc.gov/2019050155
LC ebook record available at https://lccn.loc.gov/2019050156

ISBN: 978-0-367-14342-8 (hbk)
ISBN: 978-0-367-14343-5 (pbk)
ISBN: 978-0-429-03138-0 (ebk)

Typeset in Times
by Apex CoVantage, LLC

Dedicated to my wonderful students, my inspiration and greatest helpers. You are always remembered and forever loved.

Contents

Acknowledgments

Many thanks to all whose efforts helped me write this book.

I would like to express my deep gratitude to my research assistants, student readers, and teaching assistants for their contributions, encouragement, useful critiques, and all-around awesomeness.

I would also like to thank my Key Strategies Training (KST) colleagues for their collaboration and for launching my counselor training scholarship. My grateful thanks are extended to my professors, mentors, and colleagues for their encouragement and guidance. I would also like to extend my thanks to Whitworth University, Psi Chi International Honors Society, and the Society for the Teaching of Psychology for generous grant funding to support research for this book and to Routledge for helping me bring this book into the world.

Finally, I wish to thank Casey, my loving family, and my wonderful cats for their constant love and support. Thank you for making all of this possible.

1 Introduction to Helping

> **Chapter Goals**
>
> This chapter will prepare you to:
>
> - Consider what characterizes psychological distress, including significant factors in its causes and triggers.
> - Gain an understanding of what constitutes nonprofessional helping for psychological distress and what does not.
> - Identify the different roles and occupations of nonprofessional helpers in the mental health field.

Introduction

We are each a vessel navigating the stormy seas of life. Whether floating on calm waters or fighting treacherous rapids, we occasionally find ourselves stuck in a whirlpool of crisis. Thankfully, humans are relational and interdependent beings who never have to sail alone. When drowning in emotional turmoil and stress, sometimes we need someone to throw us a life raft, to see our pain and pull us out of the whirlpool, so we can adjust our sails and restore our life flow once again. It is through these moments of being lovingly rescued by another that we learn, grow, and are transformed. We can raise each other up to be stronger and more capable navigators of our own lives.

I find inspiration from the words of Louisa May Alcott (1953) in *Little Women*: "I am not afraid of storms for I am learning to sail my ship." The thematic expression of water as a representation of our life and struggles is found everywhere. It resonates with us, for it expresses the range of human experience and how we learn to navigate our life journey. The metaphor extends further into emergency preparedness: just as we need trained lifeguards and water rescuers who can throw us a life raft, we also need trained helpers who can offer an emotional lifeline when needed.

This is what inspired me to create the LifeRAFT helping skills model and share it with you. Throughout this book, we will continue to use the life/water metaphor to elucidate the experience of distress as drowning and the helping process as water rescue.

This book will train you in how to help others save themselves from sinking into emotional turmoil by teaching you the skills of nonprofessional counseling, also called "mental health first aid" (Quinnett, 1995). Although people generally want to provide help, many people do not know what to do when they witness someone flooded by psychological distress (Myers, 2010). If they are already prepared, they are likely a mental health professional. These trained professional helpers are available to see clients only on an occasional basis, usually for just one hour per week.

Everyday people are not trained in helping skills, the interpersonal interventions that have been empirically demonstrated to help those in distress. While helping skills training is often reserved only for mental health professionals, such skills are available and appropriate for everyone to use (Hill, 2014). Although everyday people usually do not have formal helping skills training, they can do something to help. They are the ones who are in contact with people most often, and although they cannot diagnose or treat problems, they can help address crises, aid with immediate needs, and refer for additional treatment. Just as everyday people are taught basic first aid, they too can be taught the "mental health first aid" techniques that we call "helping skills."

Personal Reflection

Congratulations on your decision to become a LifeRAFT trained helper! This book will teach you how to help people in all kinds of challenging psychological situations. The first thing you must do is choose to commit to your training as an effective helper.

- What are your reasons for engaging in helping skills training?
- Is it worth it to complete LifeRAFT training? For what reasons?

We need more people who can help in this world. Cheers in advance to you!

Psychological Distress

To understand how to help someone, it is useful to first recognize what people need rescuing from. In other words, we need to understand what psychological distress is and where it comes from.

Psychological Distress Defined

For our purposes, we will define psychological distress as unpleasant thoughts, actions, and/or feelings that impact a person's ability to function in a healthy and adaptive way (Mirowsky & Ross, 2002). For example, if Annie was spending the evening with her friends, we would expect she would have a reasonably good time. If instead she experienced severe fear all evening that kept her from connecting and enjoying herself, we might label this as "psychological distress." Here, "severe fear" is a form of upset or unpleasant feelings, and "kept her from connecting and enjoying herself" indicates a negative impact on her ability to function.

Unpleasant thoughts, actions, and feelings can manifest in countless forms and are unique to each individual. In general, unpleasant thoughts are characterized by excessively broad and negative ideas about oneself or the world (Beck, 2011). "I am stupid" and "people are not to be trusted" are examples of broad, negative generalizations about oneself and the world that lead to distress.

Unpleasant actions are conceptualized as the sabotaging behaviors that make us feel bad in some regard, either immediately or after a delay (Martell, Dimidjian, Herman-Dunn, & Lewinsohn, 2010). For example, watching a sad movie when you are already sad results in increased hurt immediately, while binge eating may feel soothing in the moment but causes delayed discomforts and health problems in the long term.

Unpleasant feelings are negative emotions that cause pain and suffering. There are numerous examples of these, but the most common types include variations of sadness, anger, and fear (Greenberg, 2002). Note that "negative" is not synonymous with "bad," because these emotions serve a vital function in our lives. Instead, "negative" refers to the fact that these emotions produce uncomfortable sensations. Feeling angry when a coworker gossips behind your back does not feel good, which characterizes it as a negative feeling. This anger can even disrupt your daily routine by causing you to be irritable and curt toward others, thus impacting functioning. Although negative and disruptive, the anger may also mobilize you to confront your coworker directly to resolve the issue, thereby serving a vital function. Negative thoughts, feelings, and actions not only are unpleasant, distressful, and disruptive but can also serve an essential and valuable part of the human experience.

Causes of Psychological Distress

The causes of psychological distress can be as varied as the reactions they cause. Origins of distress, much like the distress itself, vary between individuals, and what prompts feelings of distress in one person may not in another (Durand & Barlow, 2013).

How much distress a person experiences from a given situation, or whether a situation translates into psychological distress at all, is a highly individualized and multidimensional process based on a myriad of factors. For example, Ramsey may experience psychological distress in the form of intense anger and rage after receiving a credit card bill that he is unable to pay. The cause of Ramsey's distress might seem obvious, but the nature and intensity of his distress may be different than other people who may instead feel frightened about their financial future or even inspired to make changes in the face of consequences.

The primary factors involved in causation of psychological distress are called "predispositions," meaning a person's liabilities or their likelihood to experience distress in response to situations (Abela, Sakellaropoulo, & Taxel, 2007). As a baseline tendency for situational reactions, predispositions to psychological distress include factors such as genetics, physiology, environment, behavior, emotion, and cognition. We will use the case of Ramsey to further illuminate each of these predispositions.

Genetic Factors

Genetic factors are inherited tendencies that make distress more or less likely to occur (Durand & Barlow, 2013). Ramsey's intense anger reaction to the credit card bill may be related to genes he inherited that predispose him to reacting with anger to stressors. Sudden increases in blood pressure in response to stress, for instance, have been linked to genetics and heritability (Ost, 1992), as have a variety of other functions involved with stress (AIS, 2014).

Physiological Factors

Physiological factors include how the chemicals in the brain operate and respond (Durand & Barlow, 2013). Ramsey's brain may have an imbalance of neurotransmitters or hormones that predispose him to reacting to situations with rage. Improper levels of neurotransmitters, such as serotonin and norepinephrine, as well as hormones, such as testosterone, have been linked to aggressive impulses (Moeller, 2009).

Environmental Factors

Environmental factors include anything in people's surroundings that can impact them, including their family and friends, geographical location, and cultural norms (Durand & Barlow, 2013). For example, Ramsey is part of the mainstream culture in the United States, and as a man, he experiences certain cultural expectations and stigmas regarding his reaction and expression of distress.

In general, it is considered more socially acceptable for a man to be angry than to show fear, so men are predisposed to admit and embrace anger reactions in stressful situations, as opposed to admitting they are afraid (Durand & Barlow, 2013). This predisposition may have been further reinforced by family members, particularly if Ramsey grew up in an angry or abusive household (Akande, 2000).

Behavioral, Emotional, and Cognitive Factors

While we have already explored how psychological distress itself is characterized by unpleasant behaviors, emotions, and thoughts, baseline behavioral, emotional, and cognitive characteristics can also be causes of distress.

BEHAVIORAL FACTORS

Behavioral factors include how people generally tend to conduct themselves (Durand & Barlow, 2013). Ramsey may frequently engage in actions that make a rage response more likely. Excessive alcohol use and other risky behaviors have been linked to increased likelihood of anger (Moeller, 2009).

EMOTIONAL FACTORS

Emotional factors are the baseline range and intensity with which people experience and express feelings (Durand & Barlow, 2013). Ramsey may be a particularly animated or dramatic person in his day-to-day life, which could predispose him to an even more intense reaction to stress (Greenberg, 2002).

COGNITIVE FACTORS

Cognitive factors refer to how people regularly perceive themselves and the world around them (Durand & Barlow, 2013). Ramsey may tend to see himself as a failure with money. For others who see themselves as generally responsible and view a financial error as a one-time mistake, the bill may not be as distressing. For Ramsey, however, the bill may serve to confirm his existing negative self-views, which will likely result in higher levels of distress (Beck, 2011).

Acknowledging these predispositions aids us as helpers in having compassion and understanding for people in immediate psychological distress (Batson, Ahmad, & Stocks, 2004). It is natural to attribute other people's problems as somehow their "fault," yet unpacking the complexity of predispositions helps us to see how distress naturally occurs for some people and not others. While predisposing factors do not absolve individuals of responsibility for appropriately managing themselves, they can assist helpers in understanding causes of distress and remaining sensitive to the individual's presence and the challenges they face. Maintaining awareness of predispositions is crucial when helping people stuck in a mental health predicament. It helps us to identify tendencies people may have regarding psychological distress and have compassion for those who repeatedly get stuck in seemingly similar whirlpools of distress. With these contextual factors as a backdrop, we can turn our attention to triggers that tend to invoke psychological distress reactions.

Problem Triggers

Problem triggers are immediate crisis situations that prompt distress responses. These tend to be complex and messy problems that the distressed person is not handling well. Oftentimes, there are so many stressors at one time that it can be challenging for a person to differentiate and identify exactly what is "causing" their psychological distress (Durand & Barlow, 2013), and it becomes a case of "the straw that broke the camel's back"; seemingly small problem triggers can build up over time until something unexpected results in a distress response. Although the origins of these feelings are sometimes obvious, we are more often aware only of the distress itself and the unpleasant feelings associated with it (Beck, 2011).

As a helper, it is valuable to understand common causes of distress reactions to better anticipate and recognize psychological distress when it occurs. According to the American Institute of Stress (AIS, 2014), the primary causes of stress in the United States are (1) job pressures, including coworker tension, bosses, and work overload; (2) money, including lack of funds and financial disagreements; (3) health crises, including illness and death; (4) relationships, including conflicts, separation, divorce, and loneliness; and (5) wellness challenges, including sleep deprivation, inadequate nutrition, and media overload. These are broad categories that often overlap with one another. Difficulty sleeping (i.e., wellness challenges) because of stress at work (i.e., job pressures) and loneliness (i.e., relationships) due to the death of a partner (i.e., health) are examples of causal overlaps. The saying "when it rains, it pours" is certainly true regarding problem triggers: psychological distress often includes multiple life challenges in more than one category (Durand & Barlow, 2013).

Personal Reflection

Consider how distress operates in your own life. Reflecting on your experience of distressing triggers in your life can further help you to gain empathy and understanding for psychological distress experienced by others. To identify your current sources of stress, take the Holmes–Rahe Stress Inventory (1967), available online at www.stress.org/holmes-rahe-stress-inventory.

Holmes and Rahe were psychiatrists interested in understanding how stress contributes to illness. They surveyed over 5,000 medical patients and based on their findings developed a scale of life events, weighted by their typical impact on health. By taking this inventory, you will gain a better understanding of the stressors you have faced in the past year, your anticipated level of distress, and the likely impact on your health.

After completing the Holmes–Rahe Stress Inventory, answer the following questions:

- What was your score on the Holmes–Rahe Stress Inventory? How did taking this inventory inform your understanding of your own experience of problem triggers and psychological distress?
- How did you/are you reacting to these stressors? Considering the nature and intensity of your reactions, what might you conclude about your predispositions to psychological distress?
- What new insights do you have about others' experience of predispositions, problem triggers, and psychological distress? What do you want to keep in mind about distress as you start your training as a helper?

Now that we understand what psychological distress is and what causes it, we can turn our attention to how nonprofessionals can help.

Nonprofessional Counseling

In an effort to understand nonprofessional help for psychological distress, we return to our water metaphor. You are at the beach with your friend Carrie and you spot her in deep waters struggling to stay afloat. Sensing something is wrong, you look for help but quickly recognize that no lifeguard is on duty. Perhaps you have received training in basic lifeguarding skills, so, using what you have learned, you assess the situation and decide to swim out to provide aid. You pull Carrie to safety. Out of immediate danger, Carrie needs follow-up medical care, so you facilitate a transfer to the hospital. Medical professionals help Carrie return to a healthy level of functioning to the point of being able to swim in the water again. When all is said and done, your role in the entire process was immediate and brief but a crucial element in your friend's rescue to safety.

Nonprofessional counseling (or nonprofessional helping) for psychological distress can be similarly understood. In this scenario, we will refer to the one who is providing aid as the "helper" and the person in psychological distress as the "helpee." The helper recognizes the helpee as someone in psychological distress who wants help. The helper then assesses the situation and provides immediate aid, possibly also referring the helpee for professional mental health help, if needed. For example, let's consider the same scenario, only this time Carrie needs help psychologically as opposed to physically. You are a trained nonprofessional helper and you notice your friend Carrie "drowning" in psychological distress. She is on her way to an important meeting at a restaurant where she's repeatedly suffered panic attacks. You know that Carrie has a predisposition for anxiety and was diagnosed by a psychologist with panic disorder. It is a weekend evening and no professional therapist is available to help her work through the immediate problem trigger. No one really knows what to say or do to help Carrie, but she is not alone. You, as a trained nonprofessional helper, notice Carrie's psychological distress. You assess and assist her in dealing with the situation at hand by helping her to calm her worries and engage in positive self-talk to the point that she can attend the meeting. After the meeting, Carrie needs to continue to work with a professional therapist to address the underlying mental illness, so you refer her back to her therapist to continue treatment. When all is said and done, your role in her recovery process was immediate and brief, but when she needed it, you provided a crucial element in Carrie's "rescue" in psychological health and adaptive functioning.

Definition of Nonprofessional Helping

As demonstrated in the aforementioned example, nonprofessional helping means assessing and assisting a helpee to manage immediate life concerns more effectively. There are several noteworthy components of this definition that benefit from further consideration. While untrained helpers incorrectly assume that people want immediate answers or quick fixes to their problems without understanding the issues first, this is rarely the case (Campbell, Davidson, & Davidson, 2017). Immediate answers tend not to work (Jefferson & Lee, 1992). Earlier in this chapter we explored the causes of psychological distress and how complex and multifaceted the origins of distress can be. Quick fixes fail to acknowledge how difficult problem triggers can be for a helpee to handle, particularly given the multiple predispositions that likely also play a role in the distress. Situations where problem triggers are absurdly simple, well-defined, and straightforward most often do not result in distress or require any kind of rescue. Thus, a crucial component of helping is fully assessing the helpee and their situation first and only then assisting the helpee in getting unstuck and moving forward.

Nonprofessional helping also involves aiding a helpee to manage immediate life concerns. Although nonprofessional helping may occur within an ongoing relationship or involve multiple occasions of helping over time, a key feature of nonprofessional helping is focusing on present concerns. For this reason, nonprofessional helping is also called "supportive counseling," whereby "counseling" connects the helping situation to the broader spectrum of providing aid and "supportive" differentiates it as the type that provides temporary encouragement instead of ongoing professional treatment. Note how this defining aspect differentiates nonprofessional helping from professional helping.

Professional helping, such as the work done in counseling, psychotherapy, medicine, and psychiatric treatment, involves comprehensive aid to help people cope with repeated and ongoing life difficulties and psychopathology while developing opportunities for long-term growth (Ivey, Ivey, & Zalaquett, 2016). Professional helping is also called "mental health counseling," in which "counseling" once again connects the helping to the broader spectrum of providing aid and "mental health" differentiates it as providing more comprehensive professional care.

Nonprofessional helpers lack the education and training required to engage in the deep-seated work of developing strategies for overall life changes (Ivey et al., 2016). Instead, nonprofessional helpers learn more basic processes involved in resolving immediate problem triggers and managing temporary flare-ups of psychological distress. In this way, the relationship between nonprofessional and professional helpers is complementary: nonprofessional helpers provide aid by temporarily freeing helpees from their immediate problem whirlpools, and professional helpers aid them in navigating their overall life flow.

Lastly, the definition of a nonprofessional helper includes aiding a helpee in managing "more effectively." Note once again that the focus is not on fixing but instead on encouraging the helpee to increase their level of adaptiveness in their immediate situation. This may involve resolving a given issue, reconsidering the issue from a more balanced perspective, or giving voice to unacknowledged feelings in need of attention and validation. Whatever motivates a helpee to presently manage their problem trigger more effectively than they were previously doing is part of helping.

Purpose of Nonprofessional Helping

The primary purpose of nonprofessional helping is to support and facilitate a helpee's ability to help themselves. When we enter a helping situation, this is what we are attempting to accomplish, and if we do, we can consider the helping scenario to be a success. The most important part of this purpose is the "helpee's ability to help themselves"; we do not do the work for them. Note that our job as helpers is that of supporting and facilitating the helpee in being a self-helper.

This purpose emphasizes that helpees need to be an active participant in their own rescue; helping requires work on the part of both the helper and the helpee (Kiracofe & Buller, 2009). As exemplified by a drowning victim who fights against a water rescuer and puts both victim and rescuer at risk (American Red Cross, 2018), it is challenging, if not impossible, to help someone who does not want it (Kiracofe & Buller, 2009). For example, have you ever tried to force someone to calm down? Untrained helpers sometimes attempt to do this by repeatedly commanding helpees, "Calm down, calm down." Those who have tried can attest that this approach is ineffective. In fact, it often backfires by antagonizing the helpee even more as they respond, "Don't you think that if I could calm down, I would?! Stop telling me what to do!" We cannot force helpees to receive help, nor would we want to. Instead, helping should be seen as a two-way, collaborative process that requires helpees to engage and accept help.

Nonprofessional helping also stresses the importance of respecting and maintaining helpees' power over their own lives. As much as possible, our goal is for them to work through their own problems and arrive at their own solutions. As a helper, doing the work for a helpee is inherently problematic. No matter the outcome, this will likely encourage ineffective functioning, thereby undermining the very goal of helping. For example, imagine that your friend Mateo is in psychological distress about his relationship, and he asks you if he should break up with his partner. Rather than helping him work through the issue himself, you tell Mateo that he should end the relationship, and so he does. Regardless of whether this ends up being a good decision for Mateo or not, it carries several dangers to both Mateo and your role as a helper. If, in time, Mateo believes breaking up was the wrong course of action, his trust in you and your ability to help may decrease. He may even blame you for his problems altogether. Conversely, if Mateo believes breaking up was the correct course of action, he may put too much trust in you as a helper and become dependent on your help in the future. This compromises his trust in himself, and his ability to confront problems on his own may decrease. Both of these scenarios put Mateo at risk of managing his life less effectively, which is opposite to the goal of helping.

Instead, helping requires that helpees be empowered to make their own decisions. That way, regardless of the outcome, the credit and responsibility lie with the helpee. They can celebrate their successes and learn from their missteps without compromising your role as a helper or their perceived confidence and competence in managing their own lives. In fact, by experiencing a sense of agency in a helping situation, helpees can actually raise their competence in future situations (Egan, 2014). In this way, your immediate help can produce and support long-term benefits while still maintaining ethical boundaries (Hill, 2014).

Yet helpees still need aid in distressing situations. The key to facilitating self-help is through scaffolding. "Scaffolding" is a term used in the education field to describe the most effective method for teaching students at a deeper level of self-learning (Van de Pol, Volman, & Beishuizen, 2010). Scaffolding in a helping context teaches successive levels of temporary support. In the LifeRAFT helping skills model, we call scaffolding the "microskills ramp-up," which is a concept you will learn more about throughout your helping skills training in this book. Scaffolding facilitates helpees' ability to work through a problem trigger that they would not otherwise be able to without assistance. Assistance is provided to the helpee to the extent required for them to help themselves, and support and praise are offered as they effectively manage their own problems.

Personal Reflection

Now that you understand what nonprofessional helping is and what its purpose should be, it will be helpful to explore what unique qualities you bring to helping scenarios. As you reflect on yourself as a nonprofessional helper, answer the following questions:

- Ask three people (family, friends, etc.) to identify two qualities or skills they see in you that make you an effective helper. Record what they say. How are these qualities similar and/or different to your perception of your skills?
- Overall, what do you believe are your present strengths for helping? What do you believe will be your areas for growth as a helper? How do they connect to our definition and purpose of nonprofessional helping?

Types of Nonprofessional Helpers

We have learned that anyone can be trained as a LifeRAFT helper and can apply basic mental health first aid. Psychological distress can strike anyone at any time. Everyday people in everyday situations can, at one point or another, be a helper providing aid or a helpee receiving it. There are also numerous roles and occupations whose primary job duty is to provide nonprofessional help or that regularly utilize helping skills, which we will now review.

Everyday People

Everyday people are often called on as helpers. People in any kind of informal relationship or contact—family, friends, coworkers, classmates, and even strangers—are considered everyday people. When you are in emotional distress, whom do you most want to reach out to for support? Chances are it is a friend or family member who is not a mental health professional. These are the people whom most of us rely on and seek out first when we get stuck. The hallmark of these informal relationships is that they provide emotional support, especially during times of stress and turmoil.

Regardless of one's occupation, everyone is a nonprofessional helper at some point. Even professional counselors fall into this category outside the walls of their office or clinic. For example, although I, the author of this book, am a professional counselor as part of my job, I only serve in that role at designated times. In my everyday life, it is ethically inappropriate to provide professional counseling to family, friends, or even my students in my role as a university psychology professor. I still love to help informally in those situations, but I do so as a nonprofessional helper.

Everyday people may be called on by helpees to provide support, or they may notice a situation and offer to help without needing to be asked. Recognizing that a family member or friend is in distress or even simply exhibiting changes in behavior may prompt a helper to ask, "Are you ok?" thereby providing an opportunity for helping to take place. Still other helping situations may emerge spontaneously, such as in a relationship where the emergence or disclosure of psychological distress can happen without prompting by either party.

Everyday people can also find themselves in helping situations with acquaintances or strangers: a coworker complains to you about burnout, you happen on a crying child separated from parents, a disgruntled bus passenger engages you in conversation on your commute, you overhear a classmate remark that they struggled on an exam, and so on. You likely can think of several other scenarios you have encountered. From family, friends, acquaintances, and strangers, everyday people are presented with endless opportunities to help.

People often attempt to provide aid when they can (Myers, 2010). Unfortunately, people are rarely trained in helping skills and the effectiveness of their natural instincts in these scenarios can vary (Campbell et al., 2017). In fact, there are considerable differences between helpers regarding their effectiveness, especially when considering the specific helping strategies used (Egan, 2014). Some people are generally helpful, and some are not, just as some strategies generally tend to help, and some do not. From this we can conclude that there are identifiable forms of helping that are highly effective when performed by high-quality helpers. Training in both strategies and conceptualization of a high-quality helper appear to be particularly advantageous in moving someone from being an ineffective helper to an effective one (Campbell et al., 2017). Thus, helping from everyday people can be effective, especially with helping skills training such as the LifeRAFT training you will gain from this book.

Noncredentialed Mental Health Workers

Nonprofessional helpers also include noncredentialed mental health workers. These are people who work in the field of mental health as their occupation but are not considered professional mental health providers. They are "noncredentialed" because their positions do not generally require specific degrees or certifications to perform their job duties or a professional license to practice. Examples of noncredentialed providers include behavioral health technicians, mental health assistants, life and skills coaches, residential aides, spiritual advisors, and social and human service volunteers (O*NET, 2018). Noncredentialed mental health workers can be found in a variety of human service agencies and organizations. They are typically employed by residential care facilities, nonprofit organizations, local governments, and rehabilitation centers.

Helpers in these positions are typically responsible for caring for individuals with mental or emotional conditions, under the instructions and supervision of professional mental health practitioners. They often assist with basic living tasks and self-care. Monitoring and reinforcing behavioral management plans and providing companionship are also common duties for individuals in these positions. Concerning mental health help, individuals typically interview their clients about concerns and provide supportive counseling and refer to professional practitioners when appropriate. Because noncredentialed mental health workers are most often the people responsible for the day-to-day functioning of people in distress, their primary role concerns providing ongoing nonprofessional help by addressing immediate concerns as they arise (O*NET, 2018).

With some noncredentialed providers, their clients come to their offices or clinics. An example of this would be a behavioral health technician who works at an autism clinic, who is responsible for implementing behavioral intervention plans assigned by a certified behavioral analyst. Other noncredentialed nonprofessionals connect with clients residing in hospitals, group homes, or shelters. An example of this is a mental health aide working in an inpatient hospital and assisting patients with grooming and medication management. Some providers also travel around their communities to meet with their clients. Social service volunteers, for example, deliver meals and conduct home visits for people too sick to travel or care for themselves (Bureau of Labor Statistics, 2018).

Noncredentialed mental health jobs are practically synonymous with nonprofessional helping situations, yet as with everyday people, trained providers are rare. Considered entry-level work, noncredentialed positions usually require a high school diploma, associate degree, or bachelor's degree with little to no prior experience (Bureau of Labor Statistics, 2018). They fall prey to the same dangers regarding helping effectiveness that everyday people do: some mental health workers happen to be naturally helpful and some do not (Egan, 2014). Results vary, which raises serious concerns. Noncredentialed mental health workers often work with vulnerable populations in severe levels of distress, who need competent helping and care. For example, an adolescent runaway living on the streets who is battling suicidality and drug addiction with no family support will likely make their first encounter with help at a local shelter with a noncredentialed provider. With high safety concerns and a tenuous condition for trust, a knowledgeable and savvy first encounter is essential. Noncredentialed mental health workers need training—fortunately, this book can provide the helping skills training needed to perform their job safely and successfully. If this is you, thank you for being a responsible and diligent care worker by getting appropriately trained with LifeRAFT. You are doing your clients a huge service!

Professionals in Industries Outside of Mental Health

Nonprofessional helpers often called on to aid those in distress also include professionals in industries outside of mental health. Professionals include a variety of occupations that involve a high amount of social interaction but are not specifically geared toward treating mental health, such as business, education, medicine, customer service and retail, law and public safety, government, human services, and more (O*NET, 2018). These people work with others to accomplish goals that are not directly related to psychological distress and mental illness. However, when working with people in any capacity, encounters with emotional turmoil are likely. Think about customer service workers who are all too familiar with patrons who express psychological distress in the form of discontent and anger regarding their company or services. Also consider medical physicians: although they specialize in physiological issues and are not mental health professionals per se, they are likely to encounter psychological distress when interviewing patients about physical concerns and likely trigger distress when diagnosing serious health issues (Zolnierek & DiMatteo, 2009). As a devoted cat lover, even my veterinarian encountered my psychological distress when one of my cats was sick! Thankfully, in my case, she was wonderfully supportive; however, numerous complaints about doctors' "poor bedside manner" speak directly to the issue that some medical professionals have difficulty with talking to patients in a supportive and empathic manner and need helping skills training (Zolnierek & DiMatteo, 2009).

In fact, while most professions require helping skills (Ivey et al., 2016), few industries outside mental health regularly train their professionals in such skills. Thus, professionals in disciplines outside of mental health fall prey to the same problems that everyday people and nonprofessional mental health workers do: some are naturally helpful, and some are not (Egan, 2014). It may be shocking to learn that many of those in related helping fields such as medicine and education are not trained in such skills. Professionals usually are required to take coursework in psychology as part of their training, which provides them with a valuable understanding of how people think, feel, and act. Rarely, however, are they required to take a counseling, applied psychology, or helping skills course (Zolnierek & DiMatteo, 2009). So, at best, professionals outside mental health are all theory and no practice. They have basic theoretical ideas for why people respond the way they do but no training in how to use those principles to recognize and support someone's pain. This book can bridge the gap by providing the helping skills training professionals need to support and enhance the important work they do.

Conclusion

Life is hard. We are all navigating our own course through the changing tides and stormy seas of life, and sometimes we need help along the way. I believe that everyone—not just professional counselors—can do something to offer love and support to those struggling. This is why I created the LifeRAFT helping skills training model, and I am eager to share it with you in this book.

Many have the heart of a helper but are not trained in how to actually be one. In fact, the majority of people who encounter those in pain are not professionally prepared and need to know how to appropriately handle such situations given their role and level of skill. These include everyday people, noncredentialed mental health workers, and professionals outside the field of mental health. This book is meant to fill that gap by teaching all who want to learn how to be effective helpers to do so.

A primary theme I will emphasize throughout this book is empathy for those who are struggling in distress. That begins with an understanding of what distress is, where it comes from, and how it is triggered. Now that we have a way to conceptualize these issues, we can turn our attention to learning more about how we as nonprofessionals can operate as effective helpers.

Summary

In this chapter we discussed the following:

Psychological Distress

- Understanding what psychological distress is, where it comes from, and how it is triggered facilitates our empathy and understanding for the helpees in distress whom we encounter and try to help.
- Psychological distress is characterized by unpleasant thoughts, actions, and/or feelings that impact a person's ability to function in a healthy and adaptive way.
- Predispositions, or likelihoods to experience distress, are influenced by the following factors: genetic, physiological, environmental, behavioral, emotional, and cognitive.
- Problem triggers are the immediate crisis situations that prompt a distress response; the most common of which are job pressures, money, health crises, relationships, and wellness challenges.

Nonprofessional Helping

- Nonprofessional helping is defined as assessing and assisting a helpee to manage immediate life concerns more effectively.
- The purpose of nonprofessional helping is to support and facilitate a helpee's ability to help themselves.
- Nonprofessional helpers for mental health include:
    - everyday people in informal relationships, such as family and friends;
    - noncredentialed mental health workers such as mental health technicians, life coaches, spiritual advisors, and volunteers; and
    - professionals in industries outside of mental health that involve a high degree of social interaction, such as business, education, medicine, law and public safety, government, and human services.

References

Abela, J. R., Sakellaropoulo, M., & Taxel, E. (2007). Integrating two subtypes of depression: Psychodynamic theory and its relation to hopelessness depression in early adolescents. *The Journal of Early Adolescence*, *27*(3), 363–384.

Akande, A. (2000). Effects of exposure to violence and poverty on young children: The southern African context. *Early Child Development and Care*, *163*, 61–78.

Alcott, L. M. (1953). *Little women*. Baltimore: Penguin Books.

American Institute of Stress. (2014). Stress research. *American Institute of Stress*. Retrieved from www.stress.org/stress-research/

American Red Cross. (2018). How to respond to a water emergency. *American Red Cross*. Retrieved from www.redcross.org/content/dam/redcross/atg/PDF_s/Preparedness___Disaster_Recovery/Disaster_Preparedness/Water_Safety/WouldYouKnowWhattodo.pdf

Batson, C. D., Ahmad, N., & Stocks, E. L. (2004). Benefits and liabilities of empathy-induced altruism. In A. G. Miller (Ed.), *The social psychology of good and evil* (pp. 359–385, Chapter 14, 498 Pages). New York, NY: Guilford Press.

Beck, J. S. (2011). *Cognitive therapy: Basics and beyond* (2nd ed.). New York, NY: Guilford Press.

Bureau of Labor Statistics, U.S. Department of Labor. (2018). *Occupational outlook handbook*. Retrieved from www.bls.gov/ooh/

Campbell, E. L., Davidson, K., & Davidson, S. M. (2017). Effectiveness of LifeRAFT undergraduate helping skills training model. *Psychology Teaching Review*, *23*(2), 32–41.

Durand, V. M., & Barlow, D. H. (2013). Chapter 2: An integrative approach to psychopathology. In V. M. Durand & D. H. Barlow (Eds.), *Essentials of abnormal psychology* (pp. 30–68). Belmont, CA: Wadsworth Publishing Company.

Egan, G. (2014). *The skilled helper: A problem-management and opportunity development approach to helping* (10th ed.). Belmont, CA: Brooks/Cole.

Greenberg, L. S. (2002). *Emotion-focused therapy: Coaching clients to work through feelings*. Washington, DC: American Psychological Association.

Hill, C. E. (2014). *Helping skills: Facilitating exploration, insight, and action* (4th ed.). Washington, DC: American Psychological Association.

Holmes, T. H., & Rahe, R. H. (1967). The social readjustment rating scale. *Journal of Psychosomatic Research*, *11*(2), 213–218.

Ivey, A. E., Ivey, M. B., & Zalaquett, C. P. (2016). *Essentials of intentional interviewing: Counseling in a multicultural world* (3rd ed.). Boston, MA: Cengage Learning.

Jefferson, G., & Lee, J. R. E. (1992). The rejection of advice: Managing the problematic convergence of a "troubles-telling" and a "service encounter." In *Talk at work: Interaction in institutional settings* (pp. 521–548). Cambridge: Cambridge University Press.

Kiracofe, N. M., & Buller, A. E. (2009). Mandated disciplinary counseling: Working effectively with challenging clients. *Journal of College Counseling*, *12*(1), 71–84.

Martell, C. R., Dimidjian, S., Herman-Dunn, R., & Lewinsohn, P. M. (2010). *Behavioral activation for depression: A clinician's guide*. New York, NY: Guilford Press.

Mirowsky, J., & Ross, C. E. (2002). Measurement for a human science. *Journal of Health and Social Behavior, 43*(2), 152–170. doi:2112/10.2307/3090194

Moeller, F. G. (2009). Impulse-control disorders not elsewhere classified. In B. J. Sadock, V. A. Sadock, & P. Ruiz (Eds.), *Kaplan and Sadock's comprehensive textbook of psychiatry* (9th ed., Vol. 1, pp. 2178–2186). Philadelphia, PA: Lippincott Williams & Wilkins.

Myers, D. G. (2010). Chapter 12: Helping. In D. G. Myers (Ed.), *Social psychology* (10th ed., pp. 440–480). New York: McGraw-Hill.

National Center for O*NET Development. (2018). *O*NET online*. Retrieved from www.onetonline.org

Ost, L. G. (1992). Blood and injection phobia: Background and cognitive, physiological, and behavioral variables. *Journal of Abnormal Psychology, 10*(1), 68–74.

Quinnett, P. (1995). *QPR gatekeeper training manual*. Spokane, WA: QPR Institute, Inc.

Van de Pol, J., Volman, M., & Beishuizen, J. (2010). Scaffolding in teacher: Student interaction: A decade of research. *Educational Psychology Review, 22*(3), 271–296. doi:10.1007/s10648-010-9127-6

Zolnierek, K. B. H., & DiMatteo, M. R. (2009). Physician communication and patient adherence to treatment: A meta-analysis. *Medical care, 47*(8), 826–834. doi:10.1097/MLR.0b013e31819a5acc

2 Ethical Issues in Nonprofessional Counseling

Chapter Goals

This chapter will prepare you to:

- Develop an awareness of ethical standards and the reasons why they are important.
- Apply ethical standards appropriately to helping situations.
- Recognize the value of being a multiculturally competent helper and how to integrate multiculturalism into an ethical helping practice.

Introduction

Nonprofessional helpers must learn what helping is as well as *how* it should be provided. The *how* of helping refers to ethics; helpers should strive to provide ethical care to their helpees. Ethics are behaviors and practices that conform to principles and standards in order to uphold the utmost level of respect for the people with whom individuals work (Faiver, Eisengart, & Colonna, 2004). Professional helpers belong to organizations that govern agreed-upon ethical codes of conduct. For example, master's-level counselors follow the American Counseling Association's (ACA, 2014) *Code of Ethics*, marriage and family therapists (MFTs) follow the American Association for Marriage and Family Therapy's (AAMFT, 2015) *Code of Ethics*, Masters of Social Workers (MSWs) follow the National Association for Social Workers' (NASW, 2017) *Code of Ethics*, and doctoral-level psychologists follow the American Psychological Association's (APA, 2016) *Ethical Principles of Psychologists and Code of Conduct.*

Nonprofessional counselors are not organized by the same governing bodies, nor do they have their own designated association. As such, nonprofessional counselors do not have an established code of ethics like professional counselors. Some organizations devoted to specific types of nonprofessional helping have their own codes of conduct, and these codes often mirror those of professional counselors. An example is the National Career Development Association's (NCDA, 2015) *Ethical Standards* for career coaches. Similarly, experts in other nonprofessional helping fields have provided recommendations for ethical practices in their field, such as the *Mentoring Code of Ethics* for peer mentors presented by Johnson (2007). These independent ethical codes typically highlight the same ethical obligations of professional counselors but are adapted for the appropriate scope of practice and level of skill. Drawing from these examples, it is evident that using professional counseling ethics as a guide is a helpful practice for nonprofessional counselors.

In addition, professional principles and standards provide guidance by not only describing what is ethically important for all helping professions but also defining the boundaries of professional practice. Professional counseling ethical codes describe what a professional counselor is and what is required to be considered one (AAMFT, 2015; ACA, 2014; APA, 2016; NASW, 2017). We, as nonprofessional counselors, can use these codes as a guide to define our own helping endeavors by embracing helping that lies within the boundaries of nonprofessional helping. For example, the ACA's (2014) *Code of Ethics* states that training to be a professional counselor includes "formal graduate-level counselor education" (p. 21). By this definition, we can conclude that those who do not possess this level of education are instead nonprofessional helpers.

Although nonprofessionals are not obligated by a guild to follow the same principles and standards as professionals, they should still aspire to similar values and should model their conduct on the same standards of professionals (Hill, 2014). This section will address some of the ethical issues that nonprofessional helpers encounter by highlighting important ethical principles, as well as standards of practice to uphold and follow.

Personal Reflection

Ethical helping practice comes from our personal commitment as helpers to respect and affirm the people we help (APA, 2016). Although laws and standards guide some ethical practices, the field of nonprofessional helping has few systematized guidelines and sanctions. It is on us to monitor and guide our own behavior out of our commitment to doing right by others.

Consider your commitment to ethical practice by answering the following questions:

- What is important to you about the manner in which you conduct yourself when you help people?
- For what reasons are those important to you?
- How will you maintain your commitment to monitor and guide your own behavior as a nonprofessional helper?

Ethical Principles

Ethical principles are defined as common aspirations that helpers attempt to uphold when making decisions (Hill, 2014). While there are many ethical principles that professional counselors strive for, some also apply to nonprofessionals. These primarily include autonomy and safety.

Autonomy

Autonomy refers to the helper's ethical responsibility to empower the helpee toward independent thinking and decision-making, minimizing all forms of dependency (AAMFT, 2015). Autonomy is directly reflected in our goals for helping as we strive to help clients to help themselves. For this reason, we avoid telling helpees what to do or making decisions for them. We maintain respect and dignity for the helpee's independence by facilitating their decision-making without inserting our own biases. For example, your helpee Dena asks you for help in deciding whether she should continue to reside in California or move to Florida. Perhaps you, as the helper, believe that she should stay in California. Based on the ethical principle of autonomy, it is important that you guide your helpee to discover the decision that is best for her; perhaps in this case, it results in Dena moving to Florida. Autonomy necessitates that helping is not about the helper but instead about what is best for the helpee and ensures helpees have the right to direct their own lives based on their wishes and belief systems.

Safety

Safety refers to the helper's ethical obligation to minimize risks and protect others (Baird, 2014). In professional ethical codes, this principle is often referred to by the terms "beneficence" and "nonmaleficence." Beneficence is the intent to "do good" by genuinely helping for the benefit of the client (APA, 2016), as opposed to helping for the purpose of manipulation or exploitation. Nonmaleficence is the intent to "do no harm" by not hurting or neglecting clients (APA, 2016). In nonprofessional helping roles, this objective extends to maintaining the safety of the helper and helpee, as well as the general public. For example, when a helpee is considered to be at risk of harming themselves or a third party, the ethical principle of safety requires that helpers take measures to protect any of the people at risk. This usually involves calling the police to warn them about a potential emergency. Regarding everyone, including both helper and helpee, each one of us has the right to be protected from reasonably foreseeable danger, risk, or injury.

The ethical principles of autonomy and safety are crucial to helping; sometimes, they go hand in hand. When autonomy is upheld, safety can be enhanced. A helpee who is empowered and autonomously chooses to lessen risk-taking behavior will see a corresponding increase in safety, whereas a helpee who is disempowered by being forced to stop their risk-taking behaviors may feel out of control, resulting in rebellion through increased risk-taking and becoming even more of a safety risk.

Oftentimes, however, ethical dilemmas occur when the ethical principles of autonomy and safety are at odds (Strang, Molloy, & Harrison, 1998). Calling the police to warn them about an emergency upholds the ethical principle of safety, but it undermines the principle of autonomy by taking the decision-making away from the helpee to decide whether police aid is desired. In general, the ethical principle of autonomy is upheld as the priority, as long as it does not risk the safety of the helpee or others. When autonomy puts safety at risk, safety becomes the priority to the extent needed to offer protection (Strang et al., 1998). The specific ways these principles are handled in helping situations are presented further in the next section.

Standards of Practice

Ethical principles that are translated into behavioral strategies are called "standards of practice." They describe the kinds of practices an ethical helper should and should not engage in during helping situations. Although there are numerous standards of practice for professional helpers (e.g., AAMFT, 2015; ACA, 2014; APA, 2016; NASW, 2017), the primary ethical standards pertaining to nonprofessional helpers are competence and confidentiality.

Competence

Helpers need to operate within their scope of competence, that is, the limits of what they are qualified to do based on level of education, training, and experience (APA, 2016). Competence upholds the ethical principles of both autonomy and safety; autonomy is upheld by maintaining boundaries concerning what nonprofessionals can help with, and safety is upheld by protecting helpees against receiving aid from those not qualified to give it. Included under the category of competence are helping competence and multicultural competence.

Helping Competence

Helping competence is helpers' knowledge and understanding of what constitutes effective helping, as well as their ability to carry it out. Standards of any helping practice require that helpers provide aid only within the scope of what they are qualified to provide (APA, 2016). Helpers are not professional counselors, and it would be unethical for them to try to act as if they were. Competence is not only an ethical mandate but legally sanctioned at the state level (Baird, 2014). All states have licensing boards that set credentialing requirements (Erford, 2014), and some do so for nonprofessional helpers as well (e.g., Department of Health, 2018). Requirements vary between states (Faiver et al., 2004), so be sure to contact your state's licensing board to verify that you are operating within the competency requirements of your state prior to engaging in mental health work.

Helpers are also not fortune-tellers or experts on other people's lives. Instead, helpers tend to be caring, intuitive, and compassionate individuals who can offer limited opportunities for healing and growth. In this way, helping competence directly connects to the definition of nonprofessional helping: assessing and assisting a helpee to manage immediate life concerns more effectively. Thus, nonprofessionals can exhibit helping competence by limiting their role to the goals of providing assessment and assistance for *immediate* life concerns. This ethical standard requires that helpees be referred to qualified professionals for ongoing help if their concerns are more enduring or connected to mental illness or ingrained personality characteristics.

Multicultural Competence

Multicultural competence refers to helpers' awareness of the influences and intersectionality of cultures (ACA, 2014). This intersecting of cultures, which we call "multiculturalism," includes factors such as race, ethnicity, geographical location, gender identity, sexual orientation, language, spiritual orientation, age, physical size and abilities, socioeconomic status, and many others (Ivey, Ivey, & Zalaquett, 2016). Standards of practice necessitate that helpers both recognize and value differences between people, being sensitive to the numerous negative consequences of discrimination and oppression (ACA, 2014). Without an understanding of how these contextual issues serve as a backdrop to problem triggers, helpers are rendered ill-equipped to fully empathize and offer aid to a helpee's whole self.

Psychologists Sue and Sue (2013) defined what exactly constitutes multicultural competence, specifically for the helping professions. Multicultural competence involves awareness, knowledge, and skills.

AWARENESS

Awareness means that as a helper, you should be aware of your own assumptions, values, and biases. When helping a specific person, it is important to ask yourself, "How can I genuinely connect and empathize with this person?" or "What might block me from connecting or empathizing?" For example, you may personally hold a strong value for education. It is important to explore how this personal preference may extend to your biases and assumptions about others. If you hold a bias against people with minimal education, you may inadvertently push them toward education (violating their autonomy) or blame them for their problems; this then makes you unavailable to provide psychological support. Working through your biases regarding multicultural factors will help you to sincerely appreciate all kinds of difficulties and better empathize with people, in order to help them choose how they can best manage their own lives (Beitel, Ferrer, & Cecero, 2005). Awareness of cultural and contextual issues in your own life provides you with opportunities to understand how these concepts play out in others' lives.

KNOWLEDGE

Multicultural competence through knowledge means understanding others' worldviews (Sue & Sue, 2013). People with different backgrounds have varying ways of viewing the world. Helpers should acknowledge that their ways of thinking are not the only or right ways of thinking and seek to learn about the worldviews of others; the focus then is on appreciation of differences. When helping someone, it is important to ask yourself, "What is this person's reality?" and "How can I understand it better and appreciate it more?" For example, the Latino National Survey (Fraga et al., 2006) found that the majority of people in the United States with Latin-American descent preferred the term "Hispanic" over "Latino," although this was not the case for everyone. Knowing this fact upfront gives you, as a helper, the opportunity to be sensitive to preferred terms. It is also essential to check whether that tendency is true for that particular person by asking their preferred term. Knowledge provides a solid foundation for acting in affirming and helpful ways.

SKILLS

Multicultural competence through skills means converting awareness and knowledge of differences into helpful action (Sue & Sue, 2013). In a nonprofessional context this means openly demonstrating to helpees that you recognize differences between them and yourself and that you affirm their multicultural identities. This can involve a variety of possible interventions. Some involve indirect actions, such as letting the helpee guide whether or not you shake hands or matching the helpee in their level of preferred eye contact; this is dependent on what is comfortable and accepted in their cultural context. Other interventions may also involve the words you choose to use in an effort to show respect and non-judgment, such as saying "partner" rather than "boyfriend/girlfriend" to signal openness and affirmation of varied sexual orientations. Interventions can also involve direct actions, such as explicitly pointing out differences and asking helpees about their experience. For example, a helper might say, "We're different, so I can't possibly understand what this experience is like for you. But if you'll let me try, I'd like to understand as best as I can." Or even more directly, "What is it like to share your experience of racism as an African-American with a Caucasian person like me?"

Beginning helpers can sometimes be afraid of noting differences out of fear of causing offense. While it is vital to do so carefully and empathically, multicultural competence has been demonstrated to enhance and improve helping experiences (Sue & Sue, 2013), so much so that it is a vital part of all professional counseling ethical standards (e.g., AAMFT, 2015; ACA, 2014; APA, 2016; NASW, 2017).

Confidentiality

Another nonprofessional standard of practice is confidentiality, which requires that helpers respect their helpees' right to privacy (APA, 2016). A helper's ability to keep information confidential is the foundation of a trusting relationship (ACA, 2014). Confidentiality is often not mandated for nonprofessionals but remains an important ethical standard to uphold in order to be an effective helper. If you develop a reputation for being untrustworthy or a gossip, people will quickly stop coming to you for help. Other helpers, such as nonprofessionals in mental health settings or professionals in medical settings, are often legally mandated to the same confidentiality requirements as mental health professionals (Baird, 2014). For nonprofessional helpers working in these settings, be sure to discuss confidentiality requirements with supervisors and educate yourself on your organization's policies and mandates, as requirements can often vary between states and organizations (Faiver et al., 2004). For all other helpers not mandated by local laws or policies, it is strongly recommended to adopt confidentiality as an ethical obligation and personal helping rule.

Confidentiality further upholds the ethical principles of both autonomy and safety in different ways. Keeping information private maintains autonomy, but in some cases, safety may require sharing information where appropriate. The nuances of handling confidentiality are discussed further under limits of confidentiality and informed consent.

Limits of Confidentiality

Some information is dangerous to keep secret, particularly if it puts someone at risk for harm. Limits of confidentiality include specific information that should be shared with an authority in order to uphold safety of the helper, the helpee, and bystanders. Professional therapists have specific state and local requirements regarding what they are legally mandated to report (Faiver et al., 2004). Nonprofessional helpers are often not bound to the same requirements, unless they are in a position that dictates as much. In the cases where limits of confidentiality are not determined for you by your job, it is valuable to follow guidelines set for professional mental health providers.

General guidelines for limits of confidentiality concentrate on issues of safety, specifically regarding suicide/homicide and abuse to vulnerable individuals. If you have significant reason to believe that helpees plan to harm themselves (i.e., suicide) or someone else (i.e., homicide), it is important to report these threats to the appropriate authorities. For example, if a helpee said they planned to kill someone, it would be important to call the police. Suspected abuse to children, elderly persons, or disabled persons is also information to report to authorities. These particular groups are considered vulnerable, and therefore safety is upheld by helping them stay safe (ACA, 2014).

Informed Consent

Informed consent means that helpees have a right to know what helpers are doing before they engage in a helping situation. In a professional therapy context, counselors are required to inform their clients about the treatment services they will receive and the limits of confidentiality before they agree to receiving those services (NASW, 2017). Clients are then asked to sign documentation verifying their written consent. In nonprofessional helping, informed consent follows the same premise as professional informed consent but is typically less formalized for everyday helping situations. It would, after all, be weird to ask your friend to sign a form before you talked to them about a bad day!

Nonprofessional informed consent simply translates to sharing information with helpees and asking permission before acting. Primary issues typically involve informing helpees about competence and limits to confidentiality. Regarding competence, it is important to inform a helpee that you are a nonprofessional helper. Clearly differentiate that you are not a therapist and you cannot provide counseling. For example, you might say something, such as: "I'm not a mental health professional so I can't offer you therapy. Still, I'm someone who cares and wants to offer support right now, if you'll permit me."

Regarding confidentiality, inform your helpee that you will keep what they say in confidence, with the exception of limits to confidentiality regarding safety. Helpees will often ask a helper, "If I tell you something, do you promise not to tell anyone else?" Eager nonprofessionals often respond with an emphatic "yes" in an effort to make the helpee feel safe; however, this could lead to an ethical dilemma between autonomy and safety if safety becomes a concern. There are situations where you might need to tell someone else, so you want to be honest about this with helpees while reassuring their confidence. Informed consent requires a more nuanced and genuine response at the very beginning, such as: "I respect your privacy and will keep this between us. The only exception is if I'm worried about your safety or the safety of others; then I'd need to say something. Any concerns about that? Can we agree to that?" Note that in this example, the helper begins by assuring confidentiality (i.e., "I respect your privacy and will keep this between us") to help put the helpee at ease. The helper then notes limits of confidentiality (i.e., "The only exception is if I'm worried about your safety or the safety of others; then I'd need to say something"), so the helpee understands specifically what would need to be disclosed. The helpee is then asked if there are any questions about limits of confidentiality (i.e., "Any concerns about that?"). Finally, the helper explicitly requests the helpee's verbal consent to the helping scenario and ethical terms (i.e., "Can we agree to that?"). This exemplifies a complete and appropriate example of informed consent in a nonprofessional helping scenario.

Providing the opportunity for informed consent before discussing psychological distress is particularly important for helpee autonomy. As much as we want to help, we also want helpees to know upfront what we can and cannot provide in order that they can make the best decisions for themselves. Informed consent is also an ongoing conversation throughout helping situations (Baird, 2014). Managing confidentiality issues as they arise means reminding helpees about the limits of confidentiality as they begin to disclose such information and then following through immediately with alerting authorities and carrying out recommended follow-up procedures.

Role-Play Practice

The purpose of this role-play practice is to rehearse ethical helping by beginning a helping scenario with informed consent. For this exercise, find a volunteer helpee to role-play the beginning of a helping scenario with you. Follow these steps:

1. Consider pairing with a fellow helper-in-training and take turns being the helper and helpee.
2. Video record the scenario. Note that informed consent also applies to video recording, as you need permission from your helpee prior to recording them.
3. The helper begins the session by providing informed consent:
    a. Explain that this is a role-play scenario and video recorded for training purposes. Obtain verbal permission to engage in the role-play and record the scenario.
    b. Express a desire to help the helpee with concerns.
    c. Note competence by explaining that you are a nonprofessional helper.
    d. Assure confidentiality and note limits of confidentiality.
    e. Ask the helpee if the helpee has any questions about limits of confidentiality.
    f. Request the helpee's verbal consent to the helping scenario and ethical terms. Once consent is obtained, the role-play is complete.
4. Request feedback from your role-play helpee about what you did well and what you could improve on next time. Write down your helpee's responses.
5. Review the video recording and write down what you notice that you did well and what you could improve on next time.

Conclusion

As eager as we are to begin helping, it is critical to begin with a solid understanding about what our role is and what it is not as a nonprofessional helper. For optimum helping, we have to engage in helping in a safe and ethical manner. Remain committed to the very best in order to maintain the dignity of our helpees.

We will return time and again throughout this book to ethics, particularly upholding autonomy and safety. I carry these two ideas forward in subsequent chapters, as they remain the pillars of what we stand on as nonprofessional helpers in order to provide the best care possible.

Summary

In this chapter we discussed the following:

Ethics in Nonprofessional Helping

- Ethics are behaviors and practices that conform to principles and standards to uphold the utmost level of respect for the people with whom they work.

Ethical Principles

- Ethical principles are common aspirations or goals that helpers attempt to uphold when making decisions. For nonprofessional helpers, principles include autonomy and safety.

Standards of Practice

- Standards of practice are ethical principles that are translated into active language to describe practices an ethical helper should engage in and involve:
  - competence, including helping competence and multicultural competence; and
  - confidentiality, including limits of confidentiality and informed consent.

References

American Association for Marriage and Family Therapy. (AAMFT, 2015). *AAMFT code of ethics*. Alexandria, VA: Author. Retrieved from www.aamft.org/Legal_Ethics/Code_of_Ethics.aspx?WebsiteKey=8e8c9bd6-0b71-4cd1-a5ab-013b5f855b01

American Counseling Association. (ACA, 2014). *ACA code of ethics*. Alexandria, VA: Author. Retrieved from www.counseling.org/resources/aca-code-of-ethics.pdf

American Psychological Association. (APA, 2016). Ethical principles of psychologists and code of conduct. *American Psychologist*, *57*, 1060–1073. Retrieved from www.apa.org/ethics/code/?item=8

Baird, B. N. (2014). *The internship, practicum, and field placement handbook* (7th ed.). New York: Routledge.

Beitel, M., Ferrer, E., & Cecero, J. J. (2005). Psychological mindedness and awareness of self and others. *Journal of Clinical Psychology*, *61*(6), 739–750.

Department of Health. (2018). Agency affiliated counselor: Frequently asked questions. *Washington State Department of Health*. Retrieved from www.doh.wa.gov/LicensesPermitsandCertificates/ProfessionsNewReneworUpdate/AgencyAffiliatedCounselor/FrequentlyAskedQuestions

Erford, B. T. (2014). *Orientation to the counseling profession: Advocacy, ethics, and essential professional foundations* (2nd ed.). Boston, MA: Pearson.

Faiver, C., Eisengart, S., & Colonna, R. (2004). *The counselor intern's handbook* (3rd ed.). Belmont, CA: Cengage.

Fraga, L., Garcia, J. A., Hero, R., Jones-Correa, M., Martinez-Ebers, V., & Segura, G. (2006). *Latino National Survey (LNS)*, 2006. ICPSR20862-v2. Ann Arbor, MI: Inter-University Consortium for Political and Social Research. doi:10.3886/ICPSR20862

Hill, C. E. (2014). *Helping skills: Facilitating exploration, insight, and action* (4th ed.). Washington, DC: American Psychological Association.

Ivey, A. E., Ivey, M. B., & Zalaquett, C. P. (2016). *Essentials of intentional interviewing: Counseling in a multicultural world* (3rd ed.). Boston, MA: Cengage Learning.

Johnson, W. B. (2007). *On being a mentor: A guide for higher education faculty*. Mahwah, NJ: Lawrence Erlbaum Associates Publishers.

National Association for Social Workers. (NASW, 2017). *NASW code of ethics*. Washington, DC: Author. Retrieved from www.socialworkers.org/About/Ethics/Code-of-Ethics/Code-of-Ethics-English

National Career Development Association. (NCDA, 2015). *NCDA Code of Ethics*. Retrieved from https://ncda.org/aws/NCDA/asset_manager/get_file/3395

Strang, D. G., Molloy, D. W., & Harrison, C. (1998). Capacity to choose place of residence: Autonomy vs beneficence? *Journal of Palliative Care*, *14*(1), 25–29.

Sue, D. W., & Sue, D. (2013). *Counseling the culturally diverse: Theory & practice* (6th ed.). New York, NY: John Wiley.

3 The LifeRAFT Training Approach

Chapter Goals

This chapter will prepare you to:

- Gain knowledge of the essential methods and components of nonprofessional helping skills training.
- Become aware of the essential principles of the LifeRAFT training model and how this model is distinct and valuable.
- Learn about the skills in the microskills hierarchy that you will accumulate and utilize.
- Identify the stages of the helping process. Through this, we will learn to navigate helping and consider the steps employed within the LifeRAFT training model.
- Examine research on the LifeRAFT model and microskills hierarchy as effective training methods.

Nonprofessional Helping Skills Training

In helping, as with everyday life, direction and focus are required to effectively navigate obstacles and move forward. Becoming an effective helper is challenging and requires effort and planning (Hill, 2014). We need methods that provide a framework regarding how we engage with helping, which includes how we think about it, dedicate our efforts toward it, and plan for success in each helping scenario. Below are some of the methods by which we learn to be more effective helpers. These include the methods of practice, role-playing, feedback, recording, and transcription and commentary. Each of these methods will be important to incorporate in your own LifeRAFT helping skills training and is discussed in detail below.

Practice

Practice is one of the most important components of effective helping skills training (Hill & Lent, 2006). Although instruction such as the information provided in this book is critical, it cannot effectively prepare you to be a helper without the aid of practice and rehearsal of the skills. To become an effective helper, it is important to attempt each component as you learn it and to continue rehearsing them even after your reading is complete. Much like practice is essential to maintaining and progressing in abilities such as learning a foreign language or playing an instrument, it takes many years to become an expert helper (Ivey, Ivey, & Zalaquett, 2016). So be sure to practice, practice, practice!

Research suggests that people learn best by doing (Myers, 2010), so engaging in real-life helping scenarios is an excellent method to hone your skills. While this method is not always available or ideal for beginners, there are several similar ways you can practice your newly acquired helping skills—in fact, you have already experienced a few of them in the previous chapters of this book. Below is a formal introduction to some of the methods you will use throughout this book to practice your emerging helping skills.

Modeling

One of the most valuable ways we learn is by observing others (Bandura, 1989). This process of learning behaviors by watching someone else and then imitating their actions is called "modeling" (Colman, 2015). When people model effective helping strategies for us, we learn those strategies and feel more confident and capable in our ability to help. Although modeling is not an exercise in direct practice, it is an opportunity to witness and experience helping in order that you can later imitate and integrate components into your own practice.

Models will be provided throughout this book in the form of transcripts, typically referred to as case examples, which are designed to provide descriptions of helping scenarios and helpee characteristics. These set a scene and provide additional context to a helping scenario, as well as describe skills appropriate for that situation, in order to provide a model for you to later imitate in your own helping practice. For example, when describing how to encourage a helpee to begin talking about distress, a case example of a unique scene may be provided. In this case, we will imagine your helpee to be a five-year-old boy named Kai, who is wandering around a shopping mall crying and lost from his father. You change your posture to lean down to his level and speak in a higher vocal tone more appropriate for interacting with a small child and say:

HELPER: Hi, I'm here to help you. What's wrong?
HELPEE: I'm lost, and I can't find my dad.

With case examples, actual conversations between helpers and helpees are provided in an effort to model the exact words and phrases that can be used to accomplish a particular skill. For example, when describing how to encourage a helpee to begin talking about their distress, a transcript may be provided, such as:

HELPER: How can I help you today?
HELPEE: I need to talk about the problems I'm having at home.

Note that transcripts always include the labels of helper and helpee because together they provide clarity and context to helper interventions.

Written examples of modeling will be helpful as you progress, but real-world models are also valuable. Consider seeking out mentorship in your journey to becoming an effective LifeRAFT helper. If you are enrolled in a helping skills course or workshop, ask your instructor to role-play case examples of helping for you. Watch your classmates practice their skills and write down things you want to say or try based on their unique approaches. In everyday life, watch and imitate those who help and support you. Note their word choice, style, and what makes them an effective helper to you and then try to imitate those characteristics when helping others.

Note that with both written and real-world modeling, you may have positive and negative reactions to word choices and style. This is expected and valuable; everyone's helping style is different. We want to find your helping style. Having reactions such as "I like how that was phrased" or "I would never say it like that" helps to identify what might work for you. Recognizing your preferences and how you might phrase certain interventions similarly or differently than the model will begin establishing your own helping style.

At the same time, be sure to not only scrutinize the word choice but also identify the example of the intervention in action. Techniques can be effectively modeled even when the words in the model are not ones common to you. For example, the phrase "My golly! Sounds like you're in a pickle, dear friend" might not fit your preferred word choice, helping context, or style. Yet notice this is an effort to empathize the challenge that someone is facing and a strategy to express understanding. Taking that technique and rephrasing it to better fit you might be, "This situation sounds really challenging." Notice how both achieve the same intervention but use different word choices and style to accomplish it.

Personal Reflections

Personal reflection exercises are provided throughout the book to help you think through a skill more deeply and apply it to your own life. These let you mentally imagine helping situations, with you either helping yourself or helping someone else. Self-help and imagination exercises have been found to be common and effective methods of learning how to be a helper (Hill & Lent, 2006). For example, you might be asked to imagine or recall a time when you had a disagreement with a family member or friend that left you feeling distressed afterward. What would you have wanted someone to say to help you with your distress? Using this method, you can use your imagination to generate helpful interventions that can be used on someone else. Personal reflections, like other methods of practice, provide firsthand exposure to how it feels to work with and receive helping skills.

Written Practice

Written practice exercises are also provided throughout the book with prompts for how you might respond to a particular helping situation with your newly acquired skills. For instance, a case example of a helpee might be provided with questions about how you, as the helper, might respond. For example, let's use the earlier case of Kai, the child who was separated from his father in a shopping mall. Written practice exercises might ask you, "What questions could you use to initiate a helping situation with Kai? Write out verbatim what you would say to him." Written practice provides the opportunity to select and develop specific responses but allows the process to move slowly and with minimal risk of error. Real-world conversations move quickly, and it can be difficult to think through a response before it is your turn to speak again. Written practice opportunities provide the space to think about and construct a response without the time pressures of conversation. Once written responses are constructed, it can be easier to then translate these ideas to actual helping situations.

Role-Play Practice

Practice through modeling, personal reflections, and writing exercises are all valuable methods (Hill & Lent, 2006), but none compares to the value of role-play practice (Egan, 2014). Role-play practice involves performing the roles of helper and helpee in a prearranged training setting (Baird, 2014). Role-plays typically involve two helping trainees, or a trainer and trainee, simulating a helping interaction. In these role-plays, each trainee takes a turn portraying the roles of a helper and a helpee in distress. This method offers the benefit of rehearsing helping skills in real time, with closely approximated conditions of exposure to distress and interpersonal interactions. This can all be achieved without the burden of the helpee being in actual distress. Role-plays also afford you the opportunity to experience the roles of both helper and helpee. Taking on the role of a person in distress builds empathy and understanding as well as provides additional opportunities for modeling by experiencing another helper at work (Baird, 2014).

Role-plays are most productive when participants agree on prearranged conditions. These conditions include mutual recognition that the goal of role-plays is to aid the helper's learning and skill development. Note these goals do not necessarily state that it is a priority to help the helpee. Although helping is always the goal, it is important to keep in mind that role-play helpees may or may not receive help. As discussed in Chapter 1, we know that helping, particularly from untrained helpers, is not always beneficial (Egan, 2014). Role-plays offer ideal controlled conditions for a helper to experiment with their emerging style and fully explore helping situations without concerns about protecting a fragile helpee. As the helper in role-plays, you should focus on practicing and mastering the skills being taught and incorporating those skills into your overall style and repertoire of competencies. This will likely take experimentation and repeated practice over time. To provide a safe learning environment, it is essential that both members of the role-play enter the interaction with the agreement that helping may not occur and the helpee is prepared to withstand any potential risks or ruptures (Baird, 2014).

Another prearranged condition of role-plays is that both members agree to be as "real" as possible. Once the role-play begins, both the helper and the helpee should discard the understanding that they are in a fictional situation in order to fully commit to their roles. This means avoiding the urge to "break character" or interrupt the role-play. Try not to stop the interaction to ask questions or comment on the role-play; instead, agree not to stop until the role-play is complete. Admittedly, role-plays are awkward because both members understand that the interaction is make-believe. Fabricating distress and empathy can feel odd and challenging yet embracing the discomfort and pressing forward can be a valuable learning experience. Surprisingly, many of the seemingly unusual experiences that occur in a role-play accurately represent experiences in real-life helping situations: helpers and helpees in actual distress have been known to break into nervous laughter, lose track of their thoughts and forget what to say, feel awkward and uncomfortable, or even want to discontinue an interaction (Rodríguez et al., 2018). If you can endure the challenges present in a role-play situation and gracefully navigate the discomfort without interruption, the awkwardness you encounter in real-life situations will seem far less challenging to overcome. As they say, the show must go on!

As a helpee, being "real" also requires that you fully embrace the role of a person in psychological distress. This involves adopting the words and story of distress by empathizing with others and displaying corresponding nonverbal characteristics. To the extent possible, allow yourself to experience distress in the moment. Feel what life might be like for someone going through the situation you develop (Baird, 2014). If concocting a fictitious situation presents difficulties with accessing believable distress, consider using past instances of real distress that you have since resolved or present real stressors that you can exaggerate without harming your psyche. That said, there is no expectation for you to disclose personally relevant information about yourself. If you have concerns about maintaining wellness after a role-play, it is encouraged that you share information that is fictitious and does not resemble concerns that involve yourself or close friends and family. For ideas about possible stressors or types of distress to embody during role-plays, consult "Problem Triggers" from Chapter 1.

Praise and Polish Feedback

Once a role-play is complete, you should obtain immediate feedback on your helping skills from your helpee. Feedback from your helpee's perspective can provide invaluable instruction and guidance for how your style is experienced and ways to improve in your helping skills.

Providing Feedback

Helpees should provide feedback to helpers using the "praise and polish" method. This method is an approach to offering specific supportive, genuine, and comprehensive reactions toward the helper's skills. These comments are aimed at assisting the helper to improve their helping skills by providing both positive and negative reactions.

Receiving feedback can be intimidating and helpers may feel vulnerable, so helpees should deliver feedback respectfully with a spirit of caring and support. Choose kind words and use an empathic tone when delivering feedback. Do not, however, shy away from offering your honest opinion. Helpers need to know what they are doing well and areas where they can improve. When in the role of a helpee, you have direct experience with how a helper's style feels to someone in distress. This unique perspective is invaluable. Trust that your instincts are important; if you had a reaction to something, chances are that other people will as well.

Also consider the "mum effect," a term from social psychology to describe people's natural reluctance to share negative feedback out of fear of themselves being seen negatively (Myers, 2010). Even though constructive feedback is necessary to learning and is often valued when given, people worry that giving constructive feedback will make them look uncaring or damage their relationship with the recipient. Thus, according to the mum effect, "mum" is the word. This concept captures how people rarely get honest and constructive feedback, even when they ask for it. Do your helper a favor and push through the mum effect to tell them the truth, despite that you might feel uncomfortable disclosing it.

To further illustrate, I provide a transformative example. I worked with a helper trainee who was provided with the feedback that he sat too close to his helpee and made her feel uncomfortable. She was hesitant about whether she should tell him; she wondered if it was just she who felt this way. The helpee took a chance and shared her discomfort with her helper. For the helper, this was the first time he received this feedback; however, he later discovered that he had been identified for years by others as a "close talker." He learned that his proximity made them uncomfortable but no one had the heart to tell him! After finally being told this polish during a helping role-play, he immediately began allocating more physical space with others, both in helping situations and in his everyday life. The feedback offered by his helpee generalized to his other relationships and improved them tremendously. He noted that although it was uncomfortable feedback to receive, he is forever grateful for the corrective opportunity. As the helpee providing feedback, remember to deliver your message with kindness and commit yourself to offering your honest reactions to your helper. Fight the mum effect and show your helper care and kindness through genuine and comprehensive feedback that includes both positives and negatives. You never know when it will change their helping—or all of their relationships—for the better.

Lastly, be specific in your feedback by explaining your reactions, providing examples, and identifying ways the helper can improve. Describe, in detail, what you experienced in order to offer context and clarity to your feedback. For example, saying "your body posture wasn't very inviting" is confusing and vague; instead, describing the specific instance and context makes for more useful feedback:

HELPEE: When I started talking about my mom, you crossed your legs and looked away, which felt less inviting than earlier when you were leaning in and looking at me.

Offer specific ideas for how they can improve, for example:

HELPEE: Next time, consider focusing on conveying more support through your body postures, such as leaning forward and increasing eye contact.

The praise and polish method of feedback begins with offering a praise, which is a strength or something that the helper did well and might consider doing again in future helping situations. For example, a praise may include:

HELPEE: I really like how you provided space for me to talk without interruption. Even when I stopped talking and needed a minute to think, I liked how you waited for me to do that rather than jumping in and talking again.

Next, offer a polish, which is advice for growth or something the helper might consider changing in future situations. For example, a praise may include:

HELPEE: I didn't find it as helpful when you said, "everyone feels that way." Although I appreciate your efforts to normalize what I'm going through, it felt kind of dismissive of my experience. Next time, you might change it to something like, "it's understandable that you'd feel that way," to let me know you're tracking with me.

Remember that offering both a praise and a polish are essential for comprehensive feedback. If you find yourself saying "It was good. I can't think of anything you could do differently," you need to more thoughtfully consider your experience as the helpee. There is no such thing as a perfect helping situation. There is always room for growth and ideas for improvement.

Video Recording

Another key element of helping skills training is video recording role-play practice sessions. According to Ivey et al. (2016), video recording helps to demystify your behavior in the session and develops your ability to work more effectively. Through the use of recording and, most importantly, reviewing videos, you become your own observer of the entire interaction. This allows you the opportunity to provide yourself with additional praise and polish feedback.

Video recording is easily available using computers, laptops, cell phones, and personal cameras. Check your existing tech gadgets for recording capabilities or obtain a recording device. Position the recording device so that both the helper's and the helpee's entire bodies are in the frame. See Figure 3.1 for an example.

Figure 3.1 Video Recording Frame

This perspective allows you to review body postures as well as all nonverbal gestures and movements. If the camera is positioned to catch only part of the interaction, you might miss important behaviors needing attention and review. An example of this is if you record only from the waist up, you might miss behaviors such as distracting leg swinging or nervous foot shaking. Reviewing the interaction in its entirety provides maximum opportunity for learning.

To record, first test the camera to ensure that voices are audible and clear. Consider adding an external microphone if acoustics are problematic. Set a timer on an agreed-upon length of helping session and then begin. Remember that informed consent also includes requesting and obtaining your helpee's permission to video record them prior to doing so. Never video record without participants' knowledge and permission first. This is an ethically appropriate behavior and is also legally mandated in some states (Patrick, 1989).

This book will guide you at key points in your training to fully review and analyze your helping skills using video recordings, but there is no need to limit yourself there. Helping skills experts recommend to video your practice sessions, "as frequently as possible" (Ivey et al., 2016, p. 152), both during training and in the future.

Transcribing and Commentary

A valuable component of helping skills training is transcribing and analyzing recorded role-play helping sessions. Transcribing is the act of writing down, word for word, what is said during a video-recorded role-play helping interaction. A commentary is a series of comments and explanations aimed at analyzing a transcribed role-play helping interaction.

Simply viewing video recordings can provide some helpful insights but transcribing and analyzing sessions in written commentaries provide far greater opportunities for deeper learning and growth (Ivey et al., 2016). Transcribing offers careful analysis of your actions during a role-play session. You can examine every intervention and statement you made in order to decide what you did well and what specifically you would like to improve on or do differently. Unlike other learning methods that focus on one, generalized praise and polish by your helpee, transcribing provides detailed, moment-by-moment insights from yourself with better quantity and quality of thoughtful reactions.

To create a transcription and commentary document, use the following process and format. Organize the transcript in two columns, with the left column labeled "Transcription" and the right column labeled "Commentary." See Table 3.1 as an example. In the left column, provide a transcription of everything you (the helper) and your helpee say during the session; also note any significant nonverbal behaviors in parentheses. Be sure to indicate who is speaking at the beginning of each interaction. The transcription process is time-consuming but well worth the effort. After transcription is complete, return to the beginning of the video and watch the role-play again, pausing after each helper response. In the right column, include an analysis of each helper intervention. Comment briefly on what you observe. Note your reactions to each of your interventions, your reasons behind particular interventions, your strengths, areas for growth, and/or ideas for alternative interventions or phrasing.

We have explored several helping skills training methods, including modeling, personal reflections, written exercises, and, most importantly, role-play practice. Furthermore, we examined several important aspects of role-playing, such as integrating praise and polish feedback, video recording, and transcriptions and commentaries. Throughout this book, you will be provided opportunities to engage in each of these training methods. You are also encouraged to add extra sessions to your training and practice throughout the duration of your work as a helper in order to continue to improve your skills and own your strengths as a LifeRAFT helper. Start this journey now by practicing, using the instructions below.

Table 3.1 Role-Play Transcription and Commentary

Transcription	*Commentary*
HELPER: Before we begin, I'd like to ask if I can video record this session. Do you mind?	It is important to make sure helpees give you permission to record them. I like that I appeared confident here. It seemed to put the helpee at ease.
HELPEE: Yes, that's OK with me.	
HELPER: What do you want to talk about? (Crossed legs; picked up clipboard)	I started to get nervous here and my question sounded more abrupt than I meant it to be. My fidgeting further evidenced nervousness. I would have preferred to keep my legs uncrossed and not picked up the clipboard. Maybe say instead, "What can I help you with?"
HELPEE: Well, I guess there's lots of things. I went through a difficult divorce and it was hard, but we've pulled ourselves together. The kids are doing better in school and I'm doing better. I've . . . ah . . . got a new friend. (breaks eye contact) But you know, I've been teaching for 13 years and really feel kind of bored with it. It's the same thing every day—I'm bored with it.	
HELPER: You say you're *bored* with it?	I noted the eye contact break when the helpee talked about her new friend—I thought it might be important, but I decided to ask about it later. The last thing a helpee says in a long string at the beginning of a session is often important to them, so I focused on that feeling of boredom as I started.

Role-Play Practice

The purpose of this exercise is to rehearse the components of effective helping skills training methods, including role-play practice, "praise and polish" feedback, video recording, and transcription and commentary. It is also to obtain a baseline of your natural style of communication and helping prior to any LifeRAFT training. This baseline will afford the opportunity to compare with your later work to track your training progress, so be sure to save this video for later use.

For this exercise, find a volunteer helpee to role-play a helping scenario with you and provide feedback afterward. Set a timer for at least 15 minutes and attempt to help using whatever comes naturally to you. Complete the following:

1. Consider pairing with a fellow helper-in-training and take turns being the helper and helpee.
2. Video record the scenario. Follow the ethical guidelines discussed in Chapter 2. Note that informed consent also applies to video recording, so permission is required to video record your helpee.
3. Ask your helpee to select a topic to discuss. Consult Chapter 1, "Problem Triggers," for topic ideas if you are stuck.
4. As the helper, attempt to help your helpee. Use your natural skills and communication style and engage in ways that seem appropriate to you in the moment.

5. At the end of the role-play, request feedback from your helpee about what you did well and what you could improve on next time. Write down their responses.
6. Review the recording. Create a transcription and commentary of the session; format it as described in the aforementioned discussion. Note your reactions to each of your recorded helper responses, specifically what you thought you did well and what you could improve on next time as the helper.
7. Write a summary of your overall role-play experience. Summarize your helpee's feedback and your own commentary responses by noting themes in feedback of praises and polishes. Construct a plan for strengths you want to continue to employ and areas for growth you plan to improve on next time.

Training Model

LifeRAFT Model

To be an effective helper, it is important to follow an established method of helping. Rather than relying on trial and error, which can result in bad helping or even hurting (Egan, 2014), following a prescribed method of helping offers safety and higher possibilities for success. The method we will follow to ensure good helping is an established training model I created called LifeRAFT, which stands for Life Relief through Actions, Feelings, and Thoughts. Once trained in the LifeRAFT model, you can feel confident in your skills as a trained LifeRAFT helper (Campbell, Davidson, & Davidson, 2017).

A training model is a "deliberately simplified and usually idealized and imaginary representation of a phenomenon" (Colman, 2015). Note that the LifeRAFT model is deliberately simplified and idealized, meaning that it contains a simple set of prescribed steps used to explain the helping process and train helpers. For the purpose of making exchanges more easily understandable, the model is simplified and presented in a step-by-step fashion that is unlikely to perfectly mirror real-life helping situations. Following a prescribed set of specific steps requires a highly controlled exchange, but when a helpee presents genuine distress in a real-life helping situation, the direction of the conversation cannot be perfectly predicted. Thus, real-world helpers will rarely follow LifeRAFT exactly to the letter. This is purposeful due to the value a simplified and idealized framework offers for a helper to understand and follow.

The value of LifeRAFT comes not from being a precise set of steps, but, rather, it is most useful when regarded as a general blueprint of what leads to good practice. You may drift away from some of the details in real-life situations, but if you can use the model to understand how helping works and remember its basic progression, you will be miles ahead of untrained helpers (Campbell et al., 2017).

LifeRAFT is a relatively new method of training nonprofessional helpers that is derived both from psychological theory and from empirical evidence (Campbell, 2013). Although other training models exist (e.g., Egan, 2014; Harris, Kelly, Campbell, & Hammond, 2014; Hill, 2014; Nelson-Jones, 2015), LifeRAFT is unique in providing an evidence-based model that is designed to provide instruction exclusively on how to apply counseling theories and techniques for nonprofessional helpers. In an effort to teach helping skills at a level suitable for nonprofessionals, I adapted LifeRAFT from a professional counselor model I originally co-developed with colleagues, called "Key Strategies Training for Individual Psychotherapy" (KST-IP; Harris et al., 2014). LifeRAFT offers several unique training benefits, including ethical considerations appropriate for nonprofessional helpers, a multi-theoretical basis, evidence-based techniques, and instruction beyond basic microskills training.

LifeRAFT Overview

LifeRAFT employs a nautical theme to better your understanding of the helping process and to capture your imagination in training for later retention and use. See Figure 3.2 for a visual depiction of the LifeRAFT model. As discussed in Chapter 1, distress can be understood as a helpee drowning in emotional turmoil and stuck in a whirlpool of distress. LifeRAFT guides you, as the helper, to serve as a psychological life raft to free helpees by pulling them out of the whirlpool and helping them navigate back to their life flow once again.

Helpers are trained to navigate this LifeRAFT rescue process by way of strategies, skills, stages, and steps. The nautical theme is continued through acronyms to help you memorize the components of the model. The acronym LifeRAFT helps you to remember the three strategies: Life Relief through Actions, Feelings, and Thoughts. The process involves using microskills (sorry, no clever nautical acronym here) to SWIM with your helpee through the four stages of

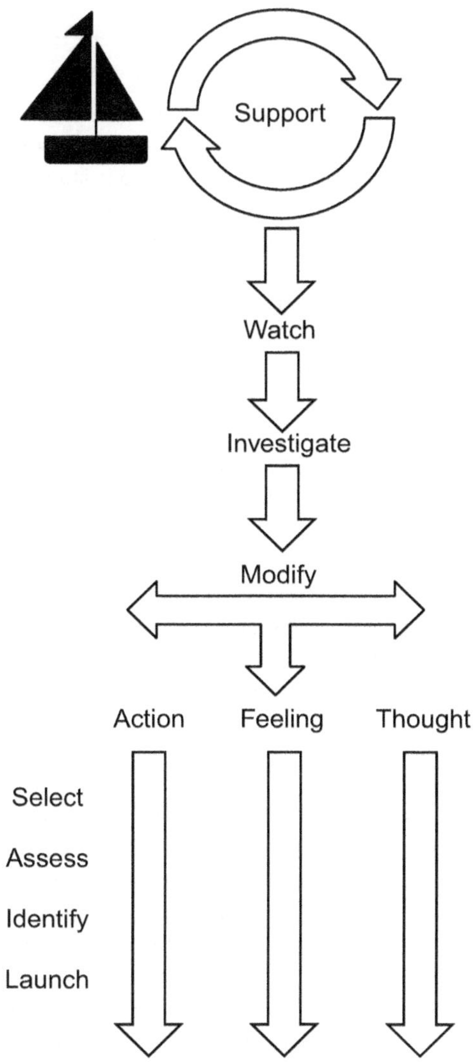

Figure 3.2 LifeRAFT Model

Table 3.2 LifeRAFT Stages

Stages (SWIM)	*Description*	*Microskills*
Support	Support your helpee by providing a foundation of empathic and nonjudgmental support, encouraging the helpee to help themselves and earning the right to influence them.	Level 1: attending, paraphrasing, reflecting feelings
Watch	Watch for warning signs of crises, assess for immediate concerns, and facilitate referrals to professional help when needed.	Level 1 Level 2: questions
Investigate	Investigate concerns to determine what is changeable, what help you can effectively provide, and prepare to move forward toward problem-solving.	Level 1 Level 2: questions, focusing
Modify	Modify concerns by engaging in a problem-solving process of selecting a focal area, assessing for problems, identifying potential improvements over problems, and launching toward improvement.	Level 1, Level 2 Level 3: information, logical consequences Level 4: confrontation, feedback Level 5: reframing, directives

helping: Support, Watch, Investigate, and Modify. Once you reach the modify stage, you SAIL through one of the strategies using four steps: Select, Assess, Identify, and Launch.

Taken together, the model proceeds as follows: A helpee is stuck in a distress whirlpool. Using microskills, you SWIM with them through four helping stages: (1) Supporting them in their distress, (2) Watching for warning signs of emergency, (3) Investigating concerns, and (4) Modifying concerns. When you get to the modify stage, you deploy your RAFT to identify a strategy of Relief through Actions, Feelings, or Thoughts. You then SAIL your helpee through the strategy using four steps: (1) Selecting and focusing on a strategy, (2) Assessing problems, (3) Identifying solutions, and (4) Launching toward solutions. Learning the LifeRAFT model involves learning microskills, SWIM stages, RAFT strategies, and SAIL steps. For a full summary of the LifeRAFT stages, see Table 3.2.

The goal of this process is for helpees to feel supported, be released from immediate distress, and feel capable of adjusting their sails to navigate the current and restore their life flow once again. If these goals are met, helping has occurred and you have provided an effective water rescue.

Now that a metaphorical overview of the model is understood, the following sections provide additional details about the strategies, skills, stages, and steps involved in working through the LifeRAFT helping skills model. The following sections provide a brief overview and introduction to the elaborated training of each component presented in subsequent chapters.

Strategies

LifeRAFT guides a nonprofessional helper in supporting someone currently in distress by focusing on the helpee's actions, feelings, or thoughts. In doing so, you will gain an understanding of how to be an effective nonprofessional helper and also an introductory understanding of three distinct professional counseling theories, which are presented as a guiding philosophy for each strategy.

Such a theoretically grounded approach is valuable for a variety of reasons. A theory in applied psychology is a set of principles organized into an explanatory framework, which is used to inform and guide the helping approach (Corey, 2009). Theories help us to identify and understand the specific nature of distress, as well as the corresponding ways to address the distress and seek a resolution.

For those who might consider a future in the professional mental health field, working with theory-based approaches also prepares you for additional training by providing initial exposure to clinical theories (Corey, 2009). Unlike simply learning about the content of the theory from a book or lecture-based course, LifeRAFT provides the opportunity to ethically use components of theories in nonprofessional practice. This information can be used as foundational experience to prepare for and make decisions about continuing training into professional clinical mental health professions.

LifeRAFT trains nonprofessional helpers to use actions, feelings, or thoughts as a theoretical strategy for change. The actions strategy draws from behavioral therapy based on Behavioral Activation Therapy (Martell, Dimidjian, Herman-Dunn, & Lewinsohn, 2010), the feelings strategy draws from Emotion-Focused Therapy (Greenberg, 2002; Greenberg & Watson, 2005), and the thoughts strategy introduces Cognitive Therapy (Beck, 2011).

Actions

The actions strategy is based on Behavioral Activation Therapy (Martell et al., 2010). It involves helping by encouraging a helpee to do something differently or commit to more effective behaviors. The LifeRAFT model suggests you use an actions-based approach with helpees when they present concerns related to stopping unwanted behaviors, meeting needs, and attaining goals. The actions strategy uses behavioral skills to identify effective actions and reward progress toward goals.

Feelings

The feelings strategy draws from Emotion-Focused Therapy (Greenberg, 2002; Greenberg & Watson, 2005). It involves encouraging helpees to feel and express their full range of emotions, in order to engage in catharsis and validation. LifeRAFT encourages you to use a feelings-based approach when helpees express concerns related to emotional expression, emotional congruence, or regulating and expanding the range and intensity of emotional expression. The feelings strategy uses emotion-based skills to explore and express adaptive over maladaptive emotions.

Thoughts

The thoughts strategy is based on Cognitive Therapy (Beck, 2011). It involves encouraging helpees to see their concerns from more functional perspectives. LifeRAFT suggests you use a thoughts-based approach when helpees' concerns involve developing rational beliefs based on objective evidence and motivated thinking that serves a useful function. The thoughts strategy employs cognitive skills to encourage the helpee to detect errors in thinking and form more accurate thoughts.

Skills

Now that we have been introduced to the LifeRAFT training model, we can now turn our attention to the skills we will use to progress through the model. Skills are the collection of distinct helping abilities you develop through training that enable you to use your training model (Egan, 2014). If your training model is your helping blueprint, your skills are each of the individual tools required for you to enact a proper helping situation. The skills we will use to conduct LifeRAFT helping are called "microskills."

Microskills Approach

Microskills are basic communication techniques that are broken down into individual skill units. Developed by counseling psychologist and helping skills expert Allen Ivey and his colleagues

(2016), microskills represent the foundation of interpersonal communication used in both counseling and everyday conversations. Examples of microskills include questions and advice, both of which are common to helping situations and professional counseling. By dissecting and categorizing our communication exchanges into individual skills, learning about microskills offers the opportunity to maximize conversational techniques for intentional helping practices.

Microskills Hierarchy

The microskills hierarchy we will use in the LifeRAFT model is an adaption of Ivey et al.'s (2016) original hierarchy and is outlined in Figure 3.3. This hierarchy is a list of microskills organized in a pyramid shape, with the skills that should be used most often at the bottom of the pyramid and the skills that should be used less frequently and after the helping scenario has progressed at the top of the pyramid. Note that the placement of each microskill on the hierarchy is intentional. This is meant to represent not only how quickly each microskill should be introduced into a helping scenario but also how often each microskill should be used throughout the scenario; microskills closer to the bottom of the pyramid should be introduced earlier and used most often throughout a helping situation.

Microskills are further categorized into listening skills and influencing skills, which will now be discussed, along with a brief introduction of each one.

Listening Skills

Listening skills are those microskills that are involved in the process of actively listening to our helpees. Listening is at the heart of helping; without it, we cannot possibly develop a connection and aid someone in distress. Active listening is not simply the act of hearing what a helpee says; rather, it is a process of intentional participation and response involving intentionally committing to understanding what the helpee is verbally and nonverbally communicating, experiencing their reality with them, and responding in ways that communicate to the helpee that you, as the helper, understand what they are saying and feel with them (Ivey et al., 2016). Throughout a helping

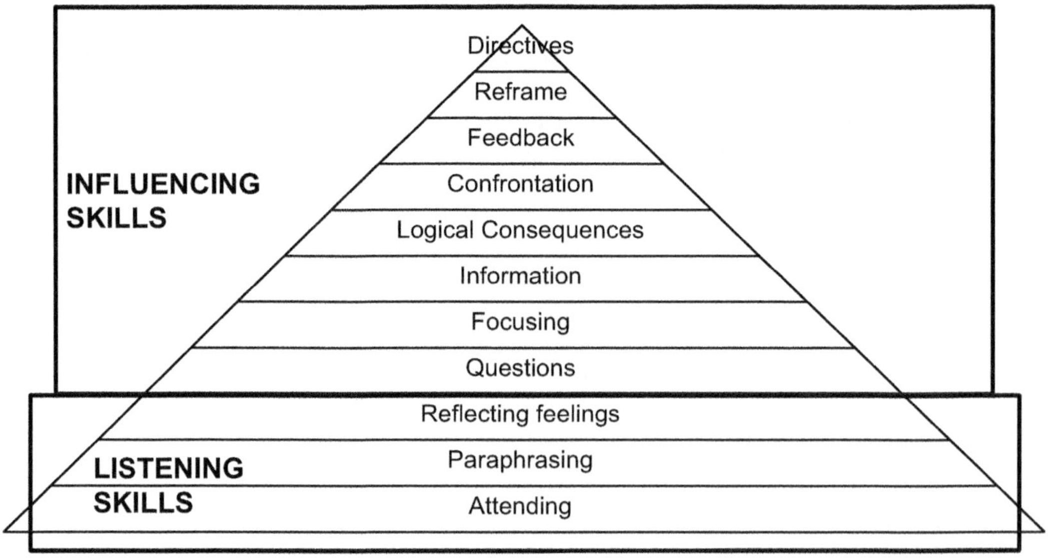

Figure 3.3 Microskills Hierarchy

situation, the helpee controls the direction of their story and disclosures, and we as helpers follow where they lead, reflecting back what we hear and witness.

Active listening is how we communicate empathy. This is the process of understanding and sharing the feelings of another person (Colman, 2015). Empathy means genuinely caring about your helpees, accepting them in full non-judgment, and communicating your care and understanding to them in a sensitive and accurate manner (Hill, 2014). It has been found to be the most important factor in whether helping is effective (Egan, 2014). Without empathy, good helping cannot take place. Thus, active listening skills are the most important skills to learn as a helper and are the skills you will use most often in helping situations.

The microskills involved in empathy-building and active listening are attending, paraphrasing, and reflecting feelings (Ivey et al., 2016).

ATTENDING

Attending represents the nonverbal and verbal behaviors that communicate support, including eye contact, vocal quality and tracking, and body language. Examples of attending behaviors include head nods and positive facial expressions, soft vocal tone, minimal verbal expressions, such as "hmm" or "uh-huh," and leaning forward. Attending gives your helpee the feeling that they are supported and listened to, as well as invites them to speak freely and openly with you in more detail.

PARAPHRASING

Paraphrasing involves shortening and clarifying the essence of what a helpee says by conveying the message back in your own words. An example paraphrase would be "I hear you saying that you're having a hard time fitting in." Paraphrasing makes helpees feel accurately heard and invites them to continue sharing.

REFLECTING FEELINGS

Reflecting feelings refers to identifying a helpee's key emotions and conveying them back to the helpee in order to clarify the helpee's affective experience. Feelings could be reflected in a statement such as "I see the hurt and fear in your eyes." This helps demonstrate that you understand and empathize with the helpee's emotional state and invite them to share their feelings in more depth.

Influencing Skills

Influencing skills are a category of microskills designed to influence the nature and direction of the conversation. Through selective attention and what you as a helper choose to emphasize, influencing skills are used to steer your helpee through what to discuss next. According to Ivey et al. (2016), influencing skills serve to guide helpees to "restory their lives, develop new ways of thinking and feeling, and take action to achieve desired goals" (p. 157). Influencing skills put the direction of helpees' disclosures more in the control of the helpers, and helpees tend to follow where they lead.

Although distinguished as influencing skills, it is important to note that listening skills can be just as influential, if not more (Ivey et al., 2016). Listening skills provide the basis for all good helping; a helper who takes too much control over guiding a helpee is not honoring their ethical purpose to support a helpee's ability to help themselves (Egan, 2014). It is vital that helpers use influencing skills sparingly and only after earning the right to do so, which is accomplished by using listening skills first. Even then, helpers should use caution and encourage helpees to set the direction of their disclosures as much as possible. Influencing skills are listed at the top of the microskills hierarchy to denote that they should be employed only after, and still less frequently than, listening skills (see Figure 3.3).

The microskills involved in influencing are questions, focusing, information, logical consequences, confrontation, feedback, reframing, and directives (Ivey et al., 2016).

QUESTIONS

Questions are defined as inquiries that are used to direct the helpee to provide certain information (Hill, 2014). Open questions draw out more information and require several words to answer them. An example of an open question is, "How are you feeling today?" Closed questions elicit specific information and can be answered in one or two words. A closed question example is, "When are you planning to meet your friend?"

FOCUSING

Focusing involves eliciting multiple perspectives to adjust the helpee's perception of an issue (Ivey et al., 2016). Helpees typically view their distress from only one lens. Focusing invites helpees to view their situation from multiple viewpoints to elicit new possibilities for change. We will learn several different angles from which to focus; one example is focusing on the present moment rather than on the past. Focusing on the present might include the following helper intervention: "Getting bullied as a child was hurtful. How do you feel talking about it now?"

INFORMATION

Information involves sharing specific facts with a helpee or teaching them specific skills to give the helpee motivation to act in new and more positive ways (Ivey et al., 2016). An example of information is, "Some people find it helpful to improve study habits by creating a plan using timed study periods with planned breaks."

LOGICAL CONSEQUENCES

Logical consequences refer to specific alternatives to a given decision with a helpee, including both positive and negative consequences that could logically result from each one (Ivey et al., 2016). In other words, we essentially develop a pro/con list with our helpee. For example, examining logical consequences might go as follows: "Let's look at what might happen if you decide to go to the party instead of studying for your exam. What positive things might result from this decision? What negative things might result?" This approach allows your helpee the opportunity to fully consider their options to choose what is best for them.

CONFRONTATION

Confrontation is defined as supportively challenging your helpee by highlighting conflicts, mixed messages, and discrepancies in verbal and nonverbal communication. Confrontation helps to empathically guide the helpee into facing opposition and reclaiming denied parts of themselves (Ivey et al., 2016). An example of confrontation is empathically stating, "You say you want to prioritize schoolwork, yet you continue to choose socializing over studying."

FEEDBACK

Feedback involves the helper transmitting reactions based on their own evaluation of the helpee (Egan, 2014). Just as we learned about how to provide feedback to fellow helpers in training, feedback toward helpees should be provided in the same way by using the praise and polish method. Recall that the praise and polish method involves offering supportive, genuine, comprehensive, and specific reactions. When used in a helping scenario, feedback is aimed at assisting the helpee to make changes by providing both positive and negative comments. An example of praise and polish feedback is, "I see how much effort you put into this and I admire your bravery for trying something new. One way you can improve next time is to engage in studying in a more conducive environment such as the library."

REFRAME

Reframing is defined as providing helpees with a new, more positive perspective on themselves and their concerns. It often involves taking a negative thought and reframing it by generating a more adaptive and balanced response (Ivey et al., 2016). For example, a helpee might say, "I'm a failure." A reframe in response would be, "I see you differently. When you say, 'I'm a failure;' I hear, 'I want to change.' That's admirable."

DIRECTIVES

Directives means providing helpees with instructions to follow specific actions (Hill, 2014), or, in other words, giving them advice. For example, "It would be helpful to write an email to your professor asking if you can set up a meeting to talk about your grade. Would you like some help with how to word the email?"

Microskills Ramp-Up

Integrating microskills into the LifeRAFT model is accomplished through the microskills ramp-up. The microskills ramp-up is a stepwise order of when and how helpers should use microskills during a helping situation. See Figure 3.4 for a depiction of this. Although microskills are effective for training helpers in what to say, microskills alone do not provide sufficient guidance to helpers in training regarding when and how to use these skills (Ridley, Mollen, & Kelly, 2011). The LifeRAFT model fills this gap in instruction through the addition of the microskills ramp-up. This ramp-up provides a structured method for using microskills.

The microskills ramp-up involves approaching a helping situation by using only listening skills first and progressing, as needed, to using influencing microskills. Influencing skills are added in a prescribed and stepwise fashion, always returning to the first levels of active listening before progressing up the levels. This is done in an effort to provide structure and direction to microskills. Thus, as a helper you begin at the first level of active listening skills (attending, paraphrasing, and reflecting feelings) and then "ramp-up" to the next level of microskills to questions and focusing. Once those are employed, you should return back to the first step of active listening. After that, you can "ramp-up" again to the next level of information and logical consequences, after which you again return to active listening, and so on. The microskills ramp-up structures responsible use of microskills, by encouraging change with more listening and less influencing at first and then gradually providing higher-level influencing skills as needed. This provides more space for helpees to guide the helping interaction and maximizes opportunities for them to help themselves.

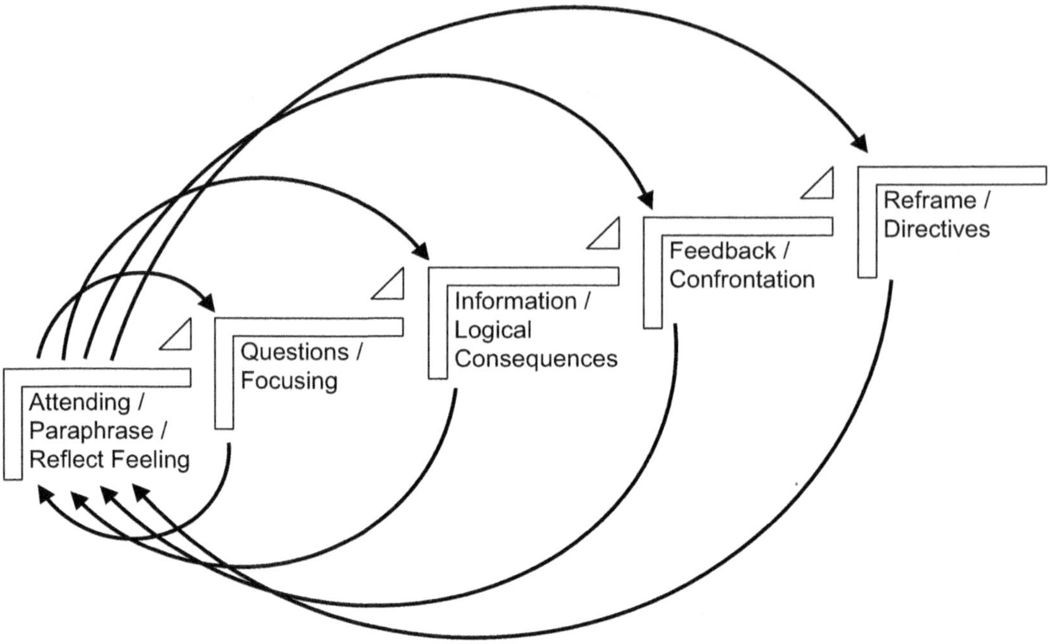

Figure 3.4 Microskills Ramp-Up

Stages

Now that we understand the metaphorical overview of the LifeRAFT model and the microskills used to navigate the process, we can turn to the stages involved in the LifeRAFT model. The four stages of the LifeRAFT model are those primary phases through which the helper should move to assist the helpee in freeing themselves from their distress and moving forward again on their own.

LifeRAFT involves four stages: (1) Support, (2) Watch, (3) Investigate, and (4) Modify (see Figure 3.5). You can remember these stages by the acronym SWIM; you SWIM with your helpee through the model. The following stages and progression of LifeRAFT described in this section are distinctive for nonprofessional helping skills training.

Stage 1: Support

Helper trainees are taught to begin a helping session by supporting the helpee through listening. This is what it means to "jump into the whirlpool of distress" with a helpee. You provide your helpee a foundation of empathic and nonjudgmental support, encourage them to help themselves, and earn the right to later exert influence as needed. Beginning only with the microskills of attending, paraphrasing, and reflection of feeling, your primary focus is to achieve and communicate that you hear what your helpee is saying, clearly see their point of view, and understand, as best as you can, the world as your helpee experiences it.

Stage 2: Watch

The second stage involves watching for warning signs and considering whether or not nonprofessional helping is appropriate or if helpees need referral to a professional. Continuing to use

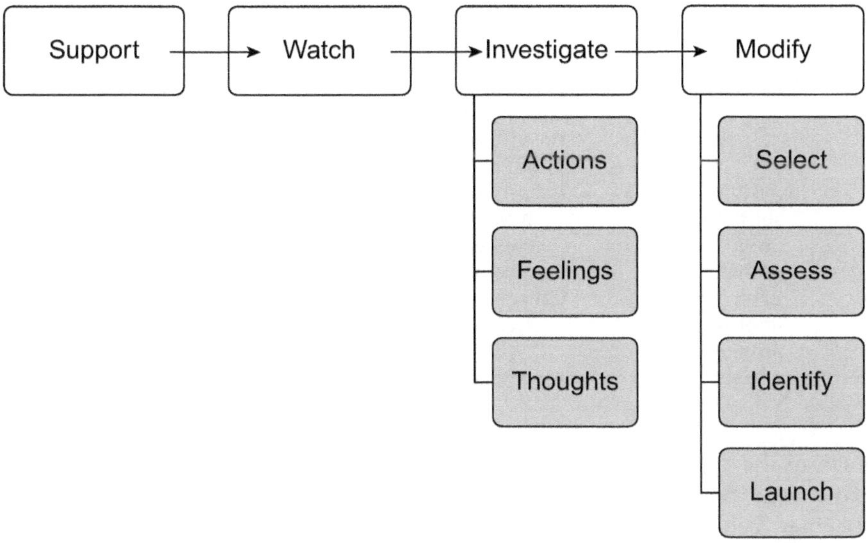

Figure 3.5 LifeRAFT Model Components

listening skills and adding the microskills of open and closed questions, you watch for warning signs of crises, assess for immediate concerns, and facilitate referrals to professional help when needed. Your goal is to ascertain whether your helpee's distress is at an appropriate level for your helping skills competence, a scope that includes nonlethal, immediate concerns that benefit from general support. Issues that benefit from professional monitoring and treatment should be referred; these include issues such as threat of harm to self or others, impaired mental status, psychosis, drugs and alcohol, or mental illness. Learning in the watch stage includes being taught how to remain calm, to use microskills to identify an appropriate professional, and to facilitate connecting your helpee with that professional when needed.

Stage 3: Investigate

The third stage of LifeRAFT is investigating concerns to determine what is changeable and what help you can effectively provide and to facilitate movement forward toward problem-solving. This involves surveying potential strategies of actions, feelings, and thoughts. Utilizing the microskills of listening skills, questions, and focusing, LifeRAFT trains you to identify your helpee's primary concern and the interplay of behaviors, emotions, and cognitions with the presenting problem. Because it's much easier and simpler to focus on one problem at a time, only one concern is chosen as a primary strategy. This approach is also recommended by underlying psychological theories. Each of the included theories asserts that the presenting issue can be addressed by focusing on one facet of the presenting issue: the behavioral, cognitive, or emotional component. The expectation is that improvements in one area will lead to similar improvements in the other two areas. For example, engaging in more functional thinking is expected to result in more adaptive feelings and effective actions.

Stage 4: Modify

The fourth step is modification through the chosen strategy of actions, feelings, or thoughts based on your helpee's ability, comfort, and interest in discussing each area, as well as your

Table 3.3 LifeRAFT Stage 4: Modify

SAIL Steps	*Description*	*Action Steps*	*Feeling Steps*	*Thought Steps*
Select	Select a focal area	Select and focus on actions	Select and focus on feelings	Select and focus on thoughts
Assess	Assess for problem	Assess ineffective actions	Assess maladaptive feelings	Assess dysfunctional thoughts
Identify	Identify potential shifts for improvement over problem	Identify potential shifts from ineffective to effective actions	Identify potential shifts from maladaptive to adaptive feelings	Identify potential shifts from dysfunctional to functional thoughts
Launch	Launch toward improvement of problem	Launch toward effective actions	Launch toward adaptive feelings	Launch toward functional thoughts

discernment of the appropriate course of action. You pick a RAFT, meaning that you select a strategy of actions, feelings, or thoughts to pursue a resolution to the helpee's concern.

Modification is the phase where basic problem-solving occurs. Most of us naturally engage in basic problem-solving steps when we encounter a problem for ourselves (Ivey et al., 2016); however, it may be so automatic that we engage in these steps without realizing we are doing so. The steps outlined in the modification stage are intended to increase awareness and intentionality around the problem-solving process, in order for helpers to be prepared to guide a helpee through the process.

Within the chosen area, the helper works with the helpee through four steps in order to guide them through solving their own problems (see Table 3.3). The steps are a four-part sequence within the modification stage that allow the process of problem-solving modification to occur. Thus, stage four involves not just one singular objective, as is the case in stages one through three; stage four (modify) is comprised of a sequence of four SAIL steps. You SAIL with your helpee through one of the strategies of the model. The SAIL steps are similar for each strategy and follow the same sequence, as outlined in Table 3.2 and discussed in the following section.

Steps

Step 1: Select

The first step involves selecting a strategy of actions, feelings, or thoughts. Using the microskills ramp-up, helpers use attending, paraphrasing, reflection of feeling, questions, and focusing to select a strategy and encourage helpees to talk specifically about how the chosen strategy impacts their concern. For example, a helpee may talk about an argument with their roommate. Applying the actions strategy, a helper might ask their helpee to discuss what actions the helpee has taken since the argument. Using a feelings approach, a helper might instead ask the helpee how they feel about the argument.

Step 2: Assess

The second step involves assessing problems in the given strategy that are holding the helpee back from resolving the present issue. Depending on the chosen strategy, this may be conceptualized as ineffective actions, maladaptive feelings, or dysfunctional thoughts. Using the microskills ramp-up, helpers are instructed to add information and logical consequences as needed in order to help guide the helpee in exploring their potential stuck points. For instance, a helpee might assess the possibility that ineffective actions such as avoidance and gossip are worsening the situation after an argument with a roommate.

Step 3: Identify

The third step involves evaluating solutions by distinguishing problematic actions, feelings, and thoughts from non-problematic ones. Helpers add more microskills, including confrontation and feedback, to guide helpees in an evaluation of problematic options as opposed to non-problematic alternatives. In the example of roommate conflict, using an actions approach would involve guiding the helpee in thinking through the ineffective results of actions, such as avoidance and gossip, and the effective results of other actions, such as apologizing and resolving the dispute.

Step 4: Launch

The fourth and final step involves launching toward a helpful and healthy resolution. Helpers add the remaining microskills, including reframing and directives as needed, to motivate their helpees toward a new perspective and a healthier direction. This is done in an effort to resolve the presenting issue. The fourth strategy most notably involves plans to engage in non-problematic choices (i.e., solutions) that have been identified previously, including effective actions, adaptive feelings, and functional thoughts. With the example of the actions approach used for helping with roommate conflict, the helper might guide the helpee in viewing their ongoing distress as a sign that they need to discontinue avoidance and self-shaming behaviors. The helper may encourage the helpee to make plans to approach the roommate in an attempt to move toward reconciliation.

Written Practice

Now that you have learned about the LifeRAFT approach, particularly the four SAIL steps, let's try applying them to your own life. Although we will learn in later chapters how to apply these steps to specific strategies of actions, feelings, and thoughts, it can be helpful to work with them broadly at first. You will notice that these four steps represent the basics of problem-solving, and oftentimes we engage in these steps without even realizing we are doing so.

This exercise will help you to become more aware and intentional in your problem-solving process. When you are more aware of these steps and how they can operate in your own life, it becomes easier to help others to adopt them as well. Try these four steps with a problem in your own life by considering a challenge, conflict, or decision you are currently facing and answering the following questions. An example is provided in italics to help guide your own responses:

- **Step 1: Select.** What is going on?
  I'm upset because I don't have a car and need reliable transportation to work.
- **Step 2: Assess.** What about your role in this situation might be a problem? What might not be working?
  I continue to rely on other methods of transportation that are unreliable. Buying a car seems like a logical course of action, but I'm scared and don't know where to start.

- **Step 3: Identify.** What might need to change? What is a possible solution or way of coping with the problem? What are the benefits of this option? What are the drawbacks?
  I need to secure reliable transportation. One possible solution is to buy my friend's car. Benefits are that my friend already offered to sell it to me, it is a convenient option, I don't need to do extra research, and it will help my friend to sell it. Drawbacks are that it's a bigger car than I wanted, it costs more than I hoped to spend, buying and selling from a friend could strain our relationship, and I might miss out on better options.
- **Step 4: Launch.** Based on this information, how do you want to move forward?
  Seems like buying my friend's car may not be the best solution for me at this time. Perhaps I should instead address my fear and uncertainty about car buying first by researching the process and finding a good fit for me.

Research Support

Before we begin training, know that the training methods presented in this book have research support. The LifeRAFT model and the microskills hierarchy have been demonstrated to benefit helpees. These approaches are empirically supported, meaning that they have been studied and that research endorses them as effective training methods (Campbell et al., 2017; Ivey et al., 2016).

LifeRAFT Research

LifeRAFT demonstrates the importance of evidence-based practice, which has been identified as a vital consideration for nonprofessionals (APA, 2013). The LifeRAFT model draws from three empirically supported psychotherapy treatments, and the effectiveness of the LifeRAFT model itself continues to be studied in order to further emphasize the importance of empirically supported practice.

LifeRAFT demonstrated empirical support in an initial pilot study. This study sought to determine whether the LifeRAFT helping model is an effective training method for undergraduate helpers. My research colleagues and I (Campbell et al., 2017) hypothesized that LifeRAFT training would demonstrate significant improvements in helping skills effectiveness compared to no training and teaching only microskills. We tested three hypotheses, and the results revealed the following:

1. Helpees reported higher effectiveness ratings for LifeRAFT role-playing scenarios, more than those for untrained and microskills-trained scenarios.
2. Helpers reported the highest levels of effectiveness for LifeRAFT-trained helping scenarios.
3. Trained LifeRAFT observers reported the highest levels of effectiveness for LifeRAFT-trained helping scenarios.

Thus, from the perspective of the helpee, helper, and a trained third-person observer, LifeRAFT training demonstrated significant improvements in helping skills effectiveness compared to no training or training in microskills.

Microskills Research

While microskills are enhanced by the LifeRAFT model, research strongly supports the usefulness of the microskills hierarchy itself. More than 450 national and international research studies have been conducted on microskills. It has been translated into 25 languages and used in more than 1,000 teaching programs. Employed with a variety of people, from beginning helpers to experienced mental health professionals, microskills have been found to be effective for training a wide variety of people to be nonprofessional helpers and professional counselors. Microskills have also been found to improve overall communication with family, friends, and coworkers (Ivey et al., 2016).

Thus, microskills have overwhelming support in the research literature, and these studies confirm findings from the perspective of the helpee, helper, and a trained third-person observer that all viewpoints agree this is an effective approach.

Research Conclusion

With the research findings on LifeRAFT and microskills, you can be confident that the combined framework offered in this book provides an excellent helping skills introduction superior to untrained helping. LifeRAFT is a helping skills training model that shows promising research results. The use of microskills has a demonstrated track record. Recent observers have noted that an approach integrating a broader model of competence with skills-based training is needed (Ridley et al., 2011), such as that provided by LifeRAFT. Future research with this model is critical to provide nonprofessionals with the highest level of helping skills training our growing field has to offer. With the research thus far, we can conclude that our helping skills training method using LifeRAFT and microskills works when trying to effectively help. You will be a better helper after reading this book, so let's get started with your training!

Summary

In this chapter we discussed the following:

Training

- Nonprofessional helping training involves practice through a variety of methods, including modeling, personal reflections, written exercises, and, most importantly, role-play practice.
- A valuable training asset is the praise and polish method, in which helpees offer the helper an evaluation of what they thought the helper did well and an area that they can improve.
- Valuable components of training also include video recording role-plays and creating a transcription and commentary of practice sessions in order for helpers to analyze their helping competencies.

Model

- LifeRAFT is an established, theoretically based training model that stands for Life Relief through Actions, Feelings, and Thoughts.
- It provides instruction on how to apply counseling theories and techniques in an introductory format that is appropriate for nonprofessionals' level of training and skill, containing strategies, skills, stages, and steps.
- LifeRAFT offers training using an approach grounded in counseling theories through the strategies of:
    - action, based on Behavioral Activation Therapy,
    - feeling, grounded in Emotion-Focused Therapy, and
    - thought, based on Cognitive Therapy.

Skills

- LifeRAFT integrates the microskills approach, which uses basic communication techniques that are broken down into individual skill units.
- Microskills are categorized into:
  - Listening skills, which include attending, paraphrasing, and reflecting feelings.
  - Influencing skills, which include questions, focusing, information, logical consequences, confrontation, feedback, reframing, and directives.

Stages

- The combined framework of the LifeRAFT model with the microskills approach trains helpers to navigate helpees through the helping stages of SWIM: (1) Support, (2) Watch, (3) Investigate, and (4) Modify.

Steps

- In the fourth stage of modify, helpers continue to guide helpees through a strategy of RAFT: Relief through Actions, Feelings, or Thoughts by employing the steps of SAIL: (1) Select, (2) Assess, (3) Identify, and (4) Launch.

Research

- The LifeRAFT model draws from three empirically supported psychotherapy treatments, and the LifeRAFT model itself has empirical support as an effective training method.
- Integration of the microskills method is strongly supported by research demonstrating the usefulness of the microskills hierarchy.
- Taken together, research findings suggest you can be confident in the LifeRAFT and microskills combined framework for effective helping skills training.

References

American Psychological Association. (APA, 2013). *APA guidelines for the undergraduate psychology major*. Washington, DC: Author. Retrieved from www.apa.org/ed/precollege/about/psymajor-guidelines.pdf

Baird, B. N. (2014). *The internship, practicum, and field placement handbook* (7th ed.). New York: Routledge.

Bandura, A. (1989). Perceived self-efficacy in the exercise of personal agency. *The Psychologist: Bulletin of the British Psychological Society, 2*, 411–424.

Beck, J. S. (2011). *Cognitive therapy: Basics and beyond* (2nd ed.). New York, NY: Guilford Press.

Campbell, E. L. (2013, April). *Key introductory strategies training: Training paraprofessionals in basic helping skills*. Symposium conducted at the annual meeting of the Western Psychological Association, Reno, NV.

Campbell, E. L., Davidson, K., & Davidson, S. M. (2017). Effectiveness of LifeRAFT undergraduate helping skills training model. *Psychology Teaching Review, 23*(2), 32–41.

Colman, A. M. (2015). *A dictionary of psychology* (4th ed.). Oxford: Oxford University Press.

Corey, G. (2009). *Theory and practice of counseling and psychotherapy* (8th ed.). Belmont, CA: Thomson/Brooks/Cole.

Egan, G. (2014). *The skilled helper: A problem-management and opportunity development approach to helping* (10th ed.). Belmont, CA: Brooks/Cole.

Greenberg, L. S. (2002). *Emotion-focused therapy: Coaching clients to work through feelings*. Washington, DC: American Psychological Association.

Greenberg, L. S., & Watson, J. C. (2005). *Emotion-focused therapy for depression.* Washington, DC: American Psychological Association.

Harris, J. E., Kelly, L. J., Campbell, E. L., & Hammond, E. S. (2014). Key strategies training: An introduction to multitheoretical practice. *Journal of Psychotherapy Integration, 24*(2), 138–152. doi:10.1037/a0037056

Hill, C. E. (2014). *Helping skills: Facilitating exploration, insight, and action* (4th ed.). Washington, DC: American Psychological Association.

Hill, C. E., & Lent, R. W. (2006). A narrative and meta-analytic review of helping skills training: Time to revive a dormant area of inquiry. *Psychotherapy, 43*(2), 154–172. doi:10.1037/0033-3204.43.2.154

Ivey, A. E., Ivey, M. B., & Zalaquett, C. P. (2016). *Essentials of intentional interviewing: Counseling in a multicultural world* (3rd ed.). Boston, MA: Cengage Learning.

Martell, C. R., Dimidjian, S., Herman-Dunn, R., & Lewinsohn, P. M. (2010). *Behavioral activation for depression: A clinician's guide*. New York, NY: Guilford Press.

Myers, D. G. (2010). Chapter 12: Helping. In D. G. Myers (Ed.), *Social psychology* (10th ed., pp. 440–480). New York: McGraw-Hill.

Nelson-Jones, R. (2015). *Basic Counseling Skills: A Helper's Manual.* (4th ed.). Thousand Oaks, CA: Sage.

Patrick, K. D. (1989). Unique ethical dilemmas in counselor training. *Counselor Education and Supervision, 28*(4), 337–341.

Ridley, C. R., Mollen, D., & Kelly, S. M. (2011). Beyond microskills: Toward a model of counseling competence. *The Counseling Psychologist, 39*(6), 825–864.

Rodríguez, J. R., López, A. B., Escolano, A. F., García-Grau, E., García, C. S., Fort, G. B., . . . Pros, M. A. (2018). Peer counselling versus role-playing: Two training methods of therapeutic skills in clinical psychology. *Psicothema, 30*(1), 21–26.

4 Stage One

Support

Chapter Goals

This chapter will prepare you to:

- Learn about support, the first stage of the LifeRAFT helping skills model, and why all helping begins with supporting.
- Become aware of when to use supporting and how to choose whether or not to engage in helping.
- Develop methods to engage in the support stage by using listening skills of attending, paraphrasing, and reflecting feelings.
- Identify what to expect as a result of supporting a helpee.

Introduction

This chapter will focus on supporting, the first stage of the LifeRAFT model. To prepare us to learn about this stage, we return to our water rescue metaphor.

Emotional distress is analogous to being swept up in a whirlpool and drowning in it. We have all been in the position of the helpee before: distressed and unsettled, we tend to ruminate on our problems and focus on the same aspects over and over again, a process that feels much like spinning helplessly in a whirlpool.

Sometimes our distress goes unnoticed, but other times it is recognized by others or we call attention to it by requesting help. We have all been in that helper situation, too: a distressed helpee looks to us for rescue as we watch them "spin" in their problems.

Frequent questions that arise from helpers are, "How can I help? What can I say or do to save this person from their despair?" Answers are not readily apparent to most of us without specialized helping skills training, as is evidenced by the fact that internet search engines and discussion boards are flooded with questions and articles regarding "what to say . . ." followed by the experience of a psychological stressor such as "when someone dies," "to someone with depression," and so forth. In response, many articles have been written for nonprofessional audiences briefly describing what to do (e.g., Campbell, 2017) or not do (e.g., Leahy, 2011) to help someone in emotional turmoil.

It is perhaps ironic that we do not know how best to help people in distress, given the fact that we have all been (and will continue to be again) in that situation and likely sought out others for help. Reflecting on that process and what was most helpful to you in those moments can be a particularly useful place to begin.

Personal Reflection

Consider help you have received in your own life. Recall times when you felt as if you were stuck in a whirlpool of emotional distress and others attempted to rescue you. Based on these experiences, answer the following questions:

- Describe a time when someone tried to help you out of emotional distress and it was helpful. What did they do that was helpful? What did you learn about helping from this experience?
- Describe a time when someone tried to help you out of emotional distress and it was unhelpful. What did they do that was unhelpful? What did you learn about helping from this experience?

When we consider what is most helpful to us when we are in distress, most people identify one of two things: people who (1) attended to their emotional needs or (2) assisted them in resolving a problem.

Attending to emotional needs is called "emotion-focused helping" (Myers, 2012). Emotion-focused helping is a method for coping with distress in which the focus is shifted away from the stressor and onto the emotional needs related to a stress reaction. Reactions to effective emotion-focused helping might include, "I felt listened to," "My helper understood what I was going through," and "My feelings were validated." Emotion-focused helping is a particularly effective strategy for circumstances in which situational influences cannot be changed (Myers, 2012). For example, emotion-focused helping may be used with a helpee, Niko, who feels grief over a friend moving away. Because the friend cannot be brought back (i.e., the stressor cannot be changed), effective helping involves attending to the sadness itself (i.e., the distress reaction), perhaps by listening and affirming Niko's feelings about the event.

Helping someone solve a problem is referred to as "problem-focused helping" (Myers, 2012). Problem-focused helping is a method to cope with distress in which the focus is placed on resolving the stressor or addressing a stressful situation directly. Reactions to effective problem-focused helping might include "I got the answer I needed," "My helper gave great advice for what to do," and "We came up with a plan." Problem-focused coping is an effective stress management strategy when situational influences are under a person's control and can be changed (Myers, 2012). For example, problem-focused helping may be used with a helpee, Sofia, who feels anger toward a noisy roommate. A helper might suggest that Sofia can cope with her anger (i.e., the distressing reaction) by directly addressing the noisy roommate (i.e., the stressor), perhaps by confronting the roommate about the noise.

Thankfully, LifeRAFT will guide you in how to engage in both emotion-focused and problem-focused helping strategies, depending on the needs of your helpee. The challenge many helpers face during the initial stage of helping is that they rush too quickly to problem-focused helping by giving advice. You may have identified times from your own experience with reactions such as "My helper just tried to tell me what to do" or "They told me things I already knew or had tried." We learned in previous chapters about the dangers of prematurely giving advice. In Chapter 1, we discussed how this method contradicts our goal to guide helpees to help themselves, and we explored in Chapter 2 how excessive advice-giving is unethical because it interferes with helpee autonomy and might lead us to make suggestions outside our scope of competence.

Guiding a helpee through their own problem-solving process is tricky and should not be rushed (Egan, 2014). The challenge with problem-focused helping is that it relies on the helpee's perceived control. People tend to seek problem-focused helping strategies only when they feel a sense of control over a situation and believe they can change either themselves or the circumstances to remedy the issue (Myers, 2012). In distress, helpees rarely feel in control. Sometimes, when a helpee is flooded in emotional distress and a helper immediately engages in problem-focused helping, it can invalidate the helpee's experience of powerlessness and increase feelings that life is beyond their control. Even in circumstances where helpees seek aid but do feel a sense of agency, they may still exhibit a preference for emotion-focused helping anyway (Connor-Smith & Flachsbart, 2007). Thus, problem-focused helping is less preferred in most helping situations, especially at the beginning. Until a better understanding of the helpee's situation is firmly established and emotional needs are met, helpers would be wise to avoid problem-solving altogether. Instead, helpers should begin by supporting.

Description of Supporting

Supporting is the first stage of the LifeRAFT helping skills model (see Figure 4.1; Support) and involves connecting and strengthening your relationship with your helpee. Research consistently suggests that the therapeutic relationship is one of the most important predictors for a positive

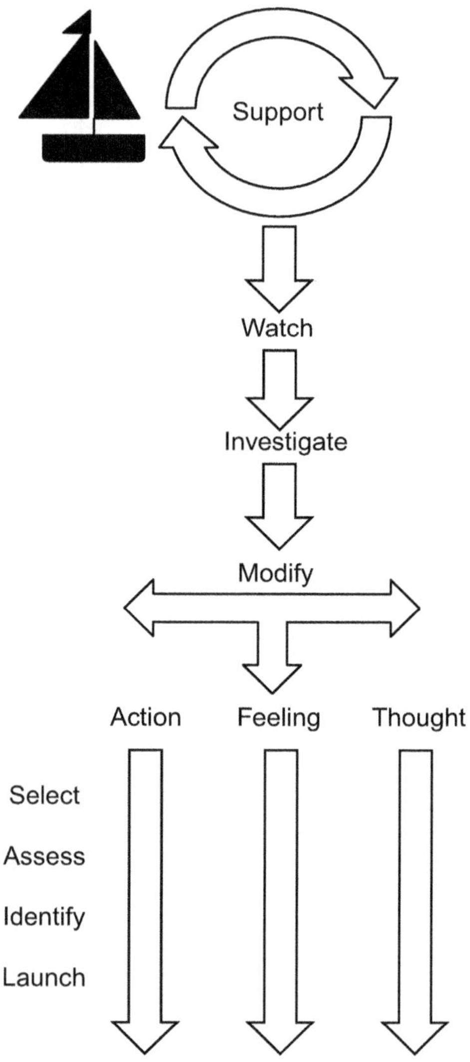

Figure 4.1 LifeRAFT Model

therapy outcome (Horvath & Bendi, 2002), as well as nonprofessional counseling scenarios (Kim et al., 2018). In both professional and nonprofessional counseling situations, there is no guarantee the helper and the helpee have a preexisting relationship. Thus, attention must be given to this relationship in every helping interaction. We will frequently talk about "earning the right" to enter into a helpee's experience and assist them with an issue; a fundamental component of earning this right is first attending to the relationship and building or reinforcing any existing connection each and every time we help.

We accomplish this by entering into the helpee's experience with them. In this case, we leap into the whirlpool with our helpees to earn the right to intervene rather than trying to snatch them out of it. They may repeat vague phrases of upset or recount the same details multiple times, and as they spin in their distress, we spin with them, listening, feeling, observing, and experiencing what they experience.

Although we may feel as if nothing is happening or we are continually covering the same information, supporting accomplishes several important goals. Supporting provides an implicit willingness to help. Rushing to judgment with quick solutions is not only disempowering and often unwelcome, it also communicates an unwillingness to fully engage in helping and instead brushes aside the issue with a quick fix (Egan, 2014). Supporting, on the other hand, shows that you are willing to expend time and energy into helping by seeking first to understand the helpee and their problems. For some, this is all the help they need (Corey, 2009). When helpees say they "just want someone to listen," they are usually communicating that they are simply in need of support. Although this process can take time and patience, it is well worth it. Supporting provides helpees a sense of safety and the feeling that they can discuss their concerns free from judgment or ridicule. This process is important for both relationship-building and for the helpee. When you focus on listening, your helpee has an opportunity to hear their own thoughts and feelings out loud, which often produces a catharsis or a release of previously blocked feelings (Breuer & Freud, 1974). New insights or courses of action may also emerge, thereby allowing the helpee to immediately work through their concern on their own. In this way, supporting establishes a foundation of emotion-focused helping, by attending to their needs and validating their emotions.

Practice Exercise

In our fast-paced world, people rarely have the opportunity to just talk without interruption. One of the most important and powerful gifts a helper can provide a helpee is simply a listening ear. In addition to building relationships, it offers helpees the opportunity to connect with themselves. Hearing ourselves talk provides new insights into ourselves, opportunity to discover our own answers, and release intense feelings that have been blocked (Corey, 2009). Although these benefits typically occur with another person listening and supporting, catharsis can also occur when a person is alone but attending to their own voice.

Try it for yourself! Choose a concern you are currently facing and find a space to be alone and talk out loud. Set a timer for ten minutes and begin talking to yourself out loud about the problem. Do not stop until the timer sounds. For added insight, video or audio record yourself talking and review the video afterward. Once you have completed this exercise, reflect on it by responding to the following questions:

- What was it like for you to talk about your concern uninterrupted? What did you gain from the experience, in terms of insights, answers, action steps, catharsis, and so forth?
- What did this experience teach you about the value of providing helpees with opportunities to talk? What was missing from your experience that highlights the value of talking to another person?

When to Support

Engaging in the supporting stage, or beginning a helping session, occurs either when a helpee approaches you with a request for help or you approach a helpee who appears in need of help. Once the two of you have agreed that you both are willing to engage, the helping situation commences.

The most common sign that supporting is needed is psychological distress, where the helpee is experiencing unpleasant thoughts, actions, and feelings that impact their ability to function in a healthy and adaptive way. The signs of this may seem obvious; however, they can be harder to discern than you might think. Research suggests that noticing signs of change in another and interpreting them as signs of distress take longer and require more conscious effort than we typically employ (Latane & Darley, 1968). In fact, people regularly mistake even forceful requests for help as innocuous events: desperate shrieks are misinterpreted as joyful squeals, assaults as roughhousing, and death as sleep (Myers, 2010). We do this because we want to assume that everything is okay, and we do not want to embarrass anyone by overreacting. So instead, we often err by not reacting to others' distress. As helpers, we need to fight against these social pressures by staying attuned to potentials for distress, risking embarrassment or appearing foolish, and checking in with people when we suspect help might be warranted.

The good news is that by reading this book you are more likely to notice people in distress, correctly interpret their behavior as signs of distress, and do something to help. People with exposure to helping skills, even simply reading about them, are more likely to stay attuned and actually engage in helping when needed (Myers, 2010). Additionally, the helping skills practice provided throughout this book will increase your likelihood even more because helping behaviors increase future helping. Nevertheless, begin to make a conscious effort and look for changes in the people around you to notice potential distress.

Deciding Whether or Not to Help

Although engaging in the support stage can often represent an implicit agreement to help, it is important to remember that you always have a choice whether or not to help someone. This is particularly true for nonprofessional helpers in their everyday lives with family and friends. Engage in careful decision-making before entering a helping situation. For nonprofessional helpers in occupations where it is their job to help, this decision may be less under your control; still, it is helpful to check in with yourself to determine if you are currently able to offer effective helping and how to best navigate the request.

Declining a Helping Request

Feelings of obligation and guilt can emerge when considering whether to decline a helpee's request for assistance. It seems cruel to watch someone struggling to stay afloat and deny them help. Yet even water rescuers are taught to "reach or throw, don't go," meaning do not fully engage in a water rescue unless you deem it safe and appropriate to do so (American Red Cross, 2018, p. 1). Throwing yourself into a "rescue" without considering your own abilities can put yourself and your helpee at additional risk.

There are legitimate reasons why you may want to be prepared to say no to helping. One important consideration is time. Studies show that people are more likely to help those in distress when they have the time to do so but decline to help when they are rushed or have competing obligations (Darley & Batson, 1973). This may strike some as selfish and run counter to our ethical obligation for beneficence to do good for our helpees (APA, 2016), but it is quite the opposite. Following the ethical obligations of professional counselors, nonprofessional helpers must also uphold *nonmaleficence* or the obligation to do no harm. Attempting to help without proper time to devote to the process can be damaging or make the helpee feel like a burden, which violates the ethical obligation for nonmaleficence. Psychologists have also noted that proper time management is an ethical imperative because of the importance of self-care (Austin, 2014). Balancing care for ourselves and others is vital to our ability to help, so sometimes we have to put ourselves and our time obligations first. It also provides excellent modeling to our helpees for how each person, ourselves included, can help themselves.

Even if we have the time, personal capacity may also be a reason to decline to help. Self-care, or taking care of your mental, emotional, spiritual, and physical well-being, is vital for helpers. Professional therapy ethical codes cite that trauma and distress undermine helping competence (APA, 2016); therefore, we as nonprofessionals can follow this example and maintain an ethical obligation to avoid overexerting ourselves. We cannot engage in helping that overwhelms our schedule or our psychological capacity. We cannot give help if we have nothing left to give.

Lastly, the nature of the problem may also limit our ability to help based on your level of competence as a helper. We will learn in Chapter 5 about how to handle emergencies and issues outside your scope of competence by referring the helpee to other help and services.

When a request is made, check in with yourself and consciously decide whether or not to help and then proceed accordingly. If you decide not to engage, be sure to communicate that clearly and kindly to your helpee. Do not assume that a person in distress will pick up on nonverbal cues or tone that subtly communicates a desire to leave. Instead, inform the helpee directly. For example:

HELPEE: I'm having a hard day. Can we talk about it?
HELPER: Thank you for asking me. I certainly would help if I could. I'm sorry, I'm not available to talk right now.

This approach expresses care and concern to the helpee by saying more than simply "no," while also maintaining appropriate boundaries for self-care.

To engage in declining a request, begin by expressing admiration and gratitude to the helpee for asking for help and for choosing you as someone they would talk to. For example, say:

HELPER: I'm proud of you for reaching out and I'm glad you feel comfortable talking to me.

Then decline the request gracefully. You can give a reason or not, depending on your comfort and preference:

HELPER: I'm sorry I can't help this time. I'm on my way to a meeting right now.

If you would like to offer the opportunity to follow-up when you are available or for them to ask in the future, let them know; otherwise, no need to add anything more.

HELPER: Can we check in tomorrow afternoon? I'm free after 1pm and would like to talk then.

Helpers can oftentimes feel the need to continue talking, but it is important at this point to stop and listen to the helpee's response. They may be understanding or upset. Either way, calmly listen and acknowledge their reaction and then reaffirm your polite decline.

HELPER: I understand you're having a tough time and I hope your day gets better. Please know I care about you and would help if I could.

Then exit the situation. If guilt emerges, remember that you are upholding autonomy by honoring this as the helpee's problem, not yours, and believe in their ability to seek out other helpers and alternate solutions. Remember that as helpers, it is unethical to take on everyone's problems ourselves. Being discerning with your time and resources is a fair and ethical choice for everyone.

Agreeing to Help

If, on the other hand, you decide that you have the time and resources to help someone, be sure to explicitly state your intentions to do so and what you are able to provide. For example:

HELPEE: I'm having a hard day. Can we talk about it?

HELPER: Yes, of course. Thanks for asking. I'm free for the next twenty minutes, if that works. We can go into the room next door.

This response not only replies to the request, it also provides specifics about what the helpee can expect.

To accept a request, begin by expressing admiration and gratitude to the helpee for asking for help and for choosing you as someone they would talk to. This helps begin to build rapport by noting your connection and also begin to empower the helpee by pointing out their strengths. For example, say:

HELPER: Thank you for being willing to share with me. I admire you for talking your way through a hard day.

Then explicitly accept their request and let them know what to expect, particularly regarding timeline. If you have other commitments or need a finite end point, let them know when you can talk and for how long:

HELPER: I need to finish writing this email and then I'll come over in ten minutes. I'm available for the next hour after that to talk.

Lastly, confirm with your helpee. Ensure that what you are able to offer works for what they need:

HELPER: Does that sound alright to you?

Be sure to follow through with what you propose. Trustworthiness is key to your identity as a helper (Kim et al., 2018), so make sure that, every step of the way, you communicate directly with your helpee and follow through on what you say you will do.

How to Support

The helping scenario begins by helpee request or by you noticing distress and offering help. Openers such as "Are you alright?" and "You seem upset. Do you want to talk about it?" are appropriate. If the helpee refuses your offer, do not force them. Let them know you are available if they want to talk later and then respect their autonomy by discontinuing your help.

If you both agree, it is important to begin by considering the physical setting. Most professional counselors accomplish this by doing therapy in a private office or clinic (O*NET, 2018). Nonprofessional helpers, however, are more likely to engage in helping in a variety of informal settings. You might find yourself in a helping situation outside, in a car, an office building, homeless shelter, school, public place, or private home. Helping can occur anywhere.

Still, try to arrange the physical space to provide optimum opportunity for safe and effective helping. Consider privacy and confidentiality by attempting to find a private and quiet space to talk that minimizes interruptions and eavesdropping. Nonprofessional helpers often find themselves attempting to help in awkward physical positions, such as standing up. During my own ill-prepared helping interactions, I have found myself becoming fatigued from standing too long, sitting on the floor, or leaning against a wall for support. These scenarios limit nonverbal attending and should be avoided. Instead, begin by locating chairs and inviting the helpee to sit with you.

Once the space is prepared, the next step is informed consent, as discussed in Chapter 2. Briefly review informed consent by noting your scope of competence, confidentiality, and limits to confidentiality. Remember to keep your informed consent casual, brief, and informative to best fit your helping situation. This might be something such as:

HELPER: I'm not a therapist, just a friend who wants to try to help. This will stay between us, unless I'm worried about the immediate safety for you or others. Sound okay?

Note that "I'm not a therapist" communicates your scope of competence by differentiating you as a nonprofessional helper to your helpee. "This will stay between us" explains confidentiality, while "except if I'm worried about the immediate safety of you or others" communicates the limits of confidentiality. Finally, "Sound okay?" elicits the helpee's consent and provides space for them to voice any concerns.

Microskills: Listening Skills

Recall that we will use the microskills hierarchy for the LifeRAFT model as outlined in Figure 4.2. The microskills hierarchy is a list of microskills organized in a pyramid shape. The bottom of the pyramid represents which skills should be used most often, while skills at the top of the list should be used only occasionally after the helping scenario has progressed (Ivey, Ivey, & Zalaquett, 2016). The placement of each microskill on the hierarchy represents not only how quickly each microskill should be introduced into a helping scenario but also how often each microskill should be used throughout the scenario. Once again, the microskills closer to the bottom of the pyramid should be introduced earlier and used most often throughout a helping situation.

We will learn more about this process in subsequent chapters with the microskills ramp-up, which is a stepwise order of when and how helpers should use microskills during a helping situation. For now, just keep in mind that we start with learning microskills at the bottom of the pyramid. We will continue to use these skills most often and return to them throughout our helping situations as the primary ingredient of helping.

As we have already discussed, microskills fall into two categories: listening skills and influencing skills. The support stage begins with listening skills, and helpers should rely on these microskills as their primary tools by using them exclusively at first. Even when other influencing skills are added later, listening skills should remain dominant. The primary reason for this is that listening skills are considered the "common factors" to professional psychotherapy, that is, they represent the consistent elements of all different therapy models that contribute to therapy success. Common factors have been found to account for around 30% of therapy outcomes, twice as much as attributable to different treatment models (Lambert, 2003). Thus, listening skills are essential to the helping process because they offer powerful tools for change, building rapport with a helpee, facilitating emotion-focused helping, and establishing a foundation that earns us the right to intervene with increasing influencing skills later.

One of the most important concepts to remember is that listening is at the heart of helping; it is our most effective and powerful helping tool. But more than listening, helping

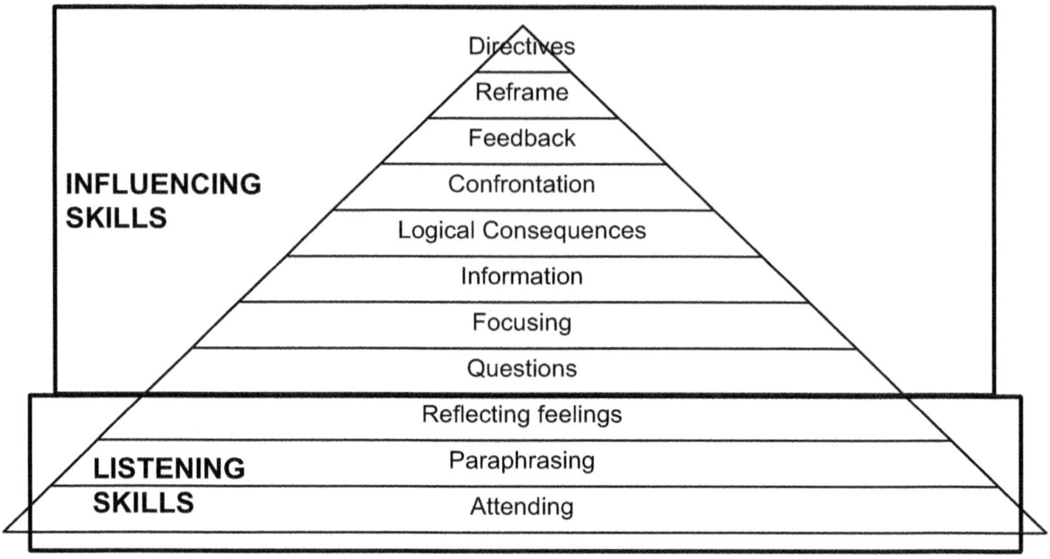

Figure 4.2 Microskills Hierarchy

requires *active* listening, which involves a process of intentional participation and response (Ivey et al., 2016). With active listening, we intentionally commit to understanding what our helpee is communicating, both verbally and nonverbally, experiencing their reality with them, and responding in ways that communicate to them that we understand and feel with them. The helpee controls the direction of their story and disclosures, and we as helpers follow where they lead, reflecting back what we hear and observe. By doing so, helpees are able to deepen their own experience and begin to disclose more detail than previously shared. Helpers can also check in with their helpees by using active listening to clarify what they hear and ensure they understand what is being said.

We also use active listening skills to enhance our relationship with the helpee and attempt to better the outcome of our helping, a process that utilizes what are known as the "facilitative conditions" for the common factors of therapy. These facilitative conditions were first proposed by Carl Rogers, a psychologist and creator of Person-Centered Therapy (1961), and include unconditional positive regard, genuineness, and empathic understanding.

Unconditional positive regard means feeling genuine care for your helpee, affirming their worth as a human being, and accepting them completely without evaluation (Rogers, 1961). Because any conditions can interfere with this process, both positive (e.g., "that's good") and negative judgments (e.g., "that's bad") are avoided. This does not mean helpers need to feel positive about every choice a helpee makes, but they must find unconditional fondness for their helpee. As helpers, it is not our place to place judgment on our helpee's choices, and doing so will simply interfere with their healing (Faiver, Eisengart, & Colonna, 2004).

Genuineness means being your real and authentic self with your helpee. Do not try to falsify care or concern for your helpees because it undermines their trust, but be honest and interact naturally with them. Of course, this does not mean you have to disclose every thought and feeling that emerges. Instead, focus on making your helping skills and style your own to bring the real you into the helping relationship (Rogers, 1961). This will be particularly important as you progress in your skills. This book will offer several examples of specific wording to use, but it is important that you find ways to navigate LifeRAFT helping according to your style to increase genuineness.

The last of Rogers' facilitative conditions, empathic understanding, is the process of comprehending and sharing the feelings of another person (Colman, 2015). Empathy means communicating your care and understanding to helpees in a sensitive and accurate manner (Hill, 2014). Empathy has been found to be the most important factor in whether helping is effective (Egan, 2014). Without empathy, good helping cannot take place.

Active listening and the facilitative conditions are what makes helping work. They are communicated via listening skills, specifically attending, paraphrasing, and reflecting feelings (Ivey et al., 2016).

Attending

Attending is defined as all forms of nonverbal communication (Ivey et al., 2016), encompassing not only body language and eye contact but also vocal sounds, tone, and quality. The face and body communicate a great deal, and researchers have noted its importance in professional counseling (Highlen & Hill, 1984), but nonprofessional helpers can harness this ability to communicate their empathy and interest through attending. However, be aware that nonverbal communication can vary greatly depending on cultural background, personal preferences, and context (Ivey et al., 2016). Thus, it is essential to note helpee reactions and adjust accordingly for each individual. The following are brief suggestions to increase positive visual communication and vocal quality:

BODY LANGUAGE

Body language includes posture, body movements, and gestures. Helpers are encouraged to sit still and avoid fidgeting, breathe deeply, and exude a sense of calm. Anxiety often expresses itself through wringing hands, shaking feet, or rocking from side to side. An anxious helper can reduce trust and increase distress in a helpee, so try to exude calm through your body language. Notice any signs of discomfort and take note of these behaviors in practice, minimizing them as much as possible. Staying relaxed will also make your helpee feel more relaxed (Egan, 2014).

Once you are sitting calmly, maintain an open body posture to demonstrate receptiveness to your helpee. Closing off your body, such as by turning part or all of your body away from the helpee or crossing your arms or legs, communicates a lack of openness to the helpee and their problems. Instead, face your helpee and keep your arms separated by resting them at your sides, on each of your legs, or on the arms of your chair. Keep your legs uncrossed at the knee or ankle and both feet planted on the floor. Hold your knees as close as is comfortable because an overly wide posture can be interpreted as aggressive or make helpees uncomfortable. This open sitting position may be uncomfortable at first, so practice is helpful. Experiment with different postures, such as leaning to one side, sitting on the edge of your chair, propping one arm up, and so forth, to see what positions work best for you.

PHYSICAL SPACE

Physical space refers to how near or far people are to each other during conversation. By manipulating the space between your helpee, you can communicate nonverbally your level of interest and involvement with them. We want to face the helpee without being too imposing;

one way to accomplish this is to "cheat out" slightly (Egan, 2014). Align your chairs so that they aren't face to face but rather angled in at about 45 degrees. This position allows you to sit with your knees facing slightly away from your helpee while your top half can remain open to them.

This still leaves the issue of physical space, that is, the distance between the chairs. Zones of physical space labeled as "typical" for middle-class US citizens include 0 to 18 inches for intimate relationships and 1.5 to 4 feet for acquaintances (Hall, 1968). These distances vary widely, but, in general, the closer our established relationship with someone, the more comfortable we are sitting close to them. When placing chairs for a helping interaction, place them at a distance that seems comfortable and appropriate for your relationship with the helpee.

Additional ways you can show interest is by reducing space, such as by moving your chair closer to your helpee, turning your body more directly toward the helpee, or by leaning forward. Leaning forward slightly is a common nonverbal request for the helpee to continue talking, as well as a sign of interest and comfort (Egan, 2014).

From there, you can watch for all of these nonverbal communication behaviors from your helpee to gauge their interest and comfort in you so you can adjust accordingly (Erford, 2014). For example, if a helpee turns away, closes off their body with crossed arms and legs, backs their chair away, or leans back, these signs would indicate they are uncomfortable, and you should provide more space by moving your chair back or angling slightly away from them. If, on the other hand, the helpee turns toward you, opens their body posture, or leans forward, this would indicate they are comfortable with the current physical space, while continual behavior of this kind might communicate a desire to be physically closer. If this is the case, you can then respond by angling your body toward them, moving your chair closer, and leaning toward them.

EYE CONTACT

Eye contact includes gaze and general eye movements. Norms regarding eye contact vary by culture, so it is once again valuable to monitor the helpee and respond in kind. In general, it is appropriate and respectful to make eye contact when people are talking, while taking care not to stare (Erford, 2014). Notice next time you have a conversation what your eyes do and be intentional about duplicating this process in helping situations. Typically, when someone is listening, they maintain more constant eye contact while the person talking makes briefer eye contact and shifts their gaze throughout their response. This is acceptable even while a person is emoting strongly, such as crying or shaking. Averting your eyes may be interpreted as discomfort or judgment, which we try to avoid. As good helpers, we will spend the majority of the helping interaction listening rather than speaking, so we focus primarily on maintaining our gaze but breaking periodically so as not to stare (Ivey et al., 2016).

FACIAL EXPRESSIONS

Facial expressions are comprised of movements such as smiling, frowning, and raising eyebrows. Avoid judgmental facial expressions such as shock, disbelief, or disgust in reaction to a helpee's distress. Instead, adopt a general facial expression of care, curiosity, and concern. Practice in front of the mirror by shifting your head to the side, furrowing your brow, and pursing your lips slightly as if to say, "I'm here for you and interested to learn more." This expression may come naturally to some while others may need to try out different expressions, understate natural movements, or exaggerate facial expressions for the right tone to come across to others. While experimenting, feedback from others is key (Hill, 2014).

Role-Play Practice

The purpose of this exercise is to rehearse attending using nonverbal skills. For this exercise, find a volunteer helpee to role-play a helping scenario with you and provide feedback afterward. Set a timer and conduct a helping scenario for at least 15 minutes, attempting to help using only nonverbal attending skills. Request that your helpee talk about an issue for 15 minutes and let them know they will not receive any verbal prompting from you, because this is an opportunity to experiment with your nonverbal skills. Complete the following:

1. Consider pairing with a fellow helper-in-training and take turns being the helper and helpee.
2. Video record the scenario, following the ethical guidelines discussed in Chapter 1, including informed consent for video recording.
3. Ask your helpee to select a topic to discuss. Consult Chapter 1, "Problem Triggers," for topic ideas.
4. As the helper, attempt to help your helpee using only nonverbal communication, such as with body language, including hand gestures, moving and manipulating the physical space, use of eye contact, and facial expressions, in ways that seem appropriate to you in the moment.
5. At the end of the role-play, request feedback from your helpee about what you did well and what you could improve on next time. Ask what nonverbal behaviors felt especially empathic and supportive and which ones were awkward or uncomfortable. Write down your helpee's responses.
6. Review the video recording. Note what you notice regarding your nonverbal communication and the ways in which your helpee responded, both verbally and nonverbally. Note what you think you did well and what you could improve on next time as the helper.

VOCAL QUALITIES

Vocal qualities are a part of attending distinct from verbal communication. Verbal communication involves words and phrases and focuses on the content of what is being spoken, while vocal qualities are the way in which the helper's voice is used, such as tone of voice, pitch, and volume (Egan, 2014). Vocal quality literally sets the tone for the helpee. New helpers tend to use their regular speaking voice or err on the side of being too businesslike in an effort to appear knowledgeable or too enthusiastic in an effort to boost the helpee's mood (Campbell, 2013). Remember that the focus is not on the helper but on communicating listening and empathy to the helpee. Do not wait for the helpee to feel safe to show their feelings but get ahead of them by inviting their distress to fully express itself in your presence through the use of your voice.

One way to do that is to imagine your helpee is already fully emoting their distress and begin by speaking to them in the tone you would use in that situation. For example, before I engage in helping, I imagine someone crying, because crying is one visual representation of emotional release that helps me to access my most empathic vocal qualities. So, I tend to begin helping situations by imagining that my helpee is already crying and speak to them in a tone of voice I would use in that situation. Accordingly, speak more softly, slow down significantly, and raise the pitch of your voice to avoid sounding too serious or lecturing (Ivey et al., 2016).

To see the difference vocal quality can make, try this: say out loud, "I understand you have something to talk to me about." First say it in your regular speaking voice. Then say it again as if you were lecturing a misbehaving child. Now say it using your most caring and empathic helper voice. Do you notice how the same sentence can have vastly different implications depending on your voice inflection? Invite your helpee to be vulnerable and share deep feelings with you through an empathic helping voice from the very beginning of the interaction.

Paraphrasing

While nonverbal communication is essential, at times active listening still requires certain verbal responses. One common verbal response that conveys listening is paraphrasing. Paraphrasing involves shortening and clarifying the essence of what a helpee says by conveying the message back in the helper's own words (Ivey et al., 2016). An example paraphrase would be, "I hear you saying that you're having a hard time fitting in." Notice how this brief statement begins with an indication of listening, "I hear you saying," and follows with a brief summarizing statement of a longer narrative, "you're having a hard time fitting in."

The purpose of paraphrasing is to make helpees feel accurately heard and invite them to continue sharing. Paraphrases also help to shorten and clarify what was said so the helper can ensure they understand what the helpee is saying and the helpee can digest their words from an outside source. This offers the helpee the opportunity to reflect on their experience in the moment to aid them in examining problems and helping themselves find solutions (Hill, 2014).

To paraphrase, wait until the helpee has stopped speaking and looks at you for a response. Start with a sentence stem that indicates you were listening. There are countless ways to phrase this, but examples include "I hear you saying," "sounds like," "seems like," "to summarize . . . ," "so this is what I heard you say," or "you seem to be saying. . . ." Be sure to switch up your sentence stems with each paraphrase so as not to sound like a broken record. After this, follow with a short and simple summary of what you heard, such as "you had a bad day" or "you and your boyfriend broke up." Paraphrases do not necessarily need to be the most recent statement shared. Instead, choose what you believe to be the most important aspect of what the helpee said and look for indications of higher energy or emotion that demonstrate strong salience from the helpee (Hill, 2014). Remember your attending skills when you deliver a paraphrase; use your most empathic body language and vocal qualities and focus on remaining calm and speaking in a soft and slow voice.

Keep your paraphrases short and simple, even though you might feel an urge to elaborate or build on the helpee's story. Also resist the urge to follow a paraphrase with a question. Your focus should be on saying just enough to keep the helpee talking and then get out of the way so they can pick up with the story where they want to and talk themselves through the distress (Hill, 2014). Listening is the key, not talking. Helpers follow the lead of the helpee at this point by riding the distress whirlpool with them. Excessive talking, directing, or even questions seize control and are ill-advised at this point, so work to keep paraphrases concise while still conveying empathy. Once the paraphrase is complete, stop talking and return to attending skills. Look at the helpee, lean forward, and even gesture with a head nod or hand to indicate you are done speaking and they are free to continue.

Written Practice

Practice writing paraphrases, noting that there is no one "right" paraphrase but instead many different paraphrases a helper could use. For each of the examples below, write three potential paraphrases you could give in response to each helpee. Be sure to try different sentence stems and summary statements with each paraphrase.

HELPEE: Everything is terrible right now. My grades are bad, I can't get myself to class, and I forgot about my last exam. I'm going to fail. What do I do? I can't drop out. My parents would kill me. I don't know if I can even salvage my grades at this point.

HELPEE: My uncle passed away last night. I still can't believe it. I miss him so much already. I get distracted for a bit and then remember and it hurts all over again. Losing someone is so hard. This is the first person close to me to pass away.

Reflecting Feelings

Reflecting feelings means identifying a helpee's key emotions and conveying them back. A statement reflecting feelings could be, "I see the hurt and fear in your eyes." Note how reflections of feelings are similar in construction to paraphrases. Like paraphrases, they begin with an indication of attending ("I see") but then follow with a brief summarization of emotions, in this case, "hurt and fear." Reflections of feelings can include feelings directly stated by the helpee, or they can be indirectly inferred through their behavior, the content of the message, or other contextual indicators (Hill, 2014). Note that often feelings go unlabeled by helpees, so while they may describe feeling a particular way, they may not name it. It is then our job as helpers to name the feeling for them (Ivey et al., 2016).

The purpose of reflecting feelings is to demonstrate that you understand and empathize with the helpee's emotional state and that you invite them to share their feelings in more depth. At times, reflecting feelings may accompany a paraphrase, such as "You had a bad day and that has left you feeling overwhelmed," in which "you had a bad day" is a paraphrase and "has left you feeling overwhelmed" is a reflection of feeling. By labeling and drawing awareness to feelings, we can assist helpees in experiencing and understanding their emotions more fully (Ivey et al., 2016). In fact, this process can be healing in and of itself because increased expression and understanding of emotions can lead to emotional regulation (Greenberg, 2002). Although the focus remains on supporting, opportunities for self-healing in this stage remain highly possible.

To reflect feelings, engage in a similar process as paraphrasing. Wait until the helpee has stopped speaking and looks at you for a response. Reflections of feeling should be constructed with the similar two-part structure: a sentence stem indicating you are attending to the helpee and a brief summary statement of the feeling you believe they are experiencing. Start with a sentence stem that indicates you were attending, such as "I hear you saying," "I see in you," "sounds like," "seems like," "your eyes suggest," "based on the facial expressions you made, I think you might be," or even just "you seem. . . ." As with paraphrasing, be sure to switch up your sentence stems with each reflection of feeling to remain conversational. Once again, follow with a short and simple label of the emotion you believe they are experiencing, such as "you are feeling a lot of anger" or "feeling sadness about this loss."

Part of the power of reflections of feeling is that they offer the helpee the experience of seeing their emotions mirrored in another person. Unlike paraphrases, reflections of feeling are far less logical and may not register when simply labeled back. In order to facilitate a helpful reflection of feeling, it is important to not only say the words but mirror the experience. Thus, you as the helper are encouraged to intensify attending skills to "wear" your helpee's feelings. For example, while you reflect the words "you seem scared," slightly widen your eyes, tense your arms, and show a bit of fear in your nonverbal communication. Avoid overdramatizing your expressions and maintain empathic attending but try on a small amount of the emotion to demonstrate to the helpee what they might be feeling (Hill, 2014).

Like paraphrases, keep reflections short and simple and resist the urge to follow with a question or additional talking. If needed, provide spaces of silence to allow the helpee to consider and fully experience the feeling before responding. Once the reflection of feeling is complete, stop talking and return to nonverbal attending once again.

Written Practice

One of the biggest challenges of reflecting feelings is possessing the expansive emotional vocabulary in order to accurately label a helpee's experience (Erford, 2014). Thus, it can be helpful to begin working now on expanding your available feeling words. We will begin with the most basic emotions and seek to grow our vocabulary from there. To that end, brainstorm feeling words that accurately describe the emotions below in terms of emotional category and intensity and fill them in the blanks below.

Intensity	*Emotional Categories*				
	Sad	*Angry*	*Scared*	*Happy*	*Surprised*
Mild					
Moderate					
Severe					

For a more complete list of feeling words, search online for "Feelings Wheels." An image search can provide you with some beautiful representations of feeling words, organized in a wheel of emotional categories.

Result of Supporting

The expected results of the support stage are that the helpee will begin to feel heard and understood, and a solid helping relationship will be created or, if a relationship already exists, effectively reaffirmed. Feelings of empathy and rapport are evidenced by helpees' increased relaxation and engagement in their body posture. Look for signs such as the helpee making increased eye contact, leaning forward, mirroring your words or gestures, and speaking slower and calmer (Ivey et al., 2016).

Given that listening skills are the most important and foundational skills in the helping process, it is important not to rush this stage. Approaching support as something to get through before the "real helping" begins represents a fundamental misunderstanding about the helping process. Supporting *is* helping; in fact, it is the most helpful part, and the skills involved should remain dominant throughout the rest of the helping situation. The time involved for support varies widely depending on the problem, people involved, and context, but when in doubt, err on the side of spending too long in the support stage (Egan, 2014).

Helpees may ask to rush the helping process (e.g., "How would you handle this if you were me?" or "Please just tell me what to do"), but resist this to avoid fostering disempowerment and dependence. Instead, respond with genuineness and listening skills, such as:

HELPER: I know you're asking for guidance, and I'm here to help you but I can't tell you what to do. Let's look at this together and try and find a solution that fits your situation.

Note in this example how listening skills of paraphrasing are used ("I know you're asking for guidance"), combined with expressions of empathy and genuineness ("I'm here to help," "Let's look at this together").

Helpees may also express disagreement with your reflections and paraphrases. Disagreements are welcomed and encouraged, because the goal is to get an accurate, empathic understanding of our helpees' situations. Although we want to try to be accurate in our restatements, adjustments are an expected and valued part of the supporting process. Remain open when helpees correct your inaccurate reflections and express gratitude and request more accurate descriptors until you both understand (Ivey et al, 2016).

The support stage reaches an end when helpees begin to exit their distress whirlpool. As they talk, it feels less as if they are spinning in the same distress narrative. Although still likely upset and feeling stuck, their description of the problem develops more direction and clarity, while as the helper, you begin to make sense of the nature of their distress (Hill, 2014). At this point, you are ready to move to LifeRAFT Stage Two: Watching.

Case Example

To show how each LifeRAFT stage can be used in practice, each chapter will conclude with a case study. This case example shows how a nonprofessional helper, a college dormitory resident assistant (Anna) works with one of her residents (Helani), who is in distress about a sudden loss of tuition funding. In this example, Anna briefly uses the support stage to build rapport and listen to Helani as she discusses her concerns.

HELPER: Hi Helani, you look sad. Would you like to talk? [Initiating help]

HELPEE: I just got really bad news and I need help figuring out what to do.

HELPER: Oh no, I'm sorry to hear that. Thank you for letting me know and I would be happy to help. I have the next half an hour free, if that works for you. We can sit right here. [Agreeing to help]

HELPEE: That works, thank you. I really need some guidance. I don't know what to do.

HELPER: Of course. You know I'm not a counselor or anything, but we can still try to figure out what to do. This will stay between us, except if I'm worried about the immediate safety of you or others. Sound okay? [Informed consent]

HELPEE: That sounds good. My parents just called and said they can't afford to pay for my school anymore. I'm already so stressed with everything I have going on and now this. What do I do?

HELPER: Oh Helani, that's awful news. You sound overwhelmed. [Paraphrase; Reflection of feeling]

HELPEE: I am. They said they could cover it and now they can't. I didn't expect to have to pay for school myself. I didn't expect this phone call.

HELPER: You started school expecting costs were taken care of and that's suddenly changed. [Paraphrase]

HELPEE: Yes, it's jarring. I feel awful that I've put my parents in a financial bind. I cringe to think how much this costs.

HELPER: Sounds like there is some hurt you feel about the cost of school. [Reflection of feeling]

HELPEE: It's not hurt so much as guilt. I feel guilty for burdening them with this. [Adjustment of reflection of feeling]

HELPER: Ah, I see. Guilt is weighing on you. [Reflection of feeling]

HELPEE: What do I do? Should I get a job? Should I drop out of school? I don't know.

HELPER: Yeah, that sounds like a difficult choice. [Paraphrase]

HELPEE: But which one should I choose? What would you do in my situation?

HELPER: I don't know. We're different people. Let's try to find what you think will work best in your situation. [Paraphrase; Resist advice]

HELPEE: But I don't know what to do. This has changed everything and I'm freaking out.

HELPER: I know, the future seems uncertain so naturally, fear comes up; this is scary. [Paraphrase; Reflection of feeling]

HELPEE: Yeah, it is. Thank you for understanding. A lot of feelings are coming up about this and I'm actually coming up with some possibilities; I just still don't know which way to go. This is a lot and I'm trying to sort all of it out.

HELPER: This is a lot and I admire you for working on it. I'm here to help walk it through with you. [Empathic statement]

As a result of the support stage, Anna has established rapport with Helani and helped her to discuss her concerns with increasing clarity and depth.

Written Practice

Here, as in following chapters, you will be asked to write statements that implement each of the skills and stages you are learning to encourage you to think about how you would implement these skills in practice. In this practice, your responses will focus on your helpee, Ivan. Ivan is a 15-year-old who frequents the nonprofit afterschool program where you volunteer. He experiences recurrent conflicts with his parents over house rules. To practice supporting, imagine that you are talking with Ivan and he makes the following statements:

- "I can't stop thinking about the argument with my parents. Seems like they don't even care. What should I do? Should I just move out or something?"
- "I didn't mean to miss curfew and I tried to explain that to them, but they just wouldn't listen."
- "I can't control what everyone else does. I told my friends I needed to get back in time for my curfew, but I don't have a car or a cell phone or anything, so I have no control. My parents just don't understand."

Given these helpee statements, write down three attending behaviors you would adopt, three paraphrases you might say, and three reflections of feeling you might offer in response to Ivan. Feel free to assume or add extra detail to Ivan's story if needed in your responses.

Role-Play Practice

The purpose of this exercise is to rehearse the support stage. For this exercise, find a volunteer helpee to role-play a helping scenario with you and provide feedback afterward. Set a timer and conduct a five-minute helping scenario, attempting to support using listening skills of attending, paraphrasing, and reflecting feelings only (no questions!). Complete the following:

1. Consider pairing with a fellow helper-in-training and take turns being the helper and helpee.
2. Video record the scenario. Follow the ethical guidelines discussed in Chapter 1, including permission to video record.
3. Ask your helpee to select a topic to discuss. Consult Chapter 1, "Problem Triggers," for topic ideas.
4. Attempt to help your helpee using only listening skills of attending, paraphrasing, and reflecting feelings.
5. At the end of the role-play, request feedback from your helpee about what you did well and what you could improve on next time. Ask what interventions felt especially empathic and supportive and which ones were awkward or uncomfortable. Write down your helpee's responses.
6. Review the video recording. Note what you observe regarding your nonverbal communication and the ways in which your helpee responded, both verbally and nonverbally. What do you think you did well, and what could you improve next time as the helper?

Summary

In this chapter we discussed the following:

Description of Supporting

- Support, the first stage of the LifeRAFT helping skills model, involves connecting and strengthening your relationship with your helpee by providing a foundation of nonjudgmental and affirmational emotion-focused helping.
- The purpose of support is to establish and build rapport, earn the right for increasing intervention, and provide a nonjudgmental space for the helpee to help themselves.

When to Support

- Supporting begins either at the helpee's request or when the helper notices a problem and offers help. Noticing problems requires intentional vigilance.
- Helpers always have the choice whether to help or not and should kindly and clearly communicate whether they accept or decline a helping request.

How to Support

- Begin supporting by agreeing to help and reviewing informed consent.
- Use the listening skills of attending, paraphrasing, and reflecting feelings.
    - Attending is nonverbal communication, such as physical space, eye contact, facial expressions, and vocal qualities.
    - Paraphrasing means shortening and clarifying the essence of what a helpee says by conveying the message back in the helper's words.
    - Reflecting feelings means identifying a helpee's key emotions and conveying them back to clarify the helpee's affective experience.

Result of Supporting

- The expected results of the support stage are that the helpee will begin to feel heard and understood and rapport will be established between them and the helper.

References

American Psychological Association. (2016). Ethical principles of psychologists and code of conduct. *American Psychologist*, *57*, 1060–1073. Retrieved from www.apa.org/ethics/code/?item=8

American Red Cross. (2018). How to respond to a water emergency. *American Red Cross*. Retrieved from www.redcross.org/content/dam/redcross/atg/PDF_s/Preparedness___Disaster_Recovery/Disaster_Preparedness/Water_Safety/WouldYouKnowWhattodo.pdf

Austin, M. W. (2014). Is time management an ethical issue? *Psychology Today*. Retrieved from www.psychologytoday.com/us/blog/ethics-everyone/201409/is-time-management-ethical-issue

Breuer, J., & Freud, S. (1974). *Studies on hysteria*. Harmondsworth: Penguin Books.

Campbell, E. L. (2013, April). *Key introductory strategies training: Training paraprofessionals in basic helping skills*. Symposium conducted at the annual meeting of the Western Psychological Association, Reno, NV.

Campbell, E. L. (2017). How to console a loved one. In *Whitworth today magazine*. Spokane, WA: Whitworth university.

Colman, A. M. (2015). *A dictionary of psychology* (Fourth ed.). Oxford: Oxford University Press.

Connor-Smith, J. K., & Flachsbart, C. (2007). Relations between personality and coping: A meta-analysis. *Journal of Personality and Social Psychology*, *93*, 1080–1107. doi:10.1037/0022-3514.93.6.1080

Corey, G. (2009). *Theory and practice of counseling and psychotherapy* (8th ed.). Belmont, CA: Thomson/Brooks/Cole.

Darley, J. M., & Batson, C. D. (1973). From Jerusalem to Jericho: A study of situational and dispositional variables in helping behavior. *Journal of Personality and Social Psychology, 27*, 100–108.

Egan, G. (2014). *The skilled helper: A problem-management and opportunity development approach to helping* (10th ed.). Belmont, CA: Brooks/Cole.

Erford, B. T. (2014). *Orientation to the counseling profession: Advocacy, ethics, and essential professional foundations* (2nd ed.). Boston, MA: Pearson.

Faiver, C., Eisengart, S., & Colonna, R. (2004). *The counselor intern's handbook* (3rd ed.). Belmont, CA: Cengage.

Greenberg, L. S. (2002). *Emotion-focused therapy: Coaching clients to work through feelings*. Washington, DC: American Psychological Association.

Hall, E. T. (1968). Proxemics. *Current Anthropology, 9*, 83–108.

Highlen, P. S., & Hill, C. E. (1984). Factors affecting client change in counseling. In S. D. Brown & R. W. Lent (Eds.), *Handbook of counseling psychology* (pp. 334–396). New York: Wiley.

Hill, C. E. (2014). *Helping skills: Facilitating exploration, insight, and action* (4th ed.). Washington, DC: American Psychological Association.

Horvath, A. O., & Bendi, R. P. (2002). The alliance. In J. C. Norcross (Ed.), *Psychotherapy relationships that work: Therapist contributions and responsiveness to patients* (pp. 37–70). New York: Oxford University Press.

Ivey, A. E., Ivey, M. B., & Zalaquett, C. P. (2016). *Essentials of intentional interviewing: Counseling in a multicultural world* (3rd ed.). Boston, MA: Cengage Learning.

Kim, S. K., Teitelman, A. M., Muecke, M., D'Antonio, P., Stringer, M., & Grisso, J. A. (2018). The perspectives of volunteer counselors of Korean immigrant women experiencing intimate partner violence. *Issues in Mental Health Nursing, 39*(10), 888–895.

Lambert, M. J. (2003). Psychotherapy outcome research: Implications for integrative and eclectic therapists. In C. Norcross & M. Goldfried (Eds.), *Handbook of psychotherapy integration* (pp. 94–129). New York: Basic Books.

Latane, B., & Darley, J. M. (1968). Group inhibition of bystander intervention in emergencies. *Journal of Personality and Social Psychology, 10*, 215–221.

Leahy, R. (2011). What not to say when your loved one is upset. *Huffington Post*. Retrieved from www.huffingtonpost.com/robert-leahy-phd/how-to-talk-to-someone-yo_b_804980.html

Myers, D. G. (2010). Chapter 12: Helping. In D. G. Myers (Ed.), *Social psychology* (10th ed., pp. 440–480). New York: McGraw-Hill.

Myers, D. G. (2012). *Exploring psychology* (9th ed.). New York: Worth Publishers.

National Center for O*NET Development. (O*NET, 2018). *O*NET online*. Retrieved from www.onetonline.org

Rogers, C. (1961). *On becoming a person*. Boston: Houghton Mifflin.

5 Stage Two
Watch

Chapter Goals

This chapter will prepare you to:

- Learn about watching, the second stage of the LifeRAFT helping skills model, and the purpose of watching.
- Become aware of when to use the watching stage and how to choose whether or not to engage in the watching stage.
- Develop methods to provide help in the watching stage using listening skills and questions.
- Identify what to expect as a result of using watching with a helpee.

Introduction

This chapter will focus on watching, the second stage of the LifeRAFT model. To prepare us to learn about our second stage of the helping process, we return to our water rescue metaphor.

Sometimes helpees get caught up in a whirlpool of emotional distress, that is, they are stuck drowning in their problems and need help getting unstuck and back to their life flow. However, upon attempting a rescue, it may become clear that a helpee is not simply stuck but is in crisis, and their immediate survival is at stake. In other words, the distress whirlpool is no longer simply a problem but rather a life-threatening emergency.

You may falsely assume if someone were truly drowning—either in water or emotional crisis—that this would be immediately apparent. However, much like water emergencies, emotional crises do not always look the way you would expect. In water, drowning is not the violent, splashing cries for help we see on television. Drowning victims are often silent and undramatic, and it can be difficult to discern there is a problem, even to the trained eye (American Red Cross, 2018). Emotional crises are similar in that they are complex and can present in a variety of ways (Bonanno, 2004). Thus, we need to learn what to look for to recognize crises when they occur.

While a helpee in crisis indicates a "full water rescue" is needed, a true mental health crisis is outside the scope of competence of a nonprofessional helper. Thus, much like a lifeguard, it is the duty of the helper to guide the helpee out of immediate harm's way and then refer them to appropriate professionals for ongoing crisis care.

Description of Watching

Psychological Crises

In order to refer a helpee in crisis, it is important to understand what constitutes a psychological crisis and how to recognize it. A crisis is actually a fairly common life event, in that almost everyone experiences one or more crises throughout their lives (Ivey, Ivey, & Zalaquett, 2016). Nevertheless, crises represent a serious deviation from normal functioning, described as "a period of psychological disequilibrium, experienced as a result of a hazardous event or situation that constitutes a significant problem that cannot be remedied by using familiar coping strategies" (Roberts, 2000, p. 7). A state of active crisis occurs when a helpee's distress exceeds their ability to cope. They may experience and exhibit physical and psychological agitation, such as changes in eating and sleeping, anxiety and/or depression, and intense preoccupation with crisis-related events or reactions.

There are many different types of crises, all vastly different from each other, and they can parallel the causes of psychological distress described in Chapter 1. In general, any life stressor can become a crisis if it causes psychological disequilibrium and extends beyond the capabilities of a person's usual coping strategies. Situational stressors such as a serious physical illness or injury, death of a loved one, divorce, job loss, criminal act, or natural disaster can trigger a crisis (Roberts, 2000).

Presentation during a crisis varies from person to person and is based on a variety of personal and contextual factors. A helpee's cultural background also affects how they react to a crisis. For example, a culture-bound reaction identified in Latinx communities is called *ataque de nervios*, which involves crying, panic, and aggression. Asians, in contrast, have a higher incidence of developing somatic symptoms in response to crises and tend to value suppression of strong emotions (Sandoval, 2002). Differences between individuals are even larger than differences between cultural groups, and thus visible responses to crises can vary widely.

For our purposes as nonprofessional helpers, a key defining feature of psychological crisis is the extent to which the crisis has impaired a helpee's ability to function and keep themselves and others safe. This information is not readily apparent and often requires some crisis assessment. We are chiefly concerned with evaluating lethality, such as suicidal and homicidal risk; helpee safety, including whether or not they are victims of violence; and psychosis, serious mental illness or under the influence of alcohol or other drugs. These crisis reactions represent serious risks to the helpee or others and must be addressed by professionals. When helpers discern a helpee is in crisis, they shift to the watching stage of LifeRAFT.

What Is Watching?

Watching is the second stage of the LifeRAFT helping skills model (see Figure 5.1; Watch). Watching means attending to potential warning signs that would signal the need for immediate intervention in cases of imminent, life-threatening concerns. The watch stage involves assessing for emergency factors that require professional intervention, directing the helpee to appropriate professionals when needed, and helping to facilitate the transition to additional help.

Not all helpees require the watching stage; in fact, most helpees will not require crisis intervention (Ivey et al., 2016). Yet it is important in all cases to begin the watching stage by assessing for harm potential. If there appears to be no immediate concerns that require professional intervention or represent issues outside of the helper's scope of competence, then helping can proceed to stage three, investigating. In some cases, however, risk assessment will yield indication that a referral is needed. In those cases, helpers should proceed completely through the watching stage and not continue to stages three and four. In cases of immediate crisis, helping typically ends with a transfer of the helpee to a professional.

When to Watch

The watching stage occurs after the supporting stage. Even when it is clear from the beginning of a helping interaction that a helpee is in crisis, helpers must still earn the right to intervene by

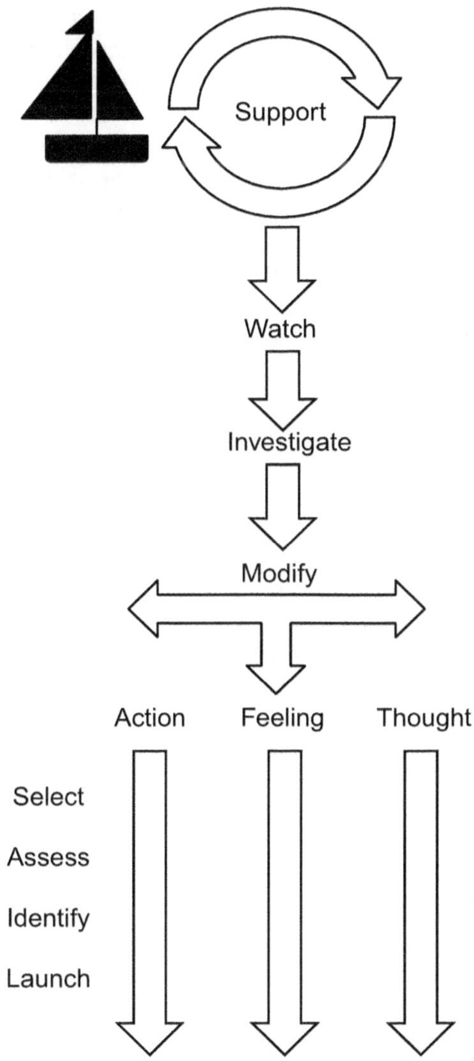

Figure 5.1 LifeRAFT Model

supporting first through the use of listening skills of attending, paraphrasing, and reflecting feeling. Once you realize a helpee is in crisis, you may feel an urge to skip the supporting stage and rush immediately to watching, but this misses the important foundation built in the supporting stage. By always beginning with supporting, we establish and strengthen our relationship with our helpee, convey to them feelings of calm and caring, and help them feel safe to continue discussing their concerns (Ivey et al., 2016). The supporting process is worth the effort because it results in better helping and greater likelihood that our interventions promote growth and healing (Egan, 2014).

The exceptions to this rule are cases of immediate danger or lethality. If the helpee, another person, or yourself is in immediate risk that cannot wait for a brief conversation, take necessary steps immediately to prioritize safety. For example, if a helpee appears to be experiencing a medical emergency such as being unconscious, bleeding, or having a seizure, call emergency services. Similarly, if a helpee is wielding a weapon, making threats toward you or others, or has left to hurt themselves or others, discontinue efforts to support and immediately call for help or protection and take measures to ensure your personal safety. In all remaining cases where the helpee discusses a crisis but is not currently experiencing or acting on it, take the time to support first before intervening.

Once the helpee begins to feel heard and understood, and rapport has been established between you and them, the watching stage can begin, should it be needed. The watching stage is needed when the helper notices signs of potential crisis that may require professional intervention in cases of imminent, life-threatening concerns. There are several crisis issues that warrant referral. The most common of these issues are described in the following sections, as are signs and symptoms to watch for. If you have suspicions that any of the following issues are present, the watching stage should fully commence. If none of the following issues appear to be present, you can continue to stage three, investigating.

Harm to Self/Suicidality

One of the most challenging and prevalent issues helpers face are suicidal crises. Suicidality involves thinking about, considering, planning, and/or intending to bring about self-inflicted death (Rudd, Joiner, Jobes, & King, 1999) and is a common symptom among people in distress, particularly those with depression. Suicide is the tenth leading cause of overall deaths in the United States and the second highest cause of death for those aged 10 to 34 (CDC, 2016). Helpers should expect to encounter helpees with suicidal ideation and be prepared to assist them (Hill, 2014).

Although suicide is a symptom of mental illness that is treatable by experts, you as a nonprofessional helper can help prevention efforts by encouraging helpees to talk about suicidality and by facilitating subsequent referrals to professional counseling. You cannot prevent suicide—no one can—but you can offer initial help needed to connect with treatment (Quinnett, 2007). With treatment, suicide is the most preventable kind of death (Rudd et al., 1999), and any positive intervention efforts can save a helpee's life and get them the professional treatment they need to never be suicidal again (Quinnett, 2007).

Helping someone who is contemplating suicide can be challenging and scary (Hill, 2014). It is important to understand that it is okay and encouraged for a helper to ask directly about suicide, as well as other crisis risks. Contrary to helper concerns, asking a helpee about suicide does not "put the idea in their head" or increase the risk of suicide—it actually lowers it. Talking directly about suicidality can lower anxiety, increase access to treatment, and lower the risk of an impulsive act (Quinnett, 2007).

Every suicidal comment and gesture must be taken seriously. Most people with suicidality are ambivalent leading up to an attempt and communicate their feelings to at least one person. People who talk about suicide do act on it, so any signs of suicidality in helpees should be explored (Quinnett, 2007).

Suicidal cues are extremely complex and can be difficult for even professional counselors to discern (Rudd et al., 1999), but you can be on the lookout for some of the basic indicators. Some of the warning signs of suicidality include verbal, behavioral, and contextual factors. In general, the more signs observed, the greater the risk (Quinnett, 2007).

Verbal warning signs include both explicit and vague expressions about death and dying. Explicit comments include statements such as "I'm going to kill myself" and "I'm going to be dead soon," whereas vague expressions include "I can't do this anymore" and "I wish I weren't here." These may be said with a serious tone or veiled through mumbling and joking in a sarcastic manner (Quinnett, 2007).

Behavioral signs may include sudden changes in behaviors such as giving away possessions, changing a will, or engaging in risky behaviors and substance abuse. Positive behavioral changes such as increased energy or displaying more positive emotions can also indicate a helpee has made peace with the decision to die (Simon, 2009).

In addition to general stressors, other contextual factors that present as warning signs may include psychiatric diagnoses and symptoms, particularly depression and feelings of hopelessness. Hopelessness may present by resisting hopeful statements from the helper (e.g., "I don't believe that") or expressive statements (e.g., "Nothing will ever get better"). Previous suicide attempts or self-injurious behaviors are also warning signs. Loss of any major relationship, especially death by suicide, increases risks, as does access to firearms (Quinnett, 2007). Additional contextual factors that increase risk of suicide include being of older age; male; non-Hispanic white or Indian/Alaska Native; divorced, widowed, or single; and gay, lesbian, bisexual, or transgender (LGBT) regarding sexual orientation and gender identity, respectively (Simon, 2009).

Danger to Others/Homicidality

Danger to others involves thinking about, considering, planning, and/or intending to become violent against another person or commit homicide (i.e., kill someone). Homicidality presents much less frequently in helping situations than suicidality, but given the comparable concern for lethality, it is important for helpers to be prepared for the possibility (Hill, 2014).

It is extremely difficult for professional counselors to predict the level of dangerousness in a client with any accuracy (Baird, 2014), so nonprofessionals are certainly not expected to predict violence in their helpees. Instead, helpers should be on the lookout and question helpees in cases where imminent violent assault seems likely.

The single best predictor for future violence is a history of past violence (Baird, 2014). Thus, if a helpee discusses handling previous upsets with violence, this should be taken seriously. Vigilance regarding verbal warning signs is also warranted, which can present as either explicit threats such as "I am going to kill her" or implicit statements such as "He better stay out of my way."

Other contextual risk factors for homicidal behaviors include being of younger age, male, low intelligence, victim of domestic violence, lack of social support, high levels of stress, and access to weapons. In cases where a helpee identifies a specific victim and availability to the victim, this implies particular danger.

Impaired Mental Status/Psychosis/Drugs and Alcohol

We will define impaired mental status as involving an altered state of consciousness that interferes with a person's immediate ability to maintain safety, care for themselves, and make effective decisions (Baird, 2014). Because alterations to mental status can vary widely in severity and many people with compromised cognitive abilities can still care for themselves, this discussion will be limited to impairments that threaten safety and well-being. This kind of impairment can be caused by severe mental illness, such as episodes of psychosis (i.e., losing touch with external reality) or the effects of drugs or alcohol (i.e., being intoxicated or high). These are considered crises when unintentional lethality or harm to self or others seems probable. For example, a helpee with alcohol intoxication may be a risk driving a vehicle or if they show signs of overdose or alcohol poisoning.

Signs of impaired mental status can be ascertained from changes in appearance and behaviors. While changes in appearance are different for different causes and substances, some general ones to look for include eyes that appear bloodshot, watery, or have trouble focusing; disheveled clothing or appearance; and body twitching, shaking, or trembling. Impaired mental status may also manifest itself in behaviors such as nonsensical, slurred, or irrational speech; appearing dazed;

difficulty standing or sitting; overly animated or sullen presentation; confusion and forgetfulness; and inappropriate speech or gestures (Baird, 2014).

Other Issues Beyond Scope of Competence

As we discussed in Chapter 2, helpees may present challenges that are beyond your scope of competence, so their situation requires referral. While we cannot cover every such situation, here are some guidelines to help you determine the level of appropriateness. Recall that scope of competence for nonprofessional counseling is limited to assessing and assisting a helpee to manage immediate life concerns more effectively. That means providing expert advice should generally be avoided and, most importantly, your helping should focus on immediate life concerns. This means that helpees requesting help with past (i.e., childhood) issues, mental illness, or deeply rooted characterological issues should be referred for professional help. That said, you *can* help address how these concerns might impact their immediate functioning. For example, a helpee with depression or bipolar disorder must be referred to their therapist to treat their diagnosis, but you can still help them work through the immediate expression of the disorder, such as helping motivate them to engage in social activities, express their sad mood and helplessness, or decrease negative self-talk and self-blame in the moment.

Personal Reflection

As you learn about crisis intervention, it will be helpful to engage in introspection about how these challenging issues impact you personally (Hill, 2014). As you reflect on helping in crisis situations concerning suicidality, homicidality, and impaired mental status, answer the following questions:

- Although many helpers have been personally affected by crisis situations similar to the ones they will help others with, other helpers have no prior experience. Prior experience does not change how helpful a helper can be (Egan, 2014); however, it can impact the feelings related to the event (Hill, 2014). How do your personal experiences (or lack thereof) impact your perspective on the crises presented in this chapter?
- Crises are some of the most difficult issues any mental health helper can face, and many helpers experience a variety of reactions to crisis (Ivey et al., 2016). What reactions do you have to talking with, asking about, and supporting helpees with these kinds of issues? What do you believe will be your strengths? What are your concerns or areas for growth?
- Support and preparation are critical for effective helping during a crisis. This chapter will help prepare you, but additional support and consultation are also essential. Identify some supervisors, professors, mentors, mental health professionals, trained nonprofessional helpers, and so forth who you can reach out to for additional guidance and support. List at least three people you can turn to for guidance with helping someone through a challenging crisis situation.

How to Watch

In cases where the helper has observed a warning sign that has led them to be concerned about a potential crisis beyond their scope of competence and requiring professional help, the supporting stage ends and the watch stage begins. If no concerns emerge during the supporting stage, helpers can skip the watching stage and move directly to the investigating stage, presented in the next chapter. Remember, all helping begins with supporting, before either watching or investigating.

Microskills: Questions

In cases where concerns are noted, the helper initiates the watching stage. Recall that LifeRAFT employs the microskills hierarchy as outlined in Figure 5.2. Microskills are organized in a pyramid shape with the skills that should be used most often placed at the bottom of the pyramid and the skills that should be used least often placed at the top of the pyramid.

We use only listening skills during the supporting stage, and we will continue to use primarily listening skills throughout helping situations because of their demonstrated value in helping and their ability to empower helpees to help themselves (Ivey et al., 2016). However, from the watching stage forward, we will also begin to intersperse influencing skills in our helping scenarios.

Influencing Skills

Influencing skills are a category of microskills designed to influence the nature and direction of what a helpee says. Through selective attention and what you as a helper choose to emphasize, influencing skills are used to steer your helpee toward what to discuss next. Influencing skills put the direction of helpees' disclosures more in the control of the helpers, and helpees tend to follow where they lead. The microskills involved in influencing are questions, focusing, information, logical consequences, confrontation, feedback, reframing, and directives (Ivey et al., 2016).

During the watching stage, we will add questions only. The reason for this is that we want to continue to listen and support our helpees, but given the potential concerns regarding crisis and need for referrals, we need to intersperse questions to guide the conversation and gather some specific information prior to moving forward. Questions offer an effective method to gather such information without blocking or disempowering the helpee's own process (Ivey et al., 2016).

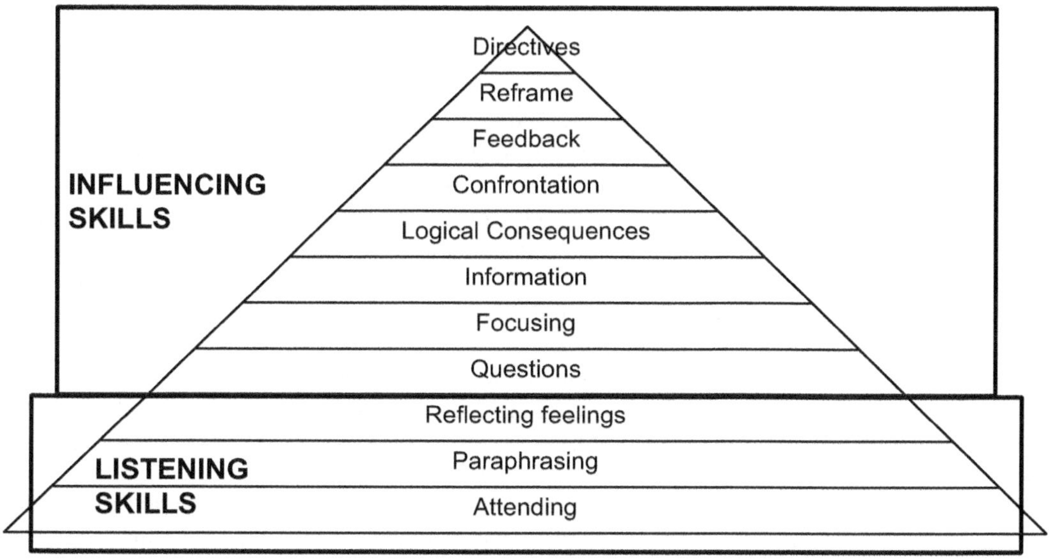

Figure 5.2 Microskills Hierarchy

Questions

Questions are defined as inquiries that are used to direct the helpee to provide certain information. Questions are an influencing skill because, unlike paraphrases and reflections of feeling, they elicit new content in a specific direction chosen by the helper (Hill, 2014). Different questions elicit helpees to continue with their disclosure in certain directions. For example, a helpee might explain that they have had several unfortunate events occur that day, including getting a speeding ticket, being late for work, and having an argument with a coworker. Helper questions such as "What was the argument with your coworker about?" versus "How did you feel about being late to work?" would prompt very different explanations from your helpee. While we need to be cautious and limit our questions to avoid dominating the direction the discussion takes, questions can be particularly effective in steering the conversation toward needed information regarding potential crises. For example, we might ask, "What did you mean when you said that you can't handle this anymore?" Given that a vague statement may imply a crisis such as suicidal risk, questions provide the opportunity to guide the conversation to further explanation and information gathering.

Questions can either be direct or indirect (Hill, 2014). Direct questions are structured as inquiries in a typical questioning fashion, with a question mark and delivered with a higher pitch at the end. Examples include "How are you?" and "Did you get a speeding ticket?" Try saying these questions aloud. Notice how you naturally use a higher vocal tone and convey an invitation for a response.

Indirect questions are inquiries that are delivered as a statement or directive, with a period and delivered with a lowered pitch at the end, similar to other kinds of statements. To use our previous examples: "Tell me about how you are doing" and "I am wondering if you got a speeding ticket." Indirect questions are one method of varying the ways you deliver questions and elicit information. Indirect questions feel slightly less interrogative than direct ones and offer the opportunity to invite more of a conversation than an interview. They also help to vary your vocal tone, because repeatedly using the raising tone necessary for questions can become irritating and interfere with the lowered, empathic tone we strive for as helpers (Egan, 2014).

In addition to being either direct or indirect, questions can further be categorized as either open or closed. Each type will be discussed in more detail in the following sections.

OPEN QUESTIONS

Open questions draw out more information and require several words to answer them. An example of a direct open question is, "How are you feeling today?" and an example of an indirect open question is, "Help me understand how you are feeling today." Notice how both the direct and indirect versions elicit the helpee to provide detail about their current mood. Open questions invite specific information to be shared with explanation. Rather than being answered in one or two words, such as a closed question (e.g., "Are you sad today?" or "I want to know if you're sad"), open questions are presented more broadly and unassumingly, inviting the helpee to expand on their response (Ivey et al., 2016).

The purpose of open questions is to guide the helpee to talk about a specific issue while also leaving room for free discussion in ways the helpee chooses. Open questions are helpful at the beginning of the watching stage because they effectively shift the conversation to (or back to) safety concerns while still providing space for the helpee to discuss the issue the way they want. Open questions are also helpful throughout the watching stage to continue to elicit details and keep the helpee talking about crisis concerns. For example, "What impact is this having on your motivation to keep going?" and "Tell me about what it looks like when you feel angry toward your ex." These questions offer shifts in the conversation and open the door to assessing for potential suicidality or homicidality, respectively, without jumping straight to asking about potential lethality.

To ask direct open questions, begin with the words *who*, *what*, *when*, or *where*. These words naturally imply questions that require an elaborated response. Continue with content you are interested in learning more about, using a curious and empathic tone, but be careful not to use an overly interrogative or probing style, such as a journalist or detective might use in uncovering a story. As helpers, we want to maintain empathy with helpees and share their pain rather than trying to get the "inside scoop." End direct questions with a higher pitch to indicate a question and use nonverbals such as making direct eye contact, leaning forward, or raising your eyebrows to invite the helpee to respond. Examples with each beginning word may include "Who were you with when this happened?" "What was your response?" "When you think about it now, what comes to mind?" and "Where did it take place?"

Use a similar approach for indirect questions, but instead begin with varied sentence stems that are either more directive in nature, such as "Tell me more about" or "Expand on what you mentioned regarding," or sentence stems that are more personal, such as "I would like to know" or "I'm wondering about. . . ." For indirect questions, you can increase your empathic tone and lower your pitch because responses do not require the same questioning tone required for direct questions.

CLOSED QUESTIONS

Closed questions elicit specific information and can be answered in one or two words. Examples of closed questions include "When are you planning to meet your friend?" and "I was wondering if you ever use drugs." Notice how direct and indirect versions of closed questions ask for very specific facts or information that can be given with one word, such as "tomorrow" and "yes." Unlike open questions, which invite the helpee to continue speaking, closed questions imply helpees should provide the requested information and then stop.

Closed questions are intended to obtain specific facts and information, particularly when a clear response is needed to a helper's inquiry (Ivey et al., 2016), but remember that closed questions also serve to encourage the helpee to stop speaking. Although this is rarely the goal in helping situations, it is sometimes warranted, particularly in the watching stage. When there is reason to be concerned about a crisis situation or need for referral, helpers may need to use closed questions to determine the level of risk. For example, specific closed questions such as "Are you thinking about killing yourself?" for assessing suicidality or "Do you think about hurting someone else?" for assessing homicidality and "Tell me where you are right now" for assessing impaired mental status are critical assessment questions. Closed questions can be vital in these cases, because they tend to provide answers that helpees may not readily disclose in response to open-ended queries. In addition, asking closed questions slows down or even halts the conversation, giving the helper the opportunity to make a subsequent referral.

To ask closed questions, typically begin with words such as *is*, *are*, *do*, or other similar stems. These words naturally imply questions that require only brief responses and no additional explanation. Follow the stem with one piece of information you wish to ask about, using a curious and empathic tone. In the case of suicide, resist the urge to ask questions indirectly (e.g., "Are you considering doing something to yourself?") or beg a certain response (e.g., "You're not going to do anything crazy, are you?"). Avoid asking multiple questions at once (e.g., "Have you had thoughts of suicide? Do you think about it now? Have you ever thought about it?"). Ask one question at a time, directly and empathically, in a balanced manner so helpees feel safe to answer truthfully (e.g., "Do you ever think about suicide?"). Given their directness, take extra effort to employ empathic attending skills by conveying as much care as possible. End direct questions with a higher pitch to indicate a question and use nonverbals such as making direct eye contact, hand gestures, and leaning forward to invite the helpee to respond.

Use a similar approach for indirect closed questions but, instead, begin with varied sentence stems. These sentence stems are the same as used for indirect open questions. They can be more directive in nature, such as "Tell me" or "Clarify for me," or sentence stems that are more personal, such as "I would like to know" or "I'm wondering about. . . ."

Open and closed questions are critical skills for the watching stage, as well as many different stages of counseling. However, although essential when needed, keep in mind that questions can be particularly problematic, because as with all influencing skills, questions put more power in the hands of the helper. With this power comes greater potential for helpees to feel insecure and judged, even when it is completely unintended (Erford, 2014). Questions can come across as judgmental and inadvertently communicate the helper's point of view. For example, the closed question "Don't you think it would help if you called your mom?" is more judgmental than "Would you like to call your mom?" Better yet would be an indirect open question like "I wonder who else you might be able to ask for support right now."

Due to its natural judgmental tone, one form of question should always be avoided: the dreaded *why* question. Questions beginning with *why* tend to put people on the defensive because they remind them of being reprimanded as children with the question "Why did you do that [insert naughty behavior here]?" (Ivey et al., 2016). Asking a helpee for their motivation is acceptable, but the "why" needs to be rephrased. Other ways to ask "Why did you do that?" can include "What led to that decision?" or "How did you come to that outcome?" These questions can elicit the same information without the potentially damaging connotations. Challenge yourself to limit the number of questions you ask and to word them as nonjudgmentally as possible. In practice role-plays, be sure to ask your helpees for feedback on this skill, as it takes practice.

Despite these issues, untrained helpers tend to use a high number of questions, particularly closed ones, in response to distress (Campbell, Davidson, & Davidson, 2017), because people are socialized to ask questions in helping situations, even though research does not indicate this as a particularly effective strategy (Erford, 2014). Instead, listening skills are most helpful and are the common factors of all effective therapies (Rogers, 1961). Usually, just a few questions can provide the gentle nudges helpees need to share essential information, so resist the urge to respond with too many questions and save them for only when they are needed.

Microskills Ramp-Up

You may recall that our LifeRAFT training model also includes the microskills ramp-up, which is the stepwise progression of when and how to use microskills during a helping situation. The microskills ramp-up is presented in Figure 5.3 and is incorporated in the watching stage to help you resist the urge to bombard your helpees with too many questions. The ramp-up asserts that, even during intense crisis situations, we use listening skills first and most often, only progressing as needed to influencing microskills in a stepwise fashion, and always returning to the first level before progressing up the steps. Thus, helpers begin at the first level of listening skills (attending, paraphrasing, and reflecting feelings) and then ramp up to the next level of microskills. This includes not only questions but also focusing, another microskill we will add later in your training. For the watching stage, we will ramp up to questions before returning to listening skills. The ramp-up dictates that once you ask a question, your next response is to return to listening skills. After that, you can ask another question, once again following that with listening skills, and so on. While this may seem robotic, the microskills ramp-up should not be seen as a prescribed formula of one listening skill to one question. Instead, consider the ramp-up as general encouragement to use listening skills most often and introduce questions only when needed.

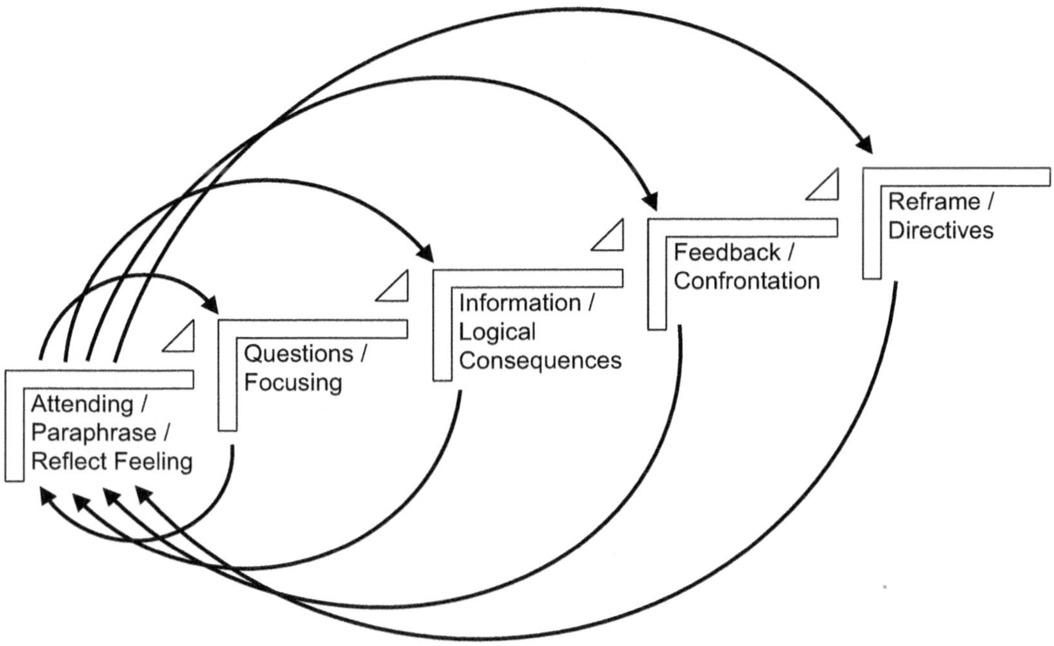

Figure 5.3 Microskills Ramp-Up

Written Practice

For each of the following examples, write out four questions you could use in response to each helpee. In the examples of Robin and Mike, warning signs are present and warrant assessing for suicidality and homicidality, respectively. Develop questions that guide your helpees to discuss potential crisis issues in more detail. Include one direct open question, indirect open question, direct closed question, and indirect closed question. Be sure to try different sentence stems with each question and aim to be as nonjudgmental in your questions as possible.

ROBIN: "My partner ended our three-year relationship yesterday. She was my whole world and really kept me going. I'm completely shattered and don't see the point of continuing alone. It's not worth it without her."

MIKE: "My neighbor is harassing and bullying me about any little noise I make, and I've had it. We've clashed before and he knows I can seriously mess him up, but he continues to bait me into fights. I've had it! He needs to be taught a lesson."

Addressing Crises

At this point, we've moved from the support stage to the watch stage, using the microskills ramp-up to ask questions when appropriate. Now we can use these skills to ask helpees about crisis concerns and refer them for help. Each of these components is explained in detail below.

Ask

The first aim of the watching stage is to ask directly about crisis concerns. Begin by eliciting more details about crisis concerns to determine if the issue is outside your scope of competence and/or representative of a crisis in need of referral. Continue using listening skills and begin to intersperse open questions to guide the conversation toward concerning material. Listening skills can help by increasing attending for crisis-laden information, such as leaning forward when your helpee describes the crisis and leaning back slightly when they divert to another topic. Paraphrases and reflections of feeling can also focus on crisis symptoms. You might say something like "I hear you saying that you have been thinking about death a lot" (paraphrase) or "You sound scared and confused, almost like you're in a fog" (reflection of feeling).

You can use questions to request helpees to explain symptoms you observe in them, such as "What is causing your slurred speech?" or "Tell me more about those bruises on your arm." Questions can be used to ask helpees to elaborate on concerning statements, such as "When you said that you never want to wake up, what did you mean by that?" and "Please help me understand what you meant about wanting to make her pay for what she did." Begin with open questions to gather more information and then, after ramping down to listening skills, ramp back up to questions and reiterate their responses by asking closed questions for direct clarification, such as "Are you saying that you want to do something to prevent yourself from ever waking up?" and "Is it the case that you want to physically hurt her?" Accompany these questions with empathic attending skills and follow them with listening skills, such as "These are intense thoughts you're dealing with" (paraphrase) or "I see how angry you are and appreciate that you're talking to me about it" (reflection of feeling). These listening skills could then be followed by another question.

For helpees who may be suicidal, the most important question to ask is the direct closed question: "Are you thinking about killing yourself?" For helpees who may be homicidal, ask a similar direct closed question, such as "Are you thinking about hurting or killing someone?" Preferably include a name if there is an identified potential victim. Remain empathically persistent and get a clear yes or no response. If helpees affirm suicidal or homicidal thoughts, additional questions might elicit whether they have a plan for how they would carry out the act, such as "Do you have a plan for how you would do it?" and "What is your plan?" Depending on their answer, you may ask whether they intend to act on it with questions like "Do you intend to follow through with this plan?" and "When/where do you intend to do this?" These questions help to define lethality (Erford, 2014). Helpees with thoughts but no specific plan or immediate intent represent a lower level of crisis while those with a plan and intent represent a higher level of crisis.

For helpees whose mental status may be impaired, screening questions from a mental status exam are helpful (Durand & Barlow, 2013). Such questions check if helpees know who they are, where they are, and when they are and can be asked in short succession: "What is your name? Where are you right now? What is the current date and time?" The more difficulty helpees have in responding to these questions, the higher their level of immediate risk. Remain empathically persistent, stay calm, and continue to use listening skills regardless of your helpee's responses. Thank them for sharing information and continuing to talk with you, because they have placed a great deal of trust in you.

Refer

The second aim of the watching stage is to refer the helpee to a professional. Familiarize yourself with referral sources ahead of time and know where to look for specific contact information. If you are acting as a helper as part of your job, it is important to consult with your supervisor to inform them that you have identified a helpee in need of more help. Handling crises and making referrals can be daunting, so all helpers should consider consulting with a trusted mentor or other helper during this process. If ever in doubt during crisis and referral situations, ask someone (Quinnett, 1995). Work with your helpee to involve their support system to talk, monitor, and remove access to dangerous situations can also be beneficial (Quinnett, 2007).

The referral procedure depends greatly on the severity of the helpee's distress. Lower-level crises include helpees who express suicidal/homicidal thoughts with no plan or intent to act on them or show slightly impaired mental status while remaining in touch with reality. If these helpees do not appear to be a danger to themselves or others, they can likely wait to schedule a regular appointment during typical business hours with a professional. In these cases, ask the helpee to agree to keep themselves safe until help is available. For example, you might ask, "Will you promise to keep yourself (and others) safe until your appointment?" Then provide the helpee with referral information and make calls with them to schedule appointments. Provide emergency information in case their situation deteriorates and risk increases.

For helpees who present with a lower level of risk, the next best option to a referral is obtaining verbal commitment from your helpee to stay safe and seek help on their own as soon as it is available, for example by asking, "Will you commit to keeping yourself safe and calling for an appointment tomorrow morning?" If they are still unwilling, the next best solution is to give them referral information and obtain a verbal commitment not to engage in lethal behaviors, such as "Will you assure me that you will keep yourself and others safe?" Sometimes helpees need time to agree to more help, and so obtaining a helpee's willingness to accept help at any time, even later in the future, is a good outcome (Quinnett, 1995).

For higher-level crises such as suicidal/homicidal plans and intent, or impaired mental status that presents a danger to themselves or others, the helpee may benefit from immediate intervention. In these cases, escort your helpee to get help or make a phone call together to someone who can help immediately. This again can be accomplished through listening and questions. For example, you could use a reflection of feeling by saying "I hear your pain and given what you're going through, I'm very worried about you. Will you please go with me now to the hospital to get help with this?" or a closed question such as "Let's call a suicide hotline together now, ok?" Continue to use listening skills as the helpee responds and considers their next steps. Remain calm and patient and give the helpee time to agree to a referral.

Nevertheless, helpees cannot be forced into accepting help, and they may decline your referrals. If they refuse and present a high level of immediate risk, it is appropriate to break confidentiality and call emergency services yourself in an effort to keep them safe. This option is available at any point that you fear for the helpee's immediate safety.

Written Practice

Effective crisis referral necessitates that you have referral sources available. These are most helpful if you have them ready and identified in advance. Some potential referrals are listed below, along with national referral information. Complete the table by researching and adding specific information for your local area. Consider using internet resources and asking others to determine resources in your area.

Type	*Crisis Reason*	*Name*	*Location*	*Phone*
Ambulance/Police	Medical, safety, or mental health emergency (on site or transportation needed)			911
Emergency Room	Medical, safety, or mental health emergency (can transport)			

Type	*Crisis Reason*	*Name*	*Location*	*Phone*
Suicide Hotlines	Immediate support for suicidality			1–800–SUICIDE 1–800–273–TALK
School or work mental health services	Mental health resources for members of your school/work			
Local mental health center	Referral source for mental health resources for community members			
Physician	Medical or mental health concerns			
Psychologist/Mental Health Counselor	Mental health concerns			
Others?				

Result of Watching

Through the watch stage, we hope to uncover potential crises and provide helpees with referral information or connect them with professionals when appropriate. Ideally, helpees will accept referrals, guarantee their safety, and commit to continued treatment, but they may be initially resistant. Often helpees need time, understanding, and support to eventually accept help (Quinnett, 1995).

In cases where a helpee is not willing to accept a referral and is unwilling to make any kind of commitment to stay safe, the important thing to keep in mind is that you are not alone and help is available, both to you as the helper and to your helpee. We cannot prevent a crisis from happening, but we can help by reaching out. As a concerned helper, you can contact any of the referral sources above, including emergency services, community mental health clinics, or medical/mental health professionals to request guidance, typically at no cost (Quinnett, 1995). Other nonprofessional helpers can also provide support, including volunteers, mentors, teachers, clergy, friends, family, or other caring people in your support network. If they do not know what to do, they may be able to direct you to someone who does. You are not alone; a caring community of helpers can stand together to address crises. Although we ordinarily maintain confidentiality, do not be afraid to let others know when safety concerns arise. When a life is at stake, we can no longer worry about breaking a trust or having our helpee angry with us. When in doubt, reach out. You could save a life.

Case Example

This case example shows how a nonprofessional helper, a father (Wayne) talks with his 20-year-old son (Kyle), who is depressed and struggling with suicidality. Prior to the beginning of this transcript, Wayne and Kyle went through the supporting stage. In this example, the helper, Wayne, briefly uses the watching stage to learn about crisis concerns and refer the helpee, Kyle, for help.

HELPER: Kyle, I love you and I'm worried about you. It sounds like the depression has gotten really intense. [Paraphrase]

HELPEE: It has, Dad. I'm really sorry. I've tried to fight it and I can't. I'm tired of fighting it and feeling this way. Every moment hurts.

HELPER: Please help me understand what you mean that you're tired of fighting it. [Open question]

HELPEE: I've been feeling this way for so long now. I can't remember what it was like to not feel depressed. Every day is a struggle and it doesn't seem like it's ever going to get any better.

HELPER: I hear how hopeless this feels for you right now. [Reflection of feeling]

HELPEE: You don't know how bad it is. I'm miserable to be around. It's even more miserable to feel this way.

HELPER: I hear you, son. Although I can't possibly know everything you're going through, thank you for helping me understand. I'm with you and want to be with you in this. [Empathic statement]

HELPEE: Thanks, but I'm backed into a corner. I can't do this anymore. I just need to escape the world.

HELPER: What would that look like to escape the world? [Open question]

HELPEE: I don't know. I just want out.

HELPER: This seems like it's hard to talk about and it's ok to take your time. [Paraphrase]

HELPEE: I don't want to feel like this anymore.

HELPER: Certainly, I don't want you to feel bad. When people are feeling depressed and hopeless like this, they sometimes wish they were dead. I'm wondering if those kinds of thoughts have come up for you? [Closed question]

HELPEE: Yes, they have. I just want to go to sleep and never wake up and not have to feel like this ever again. I hate it.

HELPER: Thank you for telling me, Kyle. I'm proud of you and appreciate you sharing where you're at. [Empathic statement] I want to make sure I understand: are you thinking about killing yourself? [Closed question]

HELPEE: Yes, sometimes I think about it. Just when things get really bad, like right now. It pops into my mind.

HELPER: Suicidal thoughts can creep in when depression gets intense. [Paraphrase]

HELPEE: Exactly. It's not all the time, but sometimes.

HELPER: I see. And in those times, do you think about how you would kill yourself? [Closed question]

HELPEE: No, not really. I just think about it magically happening somehow. I don't want to do anything; I just want to go to sleep and not wake up. Dad, I wouldn't actually do anything. I just think about it.

HELPER: I hear you that you aren't making plans to end your life. Those thoughts come in when you're hurting really bad. [Paraphrase]

HELPEE: Yes. They don't feel good. It just happens sometimes.

HELPER: How incredibly painful and upsetting. [Reflection of feeling] So you have no intention on acting on these thoughts? [Closed question]

HELPEE: No, I don't. And I won't. I worry about the future and if I feel like this for too long, I might start thinking about how I'd do it.

HELPER: That is worrisome, and I worry about that too. [Reflection of feeling] You're my son. I love you and I want you to live. [Empathic statement]

HELPEE: I can't deal with how much this hurts though.

HELPER: Kyle, we'll get through this. I can't treat you for this but can get you started with someone who can. Will you make a phone call with me right now to set up an appointment for you with a counselor? [Refer; closed question]

HELPEE: Ok, I guess. If that's what you think will help.

HELPER: I really do. I'm proud of you for this. [Empathic statement] Until the appointment, I'm also going to give you this 24-hour crisis phone number to call if you ever feel like you can't keep yourself safe: 1–800–SUICIDE.

HELPEE: I'm not going to do it. I just think about it and it sucks.

HELPER: Yes, I hear that and I'm so glad. Since you're committed to staying safe, I think you should have this just in case things took a turn for the worse. If that were to happen, will you agree to use this number to stay safe? [Paraphrase; closed question]

HELPEE: I'm not going to need it but yes, I'll agree to that. I'll also go to the counselor.

As a result of the watching stage, Wayne asked about suicidality and referred Kyle for treatment, including making an appointment with a mental health counselor and providing emergency numbers.

Written Practice

It is now your turn to try constructing responses for a watch stage helping scenario. In this practice, your responses will focus on your helpee, Maureen, a 75-year-old who has just lost her husband to cancer. To practice watching, imagine that you are talking with Maureen and she makes the following statements:

> "I can't believe my husband is gone. I have no one left now. I'm all alone."
>
> "What's the point anymore? My whole life became about taking care of him. What good am I to anyone? There's no purpose for me here anymore."
>
> "God should have taken me, too. We were supposed to go together."

- Given these helpee statements, write down three open questions and three closed questions you would ask Maureen to assess for suicidality.
- Maureen confirms that she is having suicidal thoughts but no plans or intent. What could you do and say to help facilitate referring for Maureen? Feel free to assume or add extra detail to Maureen's story if needed in your responses.

Role-Play Practice

The purpose of this exercise is to rehearse the supporting and watching stages. For this exercise, find a volunteer helpee to role-play a helping scenario with you and provide feedback afterward. Set a timer and conduct at least a ten-minute helping scenario, attempting to support using listening skills of attending, paraphrasing, and reflecting feelings only and then watch using listening skills and questions. Complete the following:

1. Consider pairing with a fellow helper-in-training and take turns being the helper and helpee.
2. Video record the scenario. Follow the ethical guidelines discussed in Chapter 1, including consent to video record.
3. Ask your helpee to select a topic to discuss. Consult Chapter 1, "Problem Triggers," for topic ideas. Ask them to, at some point, say a concerning statement such as "I don't want to live anymore." Helpees can choose what level of crisis to role-play, which they should reveal as prompted by helper interventions during the watching stage.
4. As the helper, attempt to support using listening skills of attending, paraphrasing, and reflecting feelings only and then watch using listening skills and questions.
5. At the end of the role-play, request feedback from your helpee about what you did well and what you could improve on next time. Write down your helpee's responses.
6. Review the recording. Note what you observed regarding your verbal and nonverbal communication, use of microskills, and the ways in which your helpee responded, both verbally and nonverbally. What do you think you did well and what you could improve on next time as the helper?

Summary

In this chapter we discussed the following:

Description of Watching

- Watching is the second stage of the LifeRAFT helping skills model, in which we watch for warning signs and facilitate referrals to professional help when needed.

When to Watch

- Watching begins after the supporting stage, when the helper notices or suspects warning signs of crisis or issues requiring professional help.

How to Watch

- Use listening skills of attending, paraphrasing, and reflecting feelings and questions.
- Questions include open and closed questions.
    - Open questions guide the helpee to discuss general topics of concern in more detail.
    - Closed questions serve to clarify specific information and halt conversation.
- Listening skills and questions are delivered using the microskills ramp-up, in which the helper starts with listening skills, asks a question, and actively listens to the helpee's response before asking another question.
- The process of watching involves asking about potential crisis issues such as suicidality, homicidality, and impaired mental status, as well as issues beyond your scope of competence, before then guiding the helpee to appropriate professional help.

Result of Watching

- Through the watch stage, we hope to uncover potential crises and provide helpees with referral information or connect them with professionals when appropriate.

References

American Red Cross. (2018). How to respond to a water emergency. *American Red Cross*. Retrieved from www.redcross.org/content/dam/redcross/atg/PDF_s/Preparedness___Disaster_Recovery/Disaster_Preparedness/Water_Safety/WouldYouKnowWhattodo.pdf

Baird, B. N. (2014). *The internship, practicum, and field placement handbook* (7th ed.). New York: Routledge.

Bonanno, G. (2004). Loss, trauma, and human resilience: Have we underestimated the human capacity to thrive after extremely aversive events? *American Psychologist*, *59*, 20–28.

Campbell, E. L., Davidson, K., & Davidson, S. M. (2017). Effectiveness of LifeRAFT undergraduate helping skills training model. *Psychology Teaching Review*, *23*(2), 32–41.

Centers for Disease Control and Prevention. (CDC, 2016). 10 leading causes of death by age group. *National Suicide Statistics*. Retrieved from www.cdc.gov/violenceprevention/suicide/statistics/index.html

Durand, V. M., & Barlow, D. H. (2013). Chapter 2: An integrative approach to psychopathology. In V. M. Durand & D. H. Barlow (Eds.), *Essentials of abnormal psychology* (pp. 30–68). Belmont, CA: Wadsworth Publishing Company.

Egan, G. (2014). *The skilled helper: A problem-management and opportunity development approach to helping* (10th ed.). Belmont, CA: Brooks/Cole.

Erford, B. T. (2014). *Orientation to the counseling profession: Advocacy, ethics, and essential professional foundations* (2nd ed.). Boston, MA: Pearson.

Hill, C. E. (2014). *Helping skills: Facilitating exploration, insight, and action* (4th ed.). Washington, DC: American Psychological Association.

Ivey, A. E., Ivey, M. B., & Zalaquett, C. P. (2016). *Essentials of intentional interviewing: Counseling in a multicultural world* (3rd ed.). Boston, MA: Cengage Learning.

Quinnett, P. (1995). *QPR gatekeeper training manual*. Spokane, WA: QPR Institute, Inc.

Quinnett, P. (2007). *QPR gatekeeper training for suicide prevention: The model, rationale, and theory*. Spokane, WA: QPR Institute, Inc.

Roberts, A. R. (2000). An overview of crisis theory and crisis intervention. In A. R. Roberts (Ed.), *Crisis intervention handbook* (pp. 3–30). New York: Oxford.

Rogers, C. (1961). *On becoming a person*. Boston: Houghton Mifflin.

Rudd, M. D., Joiner, T. E., Jobes, D. A., & King, C. A. (1999). Practice guidelines in the outpatient treatment of suicidality: An integration of science and a recognition of its limitations. *Professional Psychology: Research and Practice*, *30*, 437–446.

Sandoval, J. (2002). Culture, diversity, and crisis. In J. Sandoval (Ed.), *Handbook of crisis counseling, intervention, and prevention in the schools* (pp. 39–56). Mahwah, NJ: Lawrence Erlbaum Associates, Inc.

Simon, R. I. (2009). Enhancing suicide risk assessment through evidence-based psychiatry. *Psychiatric Times*, *26*(1). Retrieved from www.psychiatrictimes.com/schizophrenia/enhancing-suicide-risk-assessment-through-evidence-based-psychiatry

6 Stage Three

Investigate

Chapter Goals

This chapter will prepare you to:

- Learn about investigating, the third stage of the LifeRAFT helping skills model, and the purpose of investigating.
- Increase your awareness of when to use the investigating stage and how to engage in investigating.
- Develop methods to provide help by engaging in the investigating stage using listening skills, questions, and focusing.
- Identify what to expect as a result of completing the investigating stage with a helpee.

Introduction

This chapter will focus on investigating, the third stage of the LifeRAFT model. To prepare us to learn about the third stage of our helping process, we return to our water rescue metaphor.

We have characterized emotional distress as being swept up and trapped in a whirlpool. In the supporting stage we learned how to join with and support our stuck helpees by riding the whirlpool with them to build trust and support. We then learned how to watch for warning signs, how to identify if the helpee is drowning in crisis, and how to rescue them to safety by assessing and facilitating referrals to emergency and professional services. Now that we have joined our helpees in their distress and concluded they are not in immediate crisis, we can investigate the situation and devise a strategy for aiding them in freeing themselves from their current distress. Just as lifeguards need to assess a situation to decide what water rescue method is most appropriate (American Red Cross, 2018), so too do helpers need to investigate the conditions the helpee finds themselves in to determine the most appropriate helping skills method to use (Brooks-Harris, 2008). Just as one small physical shift can release a person from a water current, focusing on changing one area of a psychological problem can release a helpee from drowning in emotional turmoil. Investigating involves searching for one strategic shift that can be made to improve the helpee's condition. Once a strategy is identified, helpers can then use it to guide the helpee through the steps in making modifications to get unstuck from the whirlpool through a basic problem-solving process.

Description of Investigating

Investigating is the third stage of the LifeRAFT helping skills model (see Figure 6.1; Investigate). The investigating stage involves an assessment of the helpee's concerns, determining what

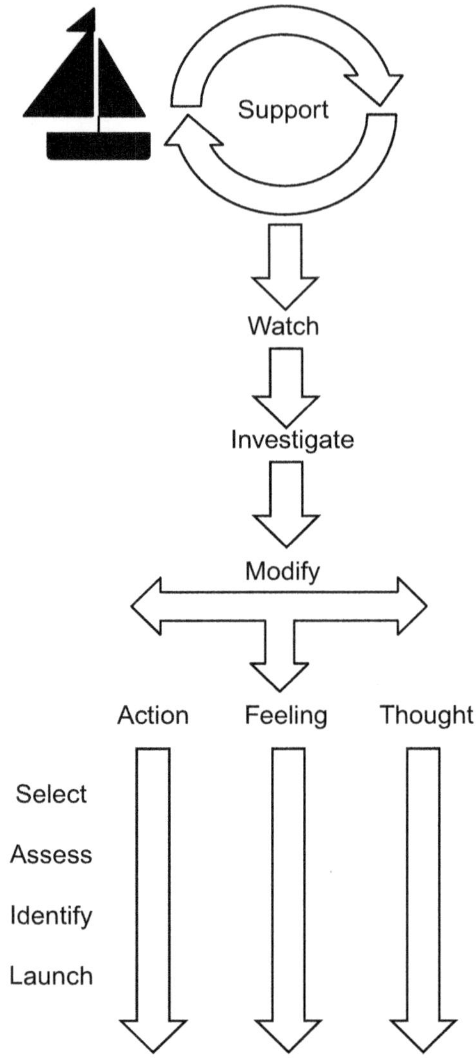

Figure 6.1 LifeRAFT Model

is changeable and what a helper can effectively provide, and then deciding how to move forward with problem-solving. When helpees are not in crisis but their distress still requires support and attention, helpers can continue LifeRAFT helping by investigating and assessing the nature of the helpee's distress. This allows us to get a better understanding of the helpee, the present situation, and the primary problem at hand, as well as which strategy might best get the helpee unstuck from their distress whirlpool.

Investigating is meant to help guide the helpee toward discussing their concerns in greater detail. Investigating is about exploring and assessing the situation on two different levels. The first is the helpee's circumstances, including the person, present, and problem. The second is the LifeRAFT strategies, including the helpee's actions, feelings, and thoughts. Both of these levels are discussed in the following sections.

Investigating Circumstances

The first task of the investigating stage is to assess the helpee's specific circumstances, including the person, present-day conditions, and the problem that ranks as most distressing. By focusing on these three areas, it helps guide the helpee to discuss areas of their life where they are able to make change to immediately improve their situation (Ivey, Ivey, & Zalaquett, 2016). It also directs the conversation to areas within a nonprofessional helper's scope of competence (APA, 2016). Assessing the person, present, and problem is further described below.

Person

Assessing the person means attending specifically to the helpee's experience of themselves (Ivey et al., 2016). This is in contrast to focusing the conversation on other people in the helpee's life or on circumstances in their environment, for example. Although these external factors are important and discussing them can provide valuable catharsis (Breuer & Freud, 1974), these benefits are better accomplished during the supporting stage of helping. During investigating, we transition to focusing on what changes the helpee can make in an effort to serve their ultimate goal of managing their immediate life concerns more effectively. Given that the only person you can change is yourself, it is best to begin the process of improving a helpee's life by focusing on the person of the helpee.

Present

Assessing the present means attending specifically to the here and now of present day, rather than focusing the conversation on what happened in the past or what might happen in the future (Ivey et al., 2016). This focus serves multiple purposes. Like focusing on the person, attending to the present also highlights changes the helpee can make now to manage their immediate life concerns more effectively. Because they cannot change the past and their impact on the future is limited to steps taken in the present, focusing on the present is the most empowering option. In addition, assessing the present also serves to maintain appropriate limits of nonprofessional counseling competence. Nonprofessional helpers can assess and assist with short-term issues. Concerns that necessitate probing into the past are typically more enduring problems connected to mental illness or ingrained personality characteristics and most often require referral to professional counselors for ongoing help (APA, 2016). By focusing on the present, you naturally limit the helping scenario to what is safe and ethically appropriate for nonprofessional helping while still offering beneficial assistance (Campbell, Davidson, & Davidson, 2017).

Problem

Assessing the problem means attending to one primary issue rather than trying to manage multiple issues at once (Ivey et al., 2016). Although distress often makes it difficult for helpees to focus on one specific event, the investigating stage requires you to start guiding helpees toward focusing and clarifying a singular issue. This serves multiple purposes. Similar to focusing on the present, it guides the helpee toward managing their immediate life concerns more effectively by isolating one area for change. Although distress often presents as a complicated mix of problems, problem-solving typically involves deconstructing the distress to identify one changeable aspect (Egan, 2014). This provides a clearer and more manageable approach for helpees to resolve their own issues. In addition, focusing on and clarifying one particular problem also helps us continue to assess and stay within our nonprofessional scope of competence and refer other issues when needed (Campbell et al., 2017).

Assessing the problem adds an additional purpose of getting a better sense of the helpee's readiness for change. Because change rarely occurs spontaneously, readiness for change represents a process or series of stages that comprise a gradual shift from a helpee being stuck in distress to adopting new ways of approaching problems. This process is called the Stages of Change or Transtheoretical Model (Prochaska, Norcross, & DiClemente, 2005) and is depicted in Figure 6.2.

The stages of change model consists of five stages: precontemplation, contemplation, preparation, action, and maintenance (Prochaska et al., 2005). The precontemplation stage is when helpees are unaware of a need for change and are therefore not considering making alterations. For example, a helpee, Norris, may be in distress about his lack of energy. He may not realize that his poor eating habits are a cause of the problem, so he is not even considering changing his diet at this time. Norris would benefit from help that simply raised his awareness of the nature of the problem and his role in it before any shift could occur. Helpees in the precontemplation stage need support to gain awareness of themselves and their concerns before they move toward considering shifts (Prochaska et al., 2005).

The contemplation stage involves recognition of a problem and considering the pros and cons of change. In our example, Norris may now realize that his eating habits are contributing to energy difficulties, yet he enjoys his food choices and is hesitant to change, so he thinks about the possibility of change without committing to anything. Helpees in the contemplation stage need support to think through and weigh out the pros and cons of their choices (Prochaska et al., 2005).

The preparation stage involves planning and taking steps toward making a change without actually engaging in modifications yet. For example, Norris may decide to change his eating and prepare for change by working with a dietitian and buying energy-dense foods. Helpees in the preparation stage need support in preparing for a successful transition (Prochaska et al., 2005).

The action stage is what people typically think of regarding change: engaging in making overt modifications of their problematic choices to new, more adaptive ones. At this point, Norris

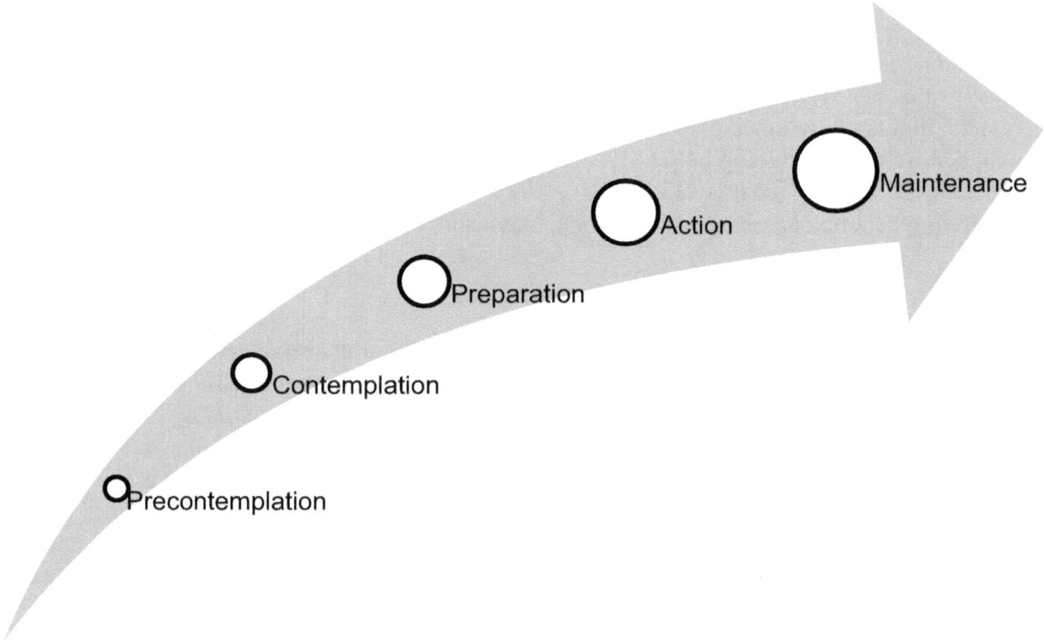

Figure 6.2 Stages of Change

changes his eating habits. Helpees in the action stage need support in strengthening their commitments and continuing to engage in healthy actions (Prochaska et al., 2005).

Stages of change do not end there; the maintenance stage involves sustaining modifications and preventing relapse. Norris might monitor his ongoing eating habits and energy level and correct himself when he reverts back to poor eating habits. Helpees in the maintenance stage need support in managing relapse and planning for preserving gains made (Prochaska et al., 2005).

By assessing your helpee's problem situation, you can begin to get a sense of their level of understanding and readiness to modify the problem. For example, a helpee in the precontemplation stage of a problem is unlikely to be ready for the action stage during your helping interaction, so pushing them to fix their problem (such as might occur in the action stage) is not likely to be helpful. Stages of change will be critical to keep in mind when choosing a strategy and figuring out how much change to expect from the overall helping scenario.

Investigating Strategies

Once a helpee is guided to focus the conversation on the person, present, or problem, our next task is to assess potential problem-solving strategies. Strategies are dimensions of functioning of actions, feelings, and thoughts (see Figure 6.3). Each strategy impacts the other and problems present as an interaction between dysfunctional thoughts, maladaptive feelings, and ineffective actions. These areas of dysfunction are shaped by a variety of contexts, including biology, interpersonal patterns, social systems, and cultural contexts (Harris, Kelly, Campbell, & Hammond, 2014). When dysfunction occurs in one area, it creates dysfunction in another; conversely, adaptiveness in one area fosters adaptiveness in another. For example, if Jayla is trying to do her homework and she has the dysfunctional thought "I am too stupid to finish my homework," she is likely to feel self-conscious. This maladaptive feeling may cause her to give up on trying to complete her homework, which is an ineffective action. Yet if Jayla completes her homework, and thus an effective action, she may instead have the functional thought "I am smart" and feel self-confident, which would be an adaptive feeling. Regardless of where the change occurs, dysfunction tends to go together, as does adaptiveness.

Focusing on the three areas of actions, feelings, and thoughts guides the helpee to discuss how their distress is expressed and impacting their life. This also directs the conversation to areas

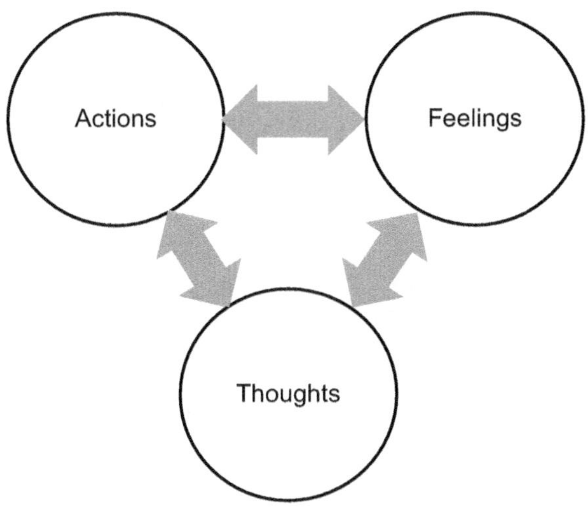

Figure 6.3 Strategies

within a nonprofessional helper's scope of competence and prepares the helper to choose a direction of how to help.

As a reminder, LifeRAFT trains nonprofessional helpers to use actions, feelings, or thoughts as a theoretical strategy for change. The action strategy is based on Behavioral Activation Therapy (Martell, Dimidjian, Herman-Dunn, & Lewinsohn, 2010), the feelings strategy draws from Emotion-Focused Therapy (Greenberg, 2002; Greenberg & Watson, 2005), and the thoughts strategy introduces Cognitive Therapy (Beck, 2011). Helpers are taught to work interactively with actions, feelings, and thoughts to promote helpee modification. You will learn more about the modification process in Chapter 7. For now, it is important to understand what each strategy is to assess a helpee's actions, feelings, and thoughts.

Actions

Actions refer to a helpee's behaviors or conduct. The action strategy is based on Behavioral Activation Therapy (Martell et al., 2010), which categorizes actions as either effective or ineffective. During the investigating stage, helpers assess for ineffective actions related to the identified problem. Martell et al. (2010) suggested that "Behaviors to decrease are those that make the client's life more difficult or interfere with managing one's needs; typically, these are avoidance patterns" (p. 65). Actions are considered ineffective when they represent behaviors that are unwanted by a helpee, or they interfere with meeting needs or attaining desired goals. Unwanted behaviors may include actions that go against a helpee's preferences or values, such as using substances, canceling on social obligations, or neglecting personal hygiene. Interference with needs and goals may present more long-term ineffectiveness, such as mismanaging anger in relationships or neglecting responsibilities in work or school.

Feelings

Feelings refer to emotions or mood. The feelings strategy draws from Emotion-Focused Therapy (Greenberg, 2002; Greenberg & Watson, 2005). It uses emotion-based skills to explore and express adaptive emotions. Unlike actions, feelings themselves are not labeled as fundamentally "adaptive" or "maladaptive." Instead, "maladaptation" refers to the way in which feelings are felt and expressed. Maladaptive feelings are those that are blocked, mismatched, or incongruent. Feelings are blocked when the helpee is unaware of or uncomfortable with a particular emotion, so it is not permitted to be felt or expressed. We sometimes refer to this as "bottling up" our feelings. Mismatches and incongruencies occur when the expressed emotion does not seem to match what might actually be experienced through nonverbal expressions, such as the helpee has clenched fists and describes feeling angry but instead labels their feelings as "sad."

Thoughts

Thoughts refer to cognitions or beliefs. The thoughts strategy is based on Cognitive Therapy (Beck, 2011) and employs cognitive skills to detect errors in thinking and form more accurate thoughts. During the investigating stage, helpers assess for dysfunctional thoughts. Dysfunctional thoughts tend to be global, rigid, excessively negative, self-sabotaging beliefs, typically about oneself. They are often related to perceiving oneself as helpless ("I am incompetent" or "I can't do anything right"); unlovable ("I am unattractive" or "I am not good enough to be loved by others"); or worthless ("I am bad" or "I am dangerous"; Beck, 2011, p. 233). Helpees may also express dysfunctional thoughts about other people ("Other people will hurt me") or the world around them ("The world is dangerous"; Beck, 2011, p. 229).

Personal Reflection

As you learn about strategies and the counseling theories connected to them, it will be helpful to engage in introspection about your own reactions. Recall that each strategy (actions, feelings, and thoughts) represents an established professional counseling theory (Beck, 2011; Greenberg, 2002; Martell et al., 2010). Although LifeRAFT will teach you to be proficient in helping drawing from each of these three methods, most trainees report a preference for one approach (Campbell, 2013). Understanding your reactions to each of these theories may begin to strengthen your connection to these approaches, identify your preferred helper orientation, and, should you choose to pursue professional counselor training, help foretell your emerging theoretical orientation. As you reflect on the strategies of actions, feelings, and thoughts, answer the following questions:

- As a helper, which strategy (actions, feelings, or thoughts) makes the most sense to you as a primary focus to change in helpees? Which strategy makes the least sense to you? Explain your answer.
- Putting yourself in the role of helpee, which strategy (actions, feelings, or thoughts) do you notice the most personal difficulty? When problems arise in your life, which one do you talk about most: ineffective actions, maladaptive feelings, or dysfunctional thoughts? Which strategy do you focus on or discuss the least? Explain your answer.
- Now that you have noted your predicted preferences for focusing on certain strategies as a helper and helpee, discuss your reactions to these preferences. What might be the reason(s) that these are your preferences? Where might they come from?

When to Investigate

Investigating typically comes after the supporting stage of helping, in cases where the watching stage is unneeded due to the absence of any crisis concerns. Recall that the supporting stage ends when helpees seem to begin to steer out of the whirlpool themselves, meaning the intensity of their distress seems to have deescalated. Although still likely upset and feeling stuck, their description of the problem develops more direction and clarity, or it takes more time and detail for them to circle back to the same information. As the helper, you begin to make sense of the nature of their distress and feel that solid rapport has been established or reaffirmed. Helpees talk about their problems with increased ease and detail and engage in more depth in exploring their issues without repeating themselves. They experience and understand their emotions more clearly and discuss their feelings in more depth (Hill, 2014). If no signs of crisis are present and no reasons for referral are given, helpers can move to the investigating stage.

In cases where the watching stage is warranted, helpers move to this stage. Your role in helping may end here if the helpee is immediately transferred to emergency services or other professional. In other cases, the crisis is resolved or plans for ongoing professional treatment are put in place; however, there remains an immediate, noncrisis issue to be addressed that is appropriate for nonprofessional counseling. For example, your helpee, Lorelai, is experiencing suicidal thoughts and might benefit from the watching stage to address the need for a referral and make an appointment with a therapist. After that, Lorelai may benefit from continued help with how to manage depression symptoms that evening or cope with anxiety about asking for time off from work to attend the therapy appointment. Once a referral is made, the immediate issue may be the referral itself: the helpee needs assistance with deciding whether to follow through with seeing a professional. In cases such as these, in which the watching stage has taken place and remaining short-term issues require further help, the investigating stage would follow.

How to Investigate

Begin investigating with our most powerful helping tool: listening. Continue to use attending, paraphrases, and reflections of feeling to keep the helpee talking. Start to attend to the details of their disclosures, namely by paying attention to their life circumstances and strategies. Although the information can be gathered largely through the use of listening skills, interspersing questions can help guide the conversation toward useful details. The microskill of focusing and the microskills ramp-up offer guidance in this process.

Microskills: Questions and Focusing

Questions and focusing are the first two influencing skills of the LifeRAFT model. Although we already learned about questions in the watching stage (Chapter 5), we will briefly review their use in a noncrisis context here before moving on to focusing.

Questions

Recall that questions are inquiries that are used to direct the helpee to provide certain information. They elicit new content in a specific direction chosen by the helper. Questions can either be direct, such as "How are you?" or indirect, such as "Tell me about how you are doing" (Hill, 2014). Direct questions are structured as inquiries in a typical questioning fashion, ending with a question mark and raised vocal pitch. Indirect questions are inquiries that are delivered as a statement or directive and end with a period and lowered vocal pitch. Alternate between direct and indirect questions to help the interaction feel more conversational and less interrogative (Egan, 2014).

Questions can also be either open, such as "What are you doing today?" or closed, such as "Are you going to the store today?" Open questions draw out more information and require several words to answer them in an effort to guide the helpee to talk more about a specific issue. Direct open questions usually begin with the words *who*, *what*, *when*, or *where*. Avoid *why* questions because they tend to sound judgmental (Erford, 2014). Indirect open questions begin with varied sentence stems stated as a directive, "Tell me more about. . . ," or a personal request, "I'm wondering about. . ." (Ivey et al., 2016). When using questions in the investigating stage, rely more on open questions, varying them between direct and indirect. The purpose of this is to encourage the helpee to maintain control over the conversation and to continue talking in greater detail.

Closed questions elicit specific information and can be answered in one or two words and then encourage the helpee to discontinue speaking. Direct closed questions typically begin with words such as *is*, *are*, *do*, or other stems that produce a similarly brief response. Indirect closed questions can begin with directives, such as "Clarify for me. . . ," or personal sentence stem like "I would like to know. . ." (Ivey et al., 2016). Closed questions should mostly be avoided in the investigating stage, because they tend to shut down conversation. Instead, reserve closed questions for instances when clarification is needed. For example, if a helpee told you how many siblings they had and you were unsure if you heard correctly, a closed question of "Did I hear you correctly that you have two siblings?" would be appropriate. Unlike the watching stage when closed questions are essential to crisis management, the investigating stage does not tend to benefit from closed questions and therefore they should be seldom used.

Focusing

The microskill of focusing is another influencing skill that involves eliciting multiple perspectives to adjust the helpee's perception of an issue. Helpees typically view their distress from only one lens, and so focusing invites them to view their situation from multiple angles to elicit new possibilities for change (Ivey et al., 2016).

We want helpees to view their situation through the lenses of person, present, and problem while focusing on their actions, feelings and thoughts. Focusing is the tool that we can use to shift the conversation to each of these areas.

Although it is a separate microskill, focusing still requires the use of the others, namely, a focusing paraphrase, reflection of feeling, or question to focus the conversation (Ivey et al., 2016). For example, a helper who wants to use focusing to understand a helpee's anger can choose to do so through the use of a paraphrase: "It seems like you had a strong reaction after talking to him"; a reflection of feeling: "You felt angry when he said that"; or question: "What was the anger toward him about?" Each of these interventions represent a different skill through the use of alternate wording, but they all serve to shift the helpee's focus to talking about their anger.

The art of focusing is that what you say influences what they say (Erford, 2014); if you talk or ask about anger, helpees will talk about anger. In the investigating stage, we most want helpees to discuss the person, present, and problem of their situations through the strategies of actions, feelings, and thoughts. These areas prepare helpees to help themselves and provide you with important information to assist them in this process. We will now learn about the different ways we can use focusing to shift the conversation to each area of life circumstances and strategies.

Focusing on Life Circumstances

Our goal is for the helpee to discuss their concerns as they pertain to themselves, the immediate present, and one particular issue. To that end, we want to guide them in discussing life circumstances of person, present, and problem.

PERSON

Guide the helpee to talk about themselves by using paraphrases, reflections of feeling, and questions that attend to the helpee, not other people. For example, avoid reflections such as "Your mother sounds angry" or questions such as "What do you believe your mom is thinking?" These examples attend to the helpee's mother; although she may be involved in the situation, trying to mind-read her situation and what she can change will not help the helpee resolve their part of the issue. Instead, focus on the person by using the helpee's name and emphasizing the word "you." Perhaps a helpee, Rachel, tells you about an argument she had with her mother. Focusing on the person, a paraphrase might be, "Rachel, I'm hearing that *you* had a disagreement with your mom." A focusing reflection of feeling might be, "*You're* hurt about what was said during the argument." If Rachel responds with detail about her mother only, a focusing indirect open question could be, "Rachel, I hear that your mom might be having a lot of reactions; I'm most concerned with what's going on for *you*."

PRESENT

Guide the helpee to talk in the present tense rather than the past or future. Avoid questions such as "What were you feeling during the argument?" and instead word your interventions in the present tense. You can emphasize the immediacy of your statement with the words "now," "currently," "in this moment," or "right now." Such a direct focusing question would be, "What are you feeling about the argument *now*?"

Past events can also be brought into the here and now to bring more realism and immediacy to the intervention (Corey, 2009). Although it may feel grammatically awkward at first, try switching to present tense, even when talking about a past event. A focusing paraphrase example might be, "So you are having a conversation with your mom and things are pleasant at first. Then they start to shift." Notice the verbs "are" and "having" rather than past tense "were" and "had." Although the situation was in the past, speak as if it is currently happening. The helpee may continue to talk in past tense at first but will typically switch to match your present tense language. This intervention gently guides the helpee to stay in the present moment and explore problem-solving in the here and now.

PROBLEM

Lead your helpee to narrow their discussion to one issue or problem. This is typically more involved than minor word changes to focus on the person or present. To focus on the problem, begin by aiding the helpee in externalizing problems. Sometimes helpees talk about themselves as the primary problem, particularly if they are feeling overwhelmed by multiple issues (Ivey et al., 2016). Discuss concerns as "*the* issue" or "*the* problem" rather than "*your* issue/problem." This wording separates the helpee from the challenges they are facing. This technique even works for intrapsychic issues such as internal choices or mental illness, for example by saying "the indecision" or "the depression." Emphasize through your word choice that the helpee is a person and the problem is the problem.

Once issues are externalized and separated from the helpee, guide them to narrow their discussion to one problem. That problem should be chosen by the helpee and is usually the most concerning, urgent, or easily manageable issue. This can once again be accomplished through a combination of paraphrasing, reflections of feeling, and questions. An example of such a paraphrase would be: "There's so much going on: the argument with your mom, difficulty sleeping, and car trouble. Sounds like the argument is of most concern to you right now." A reflection of feelings would look like: "That argument seems to be the most painful one of all; I hear your confusion about how to proceed with that." The last option is a question: "We've talked about several challenges that have come up for you and I'm curious, which one can we help you address first?" Notice the paraphrase and reflection of feeling indirectly inferred one problem, while questions can be used to directly ask the helpee where they want to focus. Once you decide upon an issue, this becomes defined as the "presenting problem," a term borrowed from professional counseling to denote what brought a client to therapy (Whiston, 2009).

Written Practice

In this practice, your responses will focus on your helpee, Bashir. Bashir is a 66-year-old employee who is sharing financial concerns with you, a human resources worker at his company. To practice investigating, imagine you have already engaged in supporting and watching and ruled out crisis issues. He shares the following with you:

"I'm having trouble making ends meet. Living paycheck to paycheck every month is so stressful. My wife stopped working a year ago and at that time, we started relying on my income. This job isn't fulfilling and before my wife got sick, we planned for me to retire by now. She likes her job and wanted to continue but couldn't. I need to keep working to make money. My wife has a lot of health issues and I don't want to worry her with anything else, so I've stopped talking to her about money. I know she is worried though. She has so much going on with her treatment. What if I can't pay for everything she needs? I'm supposed to be the strong one and provide for us through this. I can't face it, so I avoid looking at bills and won't answer the phone out of fear it's someone who wants money. I worry about what bills are going to show up in my mailbox and if I'll be able to cover them."

Given Bashir's disclosure, what could you say to focus on life circumstances? Feel free to assume or add extra detail to Bashir's story if needed in your responses.

- Focus on the person by providing a paraphrase, reflection of feeling, direct open question, and indirect open question that focuses on Bashir. Briefly explain how each of these responses accomplishes the goal of focusing on the person.
- Focus on the present by providing a paraphrase, reflection of feeling, direct open question, and indirect open question. Briefly explain how each of these responses accomplishes the goal of focusing on the present.
- Focus on the problem by providing a paraphrase, reflection of feeling, direct open question, and indirect open question. Briefly explain how each of these responses accomplishes the goal of focusing on the problem.

Focusing on Strategies

Once helpees discuss life circumstances of person, present, and problem, guide them to discuss each strategy of actions, feelings, and thoughts in turn. Though the helpee likely has an endless chain of actions, feelings, and thoughts they could discuss, you are concerned with eliciting these strategies only as they relate directly to the presenting problem. For our earlier example of Rachel, we are concerned with exploring her actions, feelings, and thoughts specifically related to the argument with her mother. The goal is for the helpee to switch between each strategy until a thorough understanding can be gathered of each area.

ACTIONS

Guide the helpee to discuss their behaviors through action-based language. Gather a mental list of what they are doing (or not doing) in response to the presenting issue. Words such as *act*, *do*, *say*, and *behave* are action-based. For example, you could use focusing questions such as "How are you acting since the argument?" or "What ways have your behaviors changed?" or "I wonder what you are doing to cope." Paraphrase and reflect feelings around any actions you hear to encourage your helpee to continue to discuss their behaviors, such as "It sounds like you have avoided your mom since the argument" and "You are staying up late worrying about this, so you are not sleeping very much."

FEELINGS

Assess the helpee's feelings regarding the presenting issue using feeling words and questions. Keep in mind that people usually have multiple emotional reactions to a presenting problem, so explore and keep track of all emotions discussed (Erford, 2014). Helpees can be asked directly about their feelings. We might ask Rachel, "How are you feeling about the argument?" or "Tell me about the emotions that have come up for you about this," or "You mentioned anger; what else is coming up?" Paraphrases are more difficult to use with emotions, so reflections of feeling are ideal. For example, "Rachel, I hear worry in your voice about what will happen next."

THOUGHTS

Guide your helpee to talk about their thoughts about the presenting issue. Thoughts are the most difficult strategy for some beginning helpers to elicit because they are so different from what a friend might ask in casual conversation (Campbell, 2013). Beck (2011) suggests that the most basic way to focus on thoughts is to ask a question like "What is going through your mind right now?" (p. 22) when a helpee talks about a presenting problem. Also ask about beliefs the presenting issue elicited about self and the world, with questions such as "With that in mind, what does that make you think about yourself?" or "What is your conclusion?" For helpees who have difficulty reporting their thoughts, it might be helpful to have them describe the distressing situation in more detail, have them imagine or visualize the event, or ask about feelings before focusing on thoughts more directly (Beck, 2011). Paraphrase and reflect feelings around any thoughts you hear to encourage your helpee to continue to discuss their cognitions. Examples of such a paraphrase and reflection of feelings, respectively, would be: "Looks like this argument with your mom has you thinking that you are a bad daughter" and "Sounds as if you are scared by the belief that you two will never speak again."

Written Practice

In this practice, let's return to your helpee, Bashir, a 66-year-old employee who is sharing financial concerns with you, a human resources worker at his company. Review his disclosure, this time with the strategies of actions, feelings, and thoughts in mind:

"I'm having trouble making ends meet. Living paycheck to paycheck every month is so stressful. My wife stopped working a year ago and at that time, we started relying on my income. This job isn't fulfilling and before my wife got sick, we planned for me to retire by now. She likes her job and wanted to continue but couldn't. I need to keep working and make money. My wife has a lot of health issues and I don't want to worry her with anything else, so I've stopped talking to her about money. I know she is worried though. She has so much going on with her treatment. What if I can't pay for everything she needs? I'm supposed to be the strong one and provide for us through this. I can't even face it, so I avoid looking at bills and won't answer the phone out of fear it's someone who wants money. I worry about what bills are going to show up in my mailbox and if I'll be able to cover them."

Given Bashir's disclosure, what could you say to focus on each of the strategies of actions, feelings, and thoughts? Feel free to assume or add extra detail to Bashir's story if needed in your responses.

- Investigate actions by providing a paraphrase, reflection of feeling, direct open question, and indirect open question. Briefly explain how each of these responses accomplishes the goal of focusing on actions.
- Investigate feelings by providing two reflections of feeling, a direct open question, and indirect open question. Briefly explain how each of these responses accomplishes the goal of focusing on feelings.
- Investigate thoughts by providing a paraphrase, reflection of feeling, direct open question, and indirect open question. Briefly explain how each of these responses accomplishes the goal of focusing on thoughts.

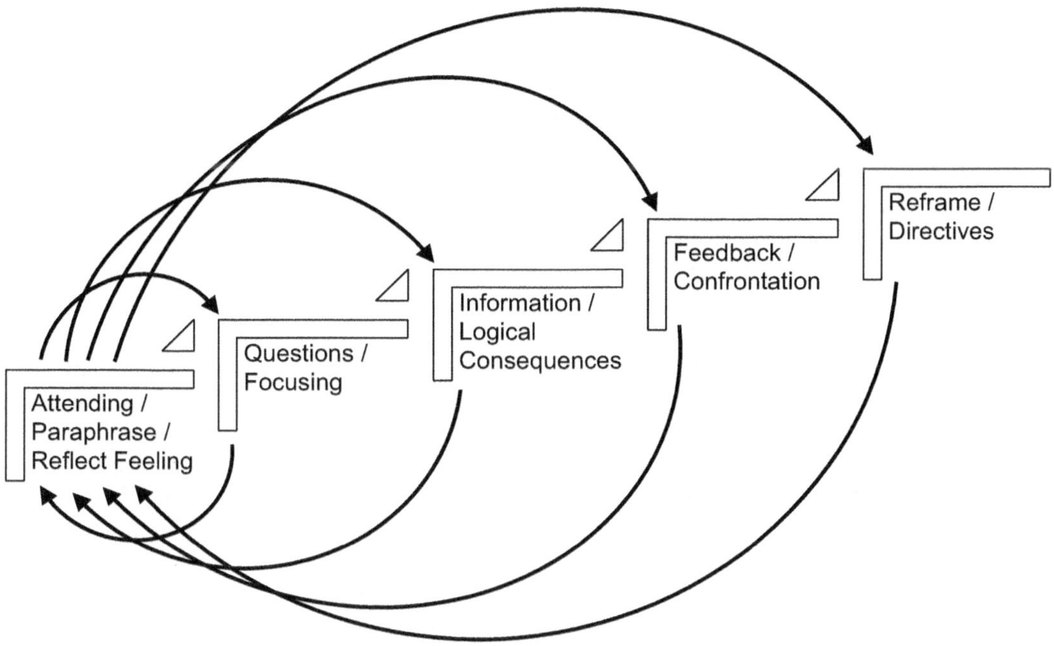

Figure 6.4 Microskills Ramp-Up

Microskills Ramp-Up

The investigating stage continues our use of the microskills ramp-up, which is a stepwise order of when and how helpers should use microskills during a helping situation. The microskills ramp-up is presented in Figure 6.4 and is incorporated in the investigating stage to help you resist the urge to bombard your helpees with too many questions. The ramp-up indicates that listening skills are used first and most often, with helpers progressing as needed to influencing microskills throughout a helping interaction in a stepwise fashion, always returning to the first level before progressing up the steps. Thus, helpers begin at the first level of listening skills of attending, paraphrasing, and reflecting feelings and then ramp up to the next level of microskills to questions and focusing.

For the investigating stage, we will ramp up to questions and focusing and then back to listening skills. The ramp-up dictates that once you ask a question, your next response is to ramp down to a listening skill of attending, paraphrasing, or reflecting feeling. After that, you can ramp up again to another question, after which you can again return to listening skills, and so on. Given the fact that focusing can be accomplished with listening skills, you are welcome to continue eliciting needed information even when ramping down. The most important takeaway is to avoid relying too heavily on questions to accomplish your assessment. Challenge yourself to gather as much information as possible using listening skills, incorporating questions sparingly. The result will be a helping interaction that remains empathic, nonjudgmental, and led by the helpee as much as possible.

Result of Investigating

The expected consequences of the investigating stage are that both the helper and the helpee will develop a deeper understanding of the helper and the distressful situation. Depth of understanding will include the helpee's circumstances, including the person, present, and presenting problem, as well as strategies of the helpee's actions, feelings, and thoughts about the problem.

A potential result of investigating may include encountering helpee resistance. Helpees may express resistance by demonstrating difficulty or unwillingness to discuss a particular area of exploration, such as displaying significant difficulty or unwillingness to talk about their emotions. This kind of resistance may be indicative of discomfort, deficits, or cultural/familial norms around talking about distress. For example, some cultures and families do not place value on fostering emotional awareness and avoid discussing emotions (Ivey et al., 2016). Be gentle when attempting to explore each of these areas and view resistances as a normal and expected part of the helping process (Hill, 2014). When helpees struggle to offer details, ask additional questions and try to reword interventions. Suggest information to fill in the gaps based on what you can infer from their nonverbals and disclosures and check on accuracy through paraphrases and reflections of feeling like "Your clenched fists suggest to me some anger." If helpees have difficulty with a particular strategy, simply note this information to be used to make decisions about which area to continue in the modifying stage.

Resistance may also indicate that the helpee is in the precontemplation stage of change or does not want to entertain solutions or problem-solving at all (Erford, 2014). Sometimes helpees just want to vent. In these cases, you might still consider noting this information and attempting to move forward to the modifying stage. Sometimes proceeding to the modifying stage using a feelings route can be beneficial as a way for the helpee to achieve emotional catharsis and validation (Campbell et al., 2017). Alternatively, consider returning to the supporting stage to allow your helpee to continue talking without helper influence. If they convey that they have achieved the catharsis they needed, such as by saying "I just needed to talk it out" or "I feel better now," consider ending the helping situation here.

The supporting stage reaches an end when the helper and helpee have an understanding of the helpee's circumstances, including the person, present, and problem, and related strategies of the helpee's actions, feelings, and thoughts regarding the problem. Once each of these areas have been verbalized by the helpee, reflected by the helper, and clear to both parties, you are ready to move to the next stage of helping: modifying.

Case Example

This case example shows how a nonprofessional helper, a 16-year-old peer mentor (Riku), talks with a 15-year-old classmate (Monica), who is angry about being reprimanded for disrupting the library. Prior to the beginning of this transcript, Riku and Monica went through the supporting stage, and Riku ruled out the need for the watching stage. In this example, the helper, Riku, briefly uses the investigating stage to learn about Monica's life circumstances and strategies.

HELPER: You sound so frustrated, Monica. [Empathic statement, reflection of feeling]

HELPEE: Riku, it's not fair! The librarian hates me and is making things up to get me in trouble.

HELPER: Seems like you see yourself as unfairly targeted. [Focusing on person, paraphrase]

HELPEE: The librarian has been kicking me out of the library since I started here. He thinks I'm a troublemaker. It's been like this for years now.

HELPER: I hear you and I'm concerned about *you*. How do *you* feel *now* about being asked to leave *today?* [Empathic statement, focusing on person and present, direct open question]

HELPEE: It sucks. I wasn't doing anything wrong. Everyone saw me get kicked out and they were laughing at me.

HELPER: Sounds like you're feeling embarrassed right now. [Focusing on person and present, reflection of feeling]

HELPEE: Of course I am. I wasn't trying to be loud or anything. I was just trying to talk to my friends. They're mad at me or something and I wanted to figure it out before it got worse.

Then I got in trouble. I almost had everything taken care of and now I've got this to deal with.

HELPER: So, there's multiple issues happening here: the conflict with friends and the trouble at the library. Which one is most upsetting for you right now? [Focusing on problem, person, present; paraphrase; direct open question]

HELPEE: The friend thing will get figured out. The library thing is going to be a problem. This keeps happening and I have to use the library for my homework.

HELPER: I see; the library is the main concern right now. Thank you for talking about it with me. [Expression of gratitude, paraphrase]

HELPEE: Sure. I don't know how to get the librarian to stop picking on me.

HELPER: Well, let's keep learning more. I'm curious about the actions you've taken since being asked to leave the library. [Focusing on actions, indirect open question]

HELPEE: I got mad and grabbed my stuff. I said some things under my breath as I walked out. The librarian heard me and told me stop. I said some more stuff. I was so mad.

HELPER: I hear that your anger came out in remarks as you left. [Focusing on actions, reflecting feelings]

HELPEE: I haven't done anything else since. I've stayed away from the library.

HELPER: Sounds like you're trying to deal by avoiding it altogether. [Focusing on actions, paraphrasing]

HELPEE: Of course I am—I don't want to get in trouble again. It sucks that the librarian is always watching for me to screw up and it's not fair.

HELPER: You sound angry, and maybe worried that this might happen again. [Focusing on feelings, reflecting feelings]

HELPEE: This can't keep happening, but I don't know how to stop it.

HELPER: Monica, it seems like you have a belief that the librarian might be singling you out. [Focusing on thoughts, paraphrase]

HELPEE: Well, doesn't it seem like that? He totally does. He hates me.

HELPER: That's so tough. When you think about what happened, what does it make you think about yourself? [Focusing on thoughts, empathic statement, direct open question]

HELPEE: I don't know. My friends probably think I'm stupid and the librarian thinks I'm a troublemaker.

HELPER: Ouch, that would be upsetting. Seems like you might believe you don't have a good reputation. [Focusing on thoughts, empathic statement, paraphrase]

HELPEE: I don't care about that so much .. . . I guess I kind of worry that I bug everybody.

HELPER: I think I understand. Makes you worry that people will see you as a pest. [Focusing on thoughts, paraphrase]

HELPEE: Yes. That would be awful.

Role-Play Practice

The purpose of this exercise is to rehearse the investigating stage. For this exercise, find a volunteer helpee to role-play a helping scenario with you and provide feedback afterward. Set a timer and conduct at least a 15-minute helping scenario, attempting to support using listening skills of attending, paraphrasing, and reflecting feelings only, and then investigate using listening skills, questions, and focusing. Note the lack of need for the watching stage. Complete the following:

1. Consider pairing with a fellow helper-in-training and take turns being the helper and helpee.

2. Video record the scenario. Follow ethical guidelines, including permission to video record.
3. Ask your helpee to select a topic to discuss. Consult Chapter 1, "Problem Triggers" for topic ideas. Helpees should avoid crises or any concerns that would highlight warning signs necessitating the watch stage.
4. As the helper, attempt to support using listening skills of attending, paraphrasing, and reflecting feelings and then investigate using listening skills, questions, and focusing.
5. At the end of the role-play, request feedback from your helpee about what you did well and what you could improve on next time. Ask what interventions felt especially empathic and supportive and which ones were awkward or uncomfortable. Write down your helpee's responses.
6. Review the video recording. Note your balance between gathering all needed information and remaining empathic and conversational. What do you think you did well and what you could improve on next time as the helper?

Summary

In this chapter we discussed the following:

Description of Investigating

- Investigating, the third stage of the LifeRAFT helping skills model, is meant to assess the helpee's concerns, determining what is changeable and what a helper can effectively provide, and deciding how to move forward with a problem-solving process.
- Investigating is about exploring and assessing the situation on two different levels:
  - the helpee's circumstances, including the person, present, and problem, and
  - strategies, including the helpee's actions, feelings, and thoughts regarding the circumstances.

When to Investigate

- Investigating typically comes after the supporting stage of helping, in cases where the watching stage is unneeded due to the absence of warning signs of any crisis concerns.
- In cases in which the watching stage has taken place and remaining short-term issues require further help, the investigating stage would follow.

How to Investigate

- Use listening skills of attending, paraphrasing, and reflecting feelings, and influencing skills of questions and focusing.
- Focusing involves eliciting multiple perspectives to adjust the helpee's perception of an issue and can be accomplished through paraphrasing, reflecting feelings, and questions.
- Listening skills, questions, and focusing are delivered using the microskills ramp-up, in which the helper starts with listening skills, moves to questions/focusing, and returns to listening skills.
- The process of investigating involves assessing person, present, and problem first; then moving to strategies of actions, feelings, and thoughts related to the problem.

Result of Investigating

- The expected consequences of the investigating stage are that an initial understanding of the helper's distress is gained by both the helper and the helpee, and they are poised to begin problem-solving through it in the next stage of helping.

References

American Psychological Association. (2016). Ethical principles of psychologists and code of conduct. *American Psychologist, 57*, 1060–1073. Retrieved from www.apa.org/ethics/code/?item=8

American Red Cross. (2018). How to respond to a water emergency. *American Red Cross*. Retrieved from www.redcross.org/content/dam/redcross/atg/PDF_s/Preparedness___Disaster_Recovery/Disaster_Preparedness/Water_Safety/WouldYouKnowWhattodo.pdf

Beck, J. S. (2011). *Cognitive therapy: Basics and beyond* (2nd ed.). New York, NY: Guilford Press.

Breuer, J., & Freud, S. (1974). *Studies on hysteria*. Harmondsworth: Penguin Books.

Brooks-Harris, J. E. (2008). *Integrative multitheoretical psychotherapy*. Boston, MA: Houghton Mifflin.

Campbell, E. L. (2013, April). *Key introductory strategies training: Training paraprofessionals in basic helping skills*. Symposium conducted at the annual meeting of the Western Psychological Association, Reno, NV.

Campbell, E. L., Davidson, K., & Davidson, S. M. (2017). Effectiveness of LifeRAFT undergraduate helping skills training model. *Psychology Teaching Review, 23*(2), 32–41.

Corey, G. (2009). *Theory and practice of counseling and Psychotherapy* (8th ed.). Belmont, CA: Thomson/Brooks/Cole.

Egan, G. (2014). *The skilled helper: A problem-management and opportunity development approach to helping* (10th ed.). Belmont, CA: Brooks/Cole.

Erford, B. T. (2014). *Orientation to the counseling profession: Advocacy, ethics, and essential professional foundations* (2nd ed.). Boston, MA: Pearson.

Greenberg, L. S. (2002). *Emotion-focused therapy: Coaching clients to work through feelings*. Washington, DC: American Psychological Association.

Greenberg, L. S., & Watson, J. C. (2005). *Emotion-focused therapy for depression*. Washington, DC: American Psychological Association.

Harris, J. E., Kelly, L. J., Campbell, E. L., & Hammond, E. S. (2014). Key strategies training: An introduction to multitheoretical practice. *Journal of Psychotherapy Integration, 24*(2), 138–152. doi:10.1037/a0037056

Hill, C. E. (2014). *Helping skills: Facilitating exploration, insight, and action* (4th ed.). Washington, DC: American Psychological Association.

Ivey, A. E., Ivey, M. B., & Zalaquett, C. P. (2016). *Essentials of intentional interviewing: Counseling in a multicultural world* (3rd ed.). Boston, MA: Cengage Learning.

Martell, C. R., Dimidjian, S., Herman-Dunn, R., & Lewinsohn, P. M. (2010). *Behavioral activation for depression: A clinician's guide*. New York, NY: Guilford Press.

Prochaska, J. O., Norcross, J. C., & DiClemente, C. C. (2005). Stages of change: Prescriptive guidelines. In G. P. Koocher, J. C. Norcross, & S. S. Hill (Eds.), *Psychologists' desk reference* (2nd ed., pp. 226–231). New York: Oxford University Press.

Whiston, S. C. (2009). *Principles and applications of assessment in counseling*. Belmont, CA: Brooks/Cole, Cengage Learning.

7 Stage Four
Modify

Chapter Goals

This chapter will prepare you to:

- Learn about modifying, the fourth stage of the LifeRAFT helping skills model, and the purpose of modifying.
- Become aware of when to use the modifying stage and how to engage in modifying.
- Develop methods to engage in and provide help in the modifying stage using all microskills through the microskills ramp-up.
- Identify what to expect as a result of engaging in modifying with a helpee.

Introduction

This chapter is about modifying, the fourth stage of the LifeRAFT model. So far, we have learned how emotional distress is akin to being swept up and getting stuck in a whirlpool. We learned about how to start by supporting the helpee in their distress and ride the whirlpool with them to build trust and rapport. We then learned how to watch for warning signs indicating that the helpee might be drowning in crisis before helping them to safety by facilitating referrals to emergency and professional services. Next, we learned to investigate or examine the situation to devise a strategy for aiding the helpee to get unstuck. We have now reached the point where we commit to a specific strategy to aid the helpee and move forward with it through the modifying stage.

Our overall goal is to aid our helpee in getting unstuck from their emotional distress and back to their life flow once again. There are likely multiple methods or paths our helpee can take to break free and get back on track, and our job is to help them choose one and move forward with it. Just as one small physical shift can release a person from a water current, focusing on changing one area of a psychological problem can release a helpee from drowning in emotional turmoil. Modifying is the stage where we commit to one approach and work through a basic problem-solving process to get the helpee unstuck and back on their way again.

Description of Modifying

Modifying is the fourth stage of the LifeRAFT helping skills model (see Figure 7.1; Modify). The modifying stage involves using the information gathered in the investigating stage to decide how to move forward with a problem-solving process and then engage in that process. This is accomplished through choosing one strategy to pursue, actions: feelings, or thoughts. Once a

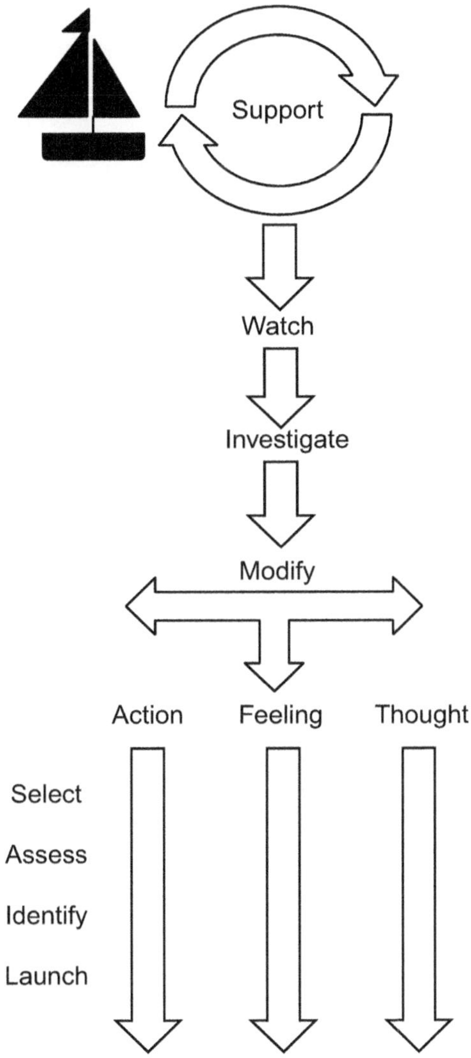

Figure 7.1 LifeRAFT Model

strategy is identified, helpers can then use it to guide the helpee through the four steps of a basic problem-solving process (see Figure 7.2).

Most of us so naturally engage in problem-solving steps when we encounter a problem that we may automatically engage in this process without realizing it (Ivey, Ivey, Zalaquett, 2016). When helpees are in distress, their capacity to reason through problem-solving may be diminished (Egan, 2014). The steps outlined in the modification stage are intended to increase awareness and intentionality around problem-solving in order for helpers to guide a helpee through the process.

In LifeRAFT, the same four steps are used regardless of the strategy chosen, but the execution is unique for each strategy. Thus, while each strategy will employ the four SAIL steps of select, assess, identify, and launch, these will be specific to our RAFT strategies of actions, feelings, and thoughts. See Table 7.1 for a summary of the LifeRAFT modify stage steps applied to each strategy. Notice how the same four steps are involved in the modifying stage and tailored

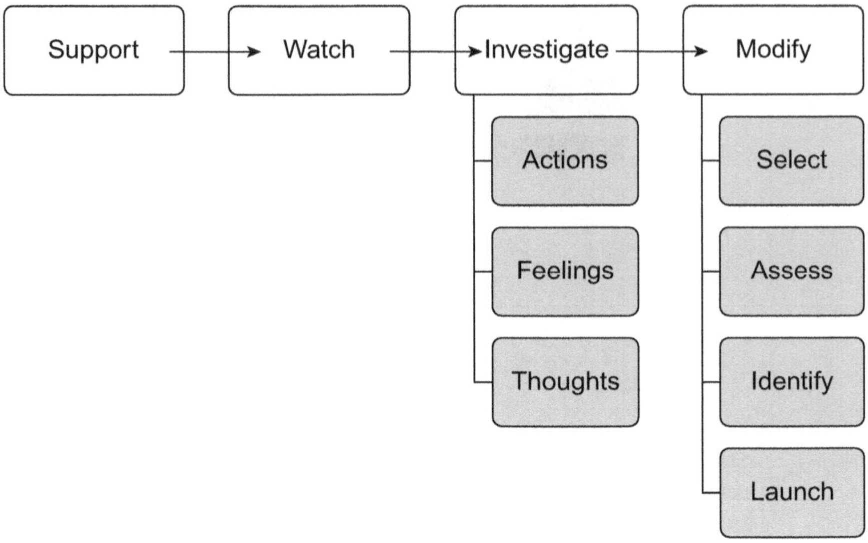

Figure 7.2 LifeRAFT Strategies and Steps

Table 7.1 LifeRAFT Modify Steps

SAIL Steps	*Description*	*Action Steps*	*Feeling Steps*	*Thought Steps*
Select	Select a focal area	Select and focus on actions	Select and focus on feelings	Select and focus on thoughts
Assess	Assess for problem	Assess ineffective actions	Assess maladaptive feelings	Assess dysfunctional thoughts
Identify	Identify potential shifts for improvement over problem	Identify potential shifts from ineffective to effective actions	Identify potential shifts from maladaptive to adaptive feelings	Identify potential shifts from dysfunctional to functional thoughts
Launch	Launch toward improvement of problem	Launch toward effective actions	Launch toward adaptive feelings	Launch toward functional thoughts

to the strategy selected. This chapter provides you with a foundation in the four steps as well as choosing a strategy. Subsequent chapters will train you in how to apply the steps to each strategy.

Benjamin Franklin (1775) is often credited as authoring the original problem-solving model in a letter he wrote to philosopher and scientist Joseph Priestley. In it, he identified three basic steps to problem-solving: first, we identify the problem, then we generate possible answers, and finally we decide what action to take. Many variations of problem-solving models have been proposed since then (e.g., Beck, 1995; Carkhuff & Anthony, 1979; Martell, Dimidjian, Herman-Dunn, & Lewinsohn, 2010), and although the number and wording of steps vary, most reflect the same themes originally proposed by Franklin. Problem-solving models have also been adapted as training models to teach others how to problem solve, such as the McMaster model of problem-based learning (Walsh, 2005), which was developed to teach students to understand a problem and address it on their own. Similarly, LifeRAFT aims to guide helpees in their own problem-solving process, rather than solving the problem for them. Similar to Franklin's (1775) approach and the McMaster model (Walsh, 2005), LifeRAFT's SAIL steps in the modifying stage provide the helper with interventions to guide the helpee in arriving at their own solutions. The SAIL steps involved in the modify stage of LifeRAFT are discussed in detail below.

Select

The first step is selecting, which involves choosing a strategy and answering the question, "What is the helpee doing within the chosen strategy?" This step involves encouraging helpees to talk specifically about how the chosen strategy impacts their concern. Although we briefly encouraged helpees to focus on each strategy during the investigating stage, we now refocus on our chosen area exclusively. The purpose of selecting is for the helper and helpee to adopt the language associated with each strategy and to begin to look at the issue from that specific lens. This allows the conversation to fix on one aspect to clarify the issue (Brooks-Harris, 2008). By focusing on one area, the conversation will become concentrated while furthering the helper and the helpee's understanding of the situation. This deeper understanding is likely to lead to more effective resolution of helpee concerns (Ivey et al., 2016).

After supporting, watching, and investigating, we begin modifying by focusing on a specific strategy for the distress. For example, applying an actions approach, a helper might ask their helpee to discuss in more detail what their behaviors have looked like since they began experiencing distress. Using a feelings approach, a helper might instead ask the helpee to describe the emotions that have emerged.

Assess

The second step involves assessing for potential problems in the given strategy that are holding the helpee back from resolving the presenting issue. Assessing serves to answer the question, "What is not working?" Depending on the chosen strategy, this may present as ineffective actions, maladaptive feelings, or dysfunctional thoughts. For instance, a helpee might determine that ineffective actions, such as pretending the problem does not exist, are worsening their situation while calming activities, such as mindfulness, are improving their situation.

The purpose of assessing is for the helper and helpee to understand the problem from the lens of one strategy only. When faced with a problem, there can be a temptation to identify aspects that need to be changed without fully understanding the entire issue first. Assessing encourages both helper and helpee to fully explore and think deeply about the situation prior to seeking solutions, which can lead to generating more thoughtful and useful answers later (Walsh, 2005).

Identify

The third step involves identifying solutions to the problem by noting problematic versus nonproblematic actions, feelings, and thoughts. Identifying serves to answer the question, "What needs to change?" Identifying is an exercise in which the helper and helpee explore problematic and nonproblematic choices. For example, a helper and helpee might look at the pros and cons of continuing to ignore a problem rather than dealing with it directly.

Identifying provides the opportunity to uncover the reasons for the helpee's reactions. Even when choices are problematic, they have reasons behind them. For example, avoiding a problem not only may make the problem worse but also might offer the benefits of temporarily relieving the discomfort of facing the problem directly or protecting against additional problems (Martell et al., 2010). Developing a pro/con list of all the consequences of reactions—good, bad, and otherwise—prepares the helpee to make an informed choice about enacting change (Egan, 2014).

Identifying also serves to reduce helpee resistance. Helpers and even professional counselors often make the false assumption that resistance is the exception to good helping and helpees will immediately accept the help given to them (Erford, 2014). This is rarely the case, and this kind of mindset will lead to frustration and failure (Egan, 2014). Instead, resistance is so common in helping scenarios that it "is to be expected in all client-counselor relationships" (Erford, 2014, p. 185). As a helper, you are encouraged to go into helping situations expecting your helpee to express at least some reluctance to adjusting themselves in response to distress.

Change is difficult and happens across a series of stages (Prochaska, Norcross, & DiClemente, 2005). If it did not happen that way, we would rarely need help in the first place. Our job as helpers is to expect resistance and work with it rather than against it (Cowan & Presbury, 2000). The identifying step gives helpees the opportunity to fully voice their support and concerns (i.e., pros and cons) for possible solutions. We further reduce resistance by empathizing with our helpee, maintaining a nonjudgmental demeanor, and showing patience through the process (Hill, 2014).

Launch

The fourth and final step involves launching toward a helpful and healthy resolution. Launching serves to answer the question, "How will the helpee change?" This most notably involves plans to engage in nonproblematic choices identified previously, including effective actions, adaptive feelings, and functional thoughts.

The purpose of launching is for the helpee to commit to some change that will help free them from their distress. The helpee makes a choice of how to address the problem. Depending on the strategy, this might be a plan to change what they are doing in response to distress, a change in their emotional expression, or a shift in their perspective on the issue. At this point in the helping scenario, the issue is either temporarily addressed or plans have been made to address it.

LifeRAFT Strategies

LifeRAFT guides you as a nonprofessional helper through how to support someone in distress by choosing a RAFT, which stands for Relief through Actions, Feelings, or Thoughts. The same four steps parallel each strategy, and each strategy is grounded in various professional counseling theories. Due to their sound clinical and research foundation, theory-based interventions are seen as optimal ways to navigate exploring helpees' experience and promoting change (Campbell, Davidson, & Davidson, 2017).

Actions, feelings, and thoughts are three fundamental, interdependent dimensions of human experience (Brooks-Harris, 2008). Because of this, focusing on any one of these dimensions can encourage change in the others. Helpers can work interactively with actions, feelings, and thoughts to promote helpee exploration and modification.

Actions

The actions strategy is based on Behavioral Activation Therapy (Martell et al., 2010), which categorizes actions as either effective or ineffective. During the investigating stage, helpers assess for ineffective actions related to the identified problem. Martell et al. (2010) suggested: "Behaviors to decrease are those that make the client's life more difficult or interfere with managing one's needs; typically, these are avoidance patterns" (p. 65). Actions are considered ineffective when they represent behaviors that are unwanted by a helpee or when they interfere with meeting needs or attaining desired goals. Unwanted behaviors may include actions that go against a helpee's preferences or values, such as using substances, canceling on social obligations, or neglecting personal hygiene. Interference with needs and goals may present more long-term ineffectiveness, such as submissiveness or mismanagement of anger in relationships or neglecting responsibilities in work or school.

Feelings

Feelings refer to emotions or mood. The feelings strategy draws from Emotion-Focused Therapy (Greenberg, 2002; Greenberg & Watson, 2005) and uses feelings-based skills to explore and express adaptive emotions. Unlike actions, feelings themselves are not labeled as adaptive or maladaptive. Instead, maladaptation refers to the way in which feelings are felt and expressed. When feelings are not fully felt, accepted, or expressed in a healthy way, they become maladaptive; maladaptive feelings are those that are blocked, mismatched, or incongruent. Feelings are blocked when the helpee is unaware or uncomfortable with a particular emotion and thus do not permit themselves to adequately feel or express it. Mismatches and incongruencies occur when the expressed emotion does not seem to match what might actually be experienced or what is conveyed through nonverbal expressions, such as a helpee describing feeling angry with clenched fists but incongruently labels their feelings as "sad."

Thoughts

Thoughts refer to cognitions or beliefs. The thoughts strategy is based on Cognitive Therapy (Beck, 2011), employing cognitive skills to detect errors in thinking and form more accurate thoughts. During the investigating stage, helpers assess for dysfunctional thoughts. Such thoughts tend to be global, rigid, excessively negative, self-sabotaging beliefs, typically about oneself. They are often related to perceiving oneself as helpless, unlovable, or worthless. These thoughts are often expressed through phrases such as "I'm incompetent" or "I can't do anything right"; "I'm unattractive" or "I'm not good enough to be loved by others"; "I'm bad" or "I'm dangerous." Helpees may also express dysfunctional thoughts about other people or the world around them through expressions like "Other people will hurt me" or "The world is dangerous" (Beck, 2011, p. 229).

Choosing a Strategy

During the investigating stage, you gathered initial information from your helpee about their actions, feelings, and thoughts related to the presenting issue. In the modifying stage, you can use this information to choose a helping strategy to follow. Subsequent chapters on the actions, feelings, and thoughts strategies will highlight additional considerations for when to use each strategy, but some basic recommendations are provided here to begin the decision-making process.

While helpee problems are always multidimensional (Hackney, 1992), and our goal as helpers is to promote holistic renewal to effective actions, adaptive feelings, and functional thoughts (Brooks-Harris, 2008), it is nevertheless essential to choose one strategy rather than attempting to address all three at once. Attempting to address all areas at once translates to an atheoretical approach that lacks direction and grounding. This kind of aimless helping is not only ineffective but can be damaging to helpees (Egan, 2014). Choosing one area provides a theoretical foundation to your helping approach, which offers ways to organize and understand problems with direction toward resolution (Halbur & Halbur, 2019). For this reason, professional counselors are ethically required to work from a theoretical orientation (e.g., ACA, 2014; APA, 2013).

Because actions, feelings, and thoughts remain part of an interconnected system, promoting change in one strategy will necessarily impact the other two strategies (Brooks-Harris, 2008). In fact, the theories that each of the LifeRAFT strategies are based on—Behavioral Therapy for actions (Martell et al., 2010), Emotion-Focused Therapy for feelings (Greenberg, 2002), and Cognitive Therapy for thoughts (Beck, 2011)—all rest on the premise that focusing on one dimension of functioning will promote overall change in the other areas. In addition, although each approach focuses on one area as the primary agent of change, the other two areas are not ignored. They continue to be discussed, explored, and validated throughout the helping situation while continuing to return to the chosen strategy as the intervention point to encourage multi-dimensional change (Harris, Kelly, Campbell, & Hammond, 2014). Although it is important to choose a strategy, it matters less which approach you choose (Egan, 2014). All three strategies are based on theoretically sound, empirically supported treatments for a wide variety of issues, and each LifeRAFT strategy has demonstrated value (Campbell et al., 2017). The decision to focus on actions, feelings, or thoughts can be based on collaborative dialogue between helper and helpee and the helper's judgment.

Choosing a strategy should be based on three considerations: your characteristics and that of your helpee, as well as the nature of their distress.

Helper Characteristics

Determining a preferred theoretical orientation to helping is an involved and lengthy process (Erford, 2014). The strategies included in LifeRAFT act as a foundation for you to begin to develop your own theoretical approach. This is a philosophy of helping that reflects your beliefs about yourself, human nature, and the process of growth and change (Halbur & Halbur, 2019). Through LifeRAFT training, most helpers find that they prefer working with one strategy over others (Campbell, 2013). One approach typically aligns better with your personality and beliefs about change. For example, if you are an action-oriented person and naturally favor problem-focused helping, you may prefer the actions strategy over feelings and thoughts. You may also be more skilled at using one strategy than the others. For example, if you have high emotional intelligence and are highly adept at working with emotions but lack the experience or vocabulary for behavioral- or cognitive-based helping, you may prefer the feelings strategy over actions and thoughts. Taking these preferences and skills into account when choosing a strategy is important to provide your helpee with the best assistance you can offer.

Helpee Characteristics

Similar to your helper characteristics, it is critical to take into account your helpee's characteristics when choosing a strategy (Campbell, 2013). Consider the helpee's preferences as well as their capabilities. Preferences may be due to personality, beliefs, experience, culture, or a wide variety of other personal qualities (Corey, 2009) and may be communicated during the investigating stage by naturally discussing one strategy over others or expressing discomfort with certain strategies (Campbell et al., 2017). For example, a helpee may avoid providing details about emotions even when directly asked about them, communicating a preference for focusing on actions or thoughts instead. Like helpers, helpees are likely more skilled at discussing and working through problems using one strategy over others. Helpees who are psychologically minded or have a high level of personal insight may prefer an insight-based approach (Myers, 2012), such as the feelings and thoughts strategies. Conversely, many helpees are non-insight-oriented due to personal preference or familiarity and would benefit from selecting actions.

Nature of Presenting Problem

Lastly, consider the nature of the presenting problem when choosing a strategy, because some problems naturally lend themselves to one strategy over another.

The actions strategy works best for problem-focused helping (Campbell, 2013), which is a method to cope with distress focusing on resolving the stressor or addressing a stressful situation directly. Problem-focused coping is an effective stress management strategy for instances in which situational influences are under a person's control and can be changed (Myers, 2012). Examples include resolving a dispute with a friend or developing an exercise schedule, because addressing these issues necessitates the use of behavioral interventions.

The feelings strategy is best for emotion-focused helping (Campbell, 2013), a method to cope with distress by shifting focus away from the stressor and onto the emotional needs related to the stress reaction. Emotion-focused helping is a particularly effective strategy for circumstances in which situational influences cannot be changed (Myers, 2012), such as grieving the loss of a loved one, or circumstances in which there may not be a situation to address, such as soothing unexplained negative moods.

The thoughts strategy works best for issues of contemplation, decision-making, and faulty thinking (Campbell, 2013). Distress sometimes revolves around uncertainties, such as which job to pursue or how to interpret the meaning of an event. Faulty thinking in extreme negative beliefs such as "everyone hates me" can also cause distress. The nature of these issues is, by definition, cognitive and can benefit from the thoughts strategy.

Written Practice

As you learn about choosing a RAFT strategy, it will be helpful to practice choosing strategies of actions, feelings, or thoughts. Given that each of the strategies derives from empirically supported treatments for a wide variety of issues, there is rarely one "right" strategy. Thus, this choice can be based on the helper's judgment, as long as you have an appropriate rationale for doing so. Remember that the rationale for choosing a strategy should be based on your characteristics as a helper, your helpee's characteristics, and the nature of the helpee's problem.

For each of the scenarios below, identify what your first choice would be for a strategy and explain your choice by addressing the three considerations for choosing a strategy. Feel free to assume or add extra detail to each story if needed in your responses.

- Charlotte is a 72-year-old woman who recently moved into the assisted living center where you work. She asks to talk to you about her distress regarding her family. She tells you that her family asked her to move to the assisted living center because they could no longer provide the help she needs. Since moving, Charlotte has refused to talk to her family or let them visit her. Charlotte expresses anger with her family and tells you she thinks her family does not care about her anymore.
- Your friend Sagan is an avid writer. He wrote a novel and has an active blog with many followers. Sagan tells you he is distressed about writer's block. Suddenly he has no idea what to write about and feels anxious and depressed about whether his "gift for writing is gone." He tells you that his ability to write is the only thing he liked about himself and he now is hyper-focused on his other negative qualities. He tells you that he has stopped writing and is uncertain about what to tell people when they ask about his current projects.
- Toby is the 8-year-old boy you are babysitting. He saw frightening images of monsters on television and now he is afraid to go to his room out of fear the monsters are there. His bedtime is approaching and although he wants to go to his room to change into his pajamas, he is nervous to enter the room.

- Now that you have noted and explained your choices for strategies for each of the aforementioned scenarios, discuss your reactions to your decision-making processes. What did you learn about your own characteristics when evaluating the scenarios? What kind of information about helpees and presenting issues do you find most and least helpful when making a strategy selection?

When to Modify

The modifying stage begins after successful resolution of the investigating stage, indicated when the helper and helpee better understand the helpee's circumstances, including the person, present, and problem, and the helpee's actions, feelings, and thoughts around the problem. Once each of these areas have been verbalized by the helpee, reflected by the helper, and clear to both parties, an initial understanding of the helper's distress is reached and both are poised to begin problem-solving through it. At this point, you as the helper can initiate the modifying stage by selecting a RAFT strategy and proceeding forward through the SAIL steps.

How to Modify

Begin the modifying stage by selecting one of the three RAFT strategies. Base your decision on your assessment of what the most fitting choice might be given the combination of your helper characteristics, your helpee's characteristics, and the nature of the helpee's problem.

Next, check your decision with your helpee by reflecting the strategy back to them as either a paraphrase or an indirect closed question. This approach is recommended over asking your helpee directly about how they would like to proceed or what kind of help they would prefer because helpees in distress may have difficulty selecting and asking for what they need (Faiver, Eisengart, & Colonna, 2004). In fact, sometimes helpees ask for one kind of helping when they actually want another kind (Campbell, 2013). For example, helpees commonly express a need for help using action-based language, regardless of their actual helping preferences, and might say something like "I just don't know what to do. I need you to help me figure out how to fix this." While words such as "do" and "fix" are action-based words, they might say this even when they just want someone to listen and validate their emotions using a feelings approach. Thus, it is preferable to investigate actions, feelings, and thoughts and make your own assessment of what the helpee is communicating to you about their needs and then reflect that strategy back to them as either a paraphrase or an indirect closed question.

The paraphrase/closed question is meant to restate what it appears the helpee wants you to help them with and offer them an opportunity to either confirm or refute the accuracy of your choice. The intention behind your paraphrase/closed question is this: "It seems as if you want me to help you using a(n) (action/feeling/thought)-based approach. Is that accurate?" However, we need to phrase it differently because it is unlikely that you can use direct LifeRAFT language with your helpee. Instead, you can phrase your check-in using language they understand that represents the essence of each approach. For an action approach, you can say, "Sounds like you are trying to figure out what to do next." The words "figure out what to do" suggest a goal of following behavioral steps for addressing the problem. For a feelings approach, you might say, "I get the sense that you're wanting to vent your feelings and get this out." Descriptors such as "vent your feelings" and "get this out" are often used for emotional coping and catharsis. For a thoughts approach, you could say, "Seems like you are trying to gain some perspective on this situation." The words "gain some perspective" suggest a shift in cognitions that is associated with a thoughts approach.

Once you and your helpee are in agreement about the chosen strategy, you can continue to work through the SAIL steps of select, assess, identify, and launch. These are accomplished largely through the use of listening skills, interspersing influencing skills sequentially according to the microskills ramp-up. Each step in the modifying stage is introduced along with its respective microskills, in accordance with the microskills ramp-up.

Select

In the first step of selecting, helpers should redirect the conversation to the chosen strategy. Encourage the helpee to discuss their presenting concern from the perspective of the strategy only. For example, your helpee, Emmanuel, is a first responder for hurricane relief victims, and he talks to you about the stress and vicarious trauma he experienced while providing aid. You determine he would benefit from an actions approach, so you begin to use listening skills and targeted questions to encourage Emmanuel to talk more about his behaviors related to the stress of his work.

Microskills

Up to this point of the interaction, helpers continue to use the microskills of attending, paraphrasing, reflection of feeling, questions, and focusing to encourage helpees to talk specifically about how the chosen strategy impacts their concern. Remember to continue employing skills according to the microskills ramp-up (see Figure 7.3).

The microskills ramp-up is the stepwise order of when and how helpers should use microskills during a helping situation. It is intended to help you resist the urge to bombard your helpees with too many influencing skills and instead focus on listening skills. Helpers progress as needed to influencing microskills throughout a helping interaction in a stepwise fashion, always returning to the first level before progressing up the steps. Thus, helpers begin at the first level of listening skills and then ramp-up to the next level of influencing skills. Microskills closer to the bottom of

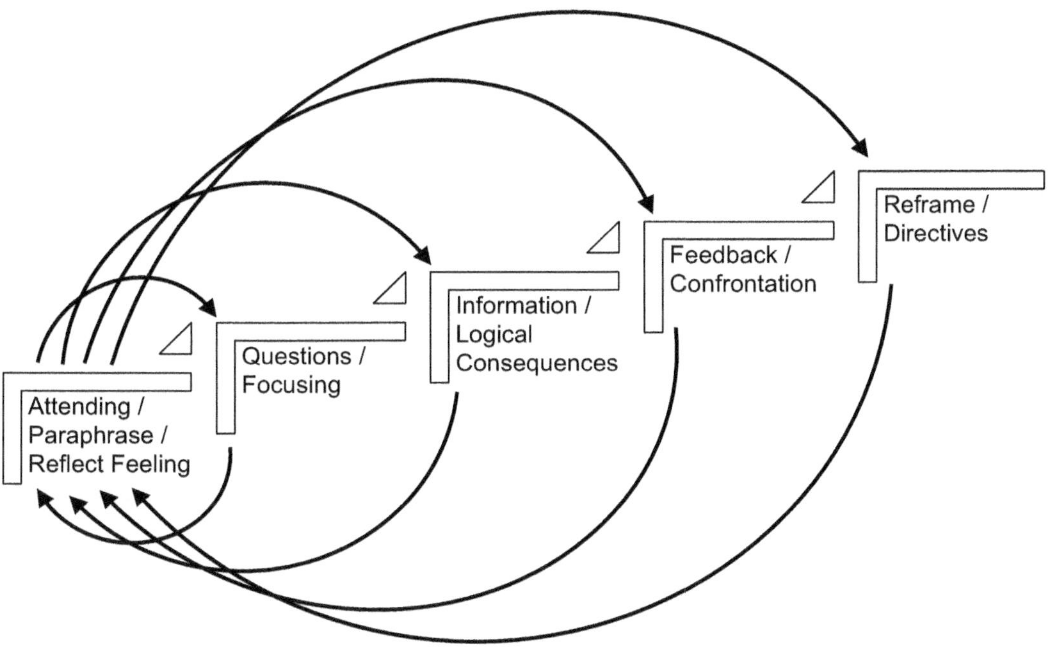

Figure 7.3 Microskills Ramp-Up

the ramp-up offer the helpee more support in coming to their own conclusions, while microskills closer to the top of the ramp-up are increasingly instructional and persuasive. The goal is for the helper to earn the right to intervene, keep the helpee talking as much as possible, and scaffold with only as much influence as is necessary for the helpee to help themselves. The result will be a helping interaction that remains empathic, nonjudgmental, and led by the helpee as much as possible by conducting an assessment through conversation rather than helper-led interview or interrogation.

Assess

The second step involves assessing problems in the given strategy that may be keeping the helpee from resolving the presenting issue. As with the other steps, the strategy may be conceptualized as ineffective actions, maladaptive feelings, or dysfunctional thoughts.

Microskills

When assessing, helpers may add the microskills of information and logical consequences as needed, following the same ramp-up sequence as before: listening skills first, then ramp-up to information or logical consequences, and finally listening skills again before returning to more influencing skills of either questions/focusing or information/logical consequences.

INFORMATION

Information involves sharing specific knowledge with a helpee and providing facts that are true for most people or situations. The purpose is to give the helpee information to encourage them to think more deeply about their own situation without taking away helpee autonomy by telling them what to do (Ivey et al., 2016). To go back to our actions-based example of Emmanuel, the hurricane relief worker, we might provide information in this way: "Some people find stress is worsened when they do not take adequate rest breaks." This is much less judgmental than saying, "You probably are not getting enough rest." Only the helpee knows what is best for them, and information offers suggestions for them to apply and explore within their own situation. In Emmanuel's case, we'd expect him to consider whether he thought he was getting sufficient rest and whether this might be related to his stress response. When we offer information about possible problems in a given strategy, the helpee can aid us in identifying their own ideas for change.

LOGICAL CONSEQUENCES

Logical consequences encourage helpees to assess potential problems by exploring specific alternatives to a given decision, particularly the positive and negative consequences that would logically result from each one (Ivey et al., 2016). In the case of the hurricane relief volunteer, Emmanuel, logical consequences could include saying, "Let's look at what might be contributing to your stress response. You mentioned that you are working through your breaks. What are some positive things that result from this decision? What negative things result?" Notice how both positive and negative consequences are elicited to allow your helpee the opportunity to fully consider the situation and decide which behaviors are problematic for them.

Helpers sometimes have trepidation about encouraging helpees to weigh both the pros and cons of change. Consider a situation where you might have strong feelings about a helpee making changes to ensure their health and safety, such as them deciding whether or not they want to discontinue their habit of stealing cars. You may be uncomfortable with the idea of weighing pros and cons in this situation, because it means guiding the helpee to consider the benefits of stealing cars as well as the drawbacks.

There is often a concern that asking a helpee about the benefits of harmful activities is seen as tacit approval of them. However, asking about consequences, both good and bad, is not an endorsement of them (Brooks-Harris, 2008). We need to fully understand discrepancies to address them. By asking about the positives and negatives to stealing cars, we can facilitate the helpee in identifying the risks to their safety while also identifying the reasons they continue to do so. For example, a helpee might identify that they steal cars not just for the money but because they know how to, and having a specialized skill set that other people do not possess makes them feel good. Knowing the real reasons behind a discrepancy may hold the key to change, so do not be afraid to explore it. To avoid swaying a discrepancy prematurely, remember not to explicitly endorse activities, for instance by saying "Stealing cars is a good idea," and remain balanced in exploring both pros and cons. You can also suggest additional pros and cons, such as "With cons of stealing cars, perhaps we could also consider the fact that you could get caught and charged with a crime."

Identify

The third step involves identifying solutions through noting problematic versus nonproblematic strategies. At this point, helpees will have noted potential problems and recognized the need for change but still likely feel resistance to making changes. In the identifying step, helpers challenge helpees to push through resistance and make changes through identifying nonproblematic strategies.

Microskills

Using the microskills ramp-up, helpers use listening skills and then ramp up to the next level of influencing skills to continue moving helpees toward change. Helpers add the use of more microskills, including confrontation and feedback, to challenge the helpee forward.

CONFRONTATION

Confrontation is defined as supportively challenging your helpee by highlighting conflicts, mixed messages, and discrepancies in verbal and nonverbal behavior. It helps to empathically guide the helpee into facing opposition and reclaiming denied parts of themselves (Ivey et al., 2016). An example of confrontation for Emmanuel would be, "You say you want to reduce your stress level and that taking breaks will help with that, and at the same time you remain hesitant to do so." This allows the helpee to wrestle directly with the discrepancy between addressing their distress and the challenges of change that are holding them back and can initiate fully weighing the pros and cons of making changes.

FEEDBACK

Feedback involves the helper transmitting reactions based on their own evaluation of the helpee (Egan, 2014). This is the stage in the helping process where we offer our opinion. This is accomplished using the praise and polish method. Recall that the praise and polish method involves offering supportive, genuine, comprehensive, and specific reactions aimed at assisting the helpee to make changes by providing both positive and negative comments. An example of praise and polish feedback for Emmanuel would be,

> I see how much you want to help the hurricane victims with every moment you have and admire your commitment to making a difference. I'm also concerned for you that without breaks, you might hurt yourself and have to stop completely.

This once again offers the helpee the opportunity to confront their resistance and consider change.

Launch

The fourth and final step involves launching toward a helpful and healthy resolution. This most notably involves plans to engage in the nonproblematic choices previously identified. The purpose is for the helpee to end the helping interaction with a method for change and a healthy perspective on themselves.

Microskills

Remember that the microskills ramp-up dictates that helpers begin with attending skills, progressing to successively more direct influencing skills as the situation demands yet always coming back to attending. In the launch step, helpers may add the remaining microskills, including reframing and directives, to motivate their helpees toward a new perspective and a healthier direction in an effort to resolve the presenting issue or get unstuck from their current predicament.

REFRAMING

Reframing is defined as providing helpees with a new, more positive perspective on themselves and their concerns. It often involves taking a negative perspective and relabeling it to a more adaptive and balanced response (Ivey et al., 2016). Reframing helps to solidify decisions to change by adding a positive angle. For example, a reframe for Emmanuel would be, "I hear you that you see taking breaks as being unhelpful for the hurricane victims; I see taking breaks as helping them by renewing your energy to be even more helpful." This helps motivate helpees to change and feel good about the changes they are making.

For many untrained helpers, reframing is their natural go-to response when people are in distress. Particularly when helpees make negative statements about themselves, helpers often feel a pull to immediately reframe. For example, when a helpee says "I'm stupid," a common reframe helper response is "No you're not! You're smart." Although this appears to be a kind response, reframing too early in a helping scenario comes off as disingenuous and unempathic because it fails to acknowledge that a helpee is feeling down and discounts their experience before seeking to understand it fully (Ivey et al., 2016). For that reason, reframes are saved for later in the microskills hierarchy, because they are more powerful when effectively timed in a helping situation. Helpers need to earn the right to offer a positive perspective by supporting the helpee in their negative frame of mind first.

DIRECTIVES

Directives involve providing helpees with instructions to follow specific actions (Hill, 2014). This is the stage in the helping process where we offer advice. For example, a directive for our hurricane relief volunteer, Emmanuel, could include "Let's start by taking a 30-minute break for lunch today. Perhaps you could set an alarm to remind you to stop working at noon. Can we agree to that?" Notice how you can make every effort to maintain helpee autonomy, even with the highest levels of influencing skills, by tentatively suggesting directives using wording such as "perhaps you could." Also note that ending directives with a question about their willingness and agreement with the directive puts the power back in the helpee's control to choose whether or not to proceed.

Note that a directive—offering direct advice—represents for many people what helping is. Now that you are engaged in helping skills training, you understand the dangers of taking away helpee autonomy and the value of encouraging helpees to help themselves. Still, the temptation to tell helpees what to do remains strong. Directives have their place and can be a valuable addition to a helping scenario (Ivey et al., 2016) but only after helpees have had a chance to explore their own solutions and you have invested the time and energy to understand their situation fully. This is precisely the reason that directives are the last microskill to be added. As helpers, we must earn the right to use them.

Result of Modifying

The expected result of the modifying stage is that the helpee's distress will be reduced and they will either be unstuck to resume their functioning or have a plan for how to do so. At this point, the helping scenario is complete, and helpers can politely thank the helpee for talking with them, offer well wishes, and exit the conversation.

Of course, the end of the modifying stage may still result in other helpee reactions that may necessitate alternate responses. At any point, a helpee might express so much resistance that it becomes clear that a return to an earlier stage is needed temporarily or for the duration of the helping scenario. We will discuss some of these situations.

When you feel tension in the helping relationship or distancing from your helpee, return to the supporting stage. For example, a helpee might shut down by discontinuing speaking or closing off body postures, appearing frustrated with you, or ending the conversation with stonewalling remarks such as "It's fine, I'll figure it out" or "Just forget it."

Crises can also emerge at any point in the conversation. If this occurs, return to the watching stage, remembering to using listening skills first and then making the transition.

If you begin to feel lost in the conversation or uncertain which direction is appropriate, return to the investigating stage to gather more information before proceeding further. We can sometimes misinterpret situations or helpees themselves may shift the focus of their distress as they talk and learn more about their own distress. Additionally, helpees sometimes need to work through one or more different strategies before resolving their distress. For example, once a helpee goes through the modifying stage with feelings, they may now be ready and desire assistance in making behavioral changes, suggesting that going through the modifying stage a second time using the actions approach may now be useful.

Keep in mind that a helpee's distress is unlikely to be fully resolved, even at the end of the helping scenario and that our goal is not to "fix" them but to help them help themselves. A shift of any kind can plant seeds for change and improvement, and simply talking with a caring helper with no visible shift can still be therapeutic (Egan, 2014).

While you now have learned about all the LifeRAFT stages, microskills, and steps, ideally you do not need to work through all of them in every helping situation. The hope is that you only proceed through the LifeRAFT model as far as helpees need before resolving the distress themselves. The helping situation ends whenever the helpee ends it, typically by suggesting that they got the help they needed. This is evidenced by them thanking you for your help, explicitly stating or demonstrating improvement in functioning, and ending the interaction or changing the subject. When in doubt, it is appropriate to ask a question such as "Did you get what you needed?" to determine if they are ending the helping situation.

Case Example

The modifying stage differs significantly between the strategies of actions, feelings, and thoughts, so you will read more case examples as you learn about each strategy in subsequent chapters. For now, this case example will focus only on the beginning of the modifying stage of selecting a RAFT strategy.

This case example shows how a nonprofessional helper, a care worker at a reproductive support center (Deon), talks with a pregnant woman (Faith) who is scared about how to raise her child alone. Prior to the beginning of this transcript, Deon and Faith went through the supporting stage and Deon addressed watching stage concerns. In this example, Deon briefly uses the investigating stage to learn about Faith's life circumstances and strategies and then chooses a strategy to pursue.

HELPER: You sound really scared, Faith. [Empathic statement, reflection of feeling]

HELPEE: Of course I am. I've decided I don't want to give my baby up for adoption or have an abortion, but the father doesn't want to be involved so it looks like I'm raising this baby alone.

HELPER: Sounds like you've thought through your options and made some decisions. [Focusing on person, paraphrase]

HELPEE: Some but not all. How are my extended family and friends going to react to this? What will they think?

HELPER: I hear you and we can keep talking about that. Right now, I'm concerned about *you*. How do *you* feel about this right now?" [Empathic statement, focusing on person and present, direct open question]

HELPEE: It's so huge. I'm not married and have so little. This isn't the way it was supposed to happen. Now that it's here, I don't know if I'm going to do a good job.

HELPER: Faith, you're feeling pretty overwhelmed right now. [Focusing on person and present, reflection of feeling]

HELPEE: I have a lot to figure out and all of it just keeps whirling in my head. I can't focus. I'm scared I can't do this.

HELPER: So that's the primary hurdle you're facing right now: fear and doubts about what the future will look like. [Paraphrase]

HELPEE: Exactly. I feel like I'm in a fog, or paralyzed, and I just don't know what my next step is.

HELPER: You've put so much effort into this already, and I know talking about it can't be easy for you. I'm curious about the actions you've taken since you've found out. [Focusing on actions, indirect open question]

HELPEE: I got really scared and stayed home and cried a lot at first. Then I contacted the father and he said he didn't want to be involved. That scared me even more. I don't want to be on my own.

HELPER: So, you felt scared and so you stayed home, cried, and contacted the father. [Focusing on feelings, focusing on actions]

HELPEE: Then I made the decision to keep the baby and now I'm here.

HELPER: That was a big step and I appreciate you coming here and talking to me. [Focusing on actions]

HELPEE: This is so scary. I can't possibly do this on my own.

HELPER: Ah, I can hear how those fears are coming back again. [Focusing on feelings, reflecting feelings]

HELPEE: Yes.

HELPER: Faith, what are you most afraid of? [Focusing on thoughts, direct open question]

HELPEE: I can barely take care of myself. How am I going to take care of a baby? No one will talk to me again when they find out. I'm alone and I'm going to mess this up just like I do with everything else in my life.

HELPER: Ouch, those are some tough thoughts going through your mind. No wonder you feel overwhelmed. I hear worries like, "I can't raise a baby," "I mess things up," and "people will abandon me." [Reflection of feeling, focusing on thoughts]

HELPEE: This is the kind of stuff that's constantly cycling in my head. I can't think.

HELPER: I can imagine it's hard to focus. Seems like it would be helpful to clear out some of the chatter in your mind to get to a healthier perspective? [Choosing a strategy, suggesting thoughts]
HELPEE: Yes. I think that would really help.

Role-Play Practice

The purpose of this exercise is to rehearse the beginning of the modifying stage and select a strategy. For this exercise, find a volunteer helpee to role-play a helping scenario with you and provide feedback afterward. Set a timer and conduct at least a 15-minute helping scenario, attempting to support using listening skills of attending, paraphrasing, and reflecting feelings only, then investigating using listening skills, questions, and focusing, and finally choosing a strategy. Complete the following:

1. Consider pairing with a fellow helper-in-training and take turns being the helper and helpee.
2. Video record the scenario. Follow the ethical guidelines discussed in Chapter 1, including consent to video record.
3. Ask your helpee to select a topic to discuss. Consult Chapter 1, "Problem Triggers," for topic ideas. Helpees should avoid crises or any concerns that would highlight warning signs necessitating the watch stage.
4. As the helper, attempt to support using the listening skills of attending, paraphrasing, and reflecting feelings and then investigate using listening skills, as well as questions, and focusing. Based on the information provided, choose a strategy to pursue and reflect it to your helpee.
5. At the end of the role-play, request feedback from your helpee about what you did well and what you could improve on next time. Ask what interventions felt especially empathic and supportive and which ones were awkward or uncomfortable. Write down your helpee's responses.
6. Review the video. Note your balance between gathering all needed information and remaining empathic and conversational. What do you think you did well and what you could improve on next time as the helper?

Summary

In this chapter we discussed the following:

Description of Modifying

- Modifying, the fourth stage of the LifeRAFT helping skills model, involves deciding how to move forward with a problem-solving process and then engaging in that process.
- Modifying involves choosing from the strategies of actions, feelings, or thoughts and then guiding the helpee through a basic problem-solving process of four steps: select, assess, identify, and launch.

When to Modify

- Modifying is used after the investigating stage of helping. It begins when the helper has gathered enough information during investigating to distinguish a specific problem to modify and accurately choose a strategy to pursue a problem-solving process.

How to Modify

- To choose a strategy, use listening skills of attending, paraphrasing, and reflecting feelings, and influencing skills of questions and focusing.
- Using the chosen strategy and applying the microskills ramp-up, helpers progress through four steps:
  - The select step uses attending, paraphrasing, reflection of feeling, questions, and focusing to encourage helpees to talk specifically about how the chosen strategy impacts their concern.
  - The assess step involves assessing which problems prevent the helpee from resolving the presenting issue. These problems are categorized as ineffective actions, maladaptive feelings, or dysfunctional thoughts. Using the microskills ramp-up, helpers add information and logical consequences to guide helpees to identify their stuck points.
  - The identify step uses feedback and confrontation to challenge helpees to push through resistance and identify solutions by evaluating problematic choices as opposed to non-problematic choices.
  - The launch step aims to propel helpees toward a healthy resolution of their presenting concern. Helpers use the remaining microskills, including reframing and directives, to motivate their helpees toward a new perspective and a healthier direction in an effort to resolve the presenting issue.

Result of Modifying

- The expected outcome of the modifying stage is that the helpee's distress will be reduced and they will either be unstuck to resume their functioning or have a plan for how to do so.
- If resolution does not occur, helpers also have the option to discontinue the helping situation, return to a previous stage of helping either temporarily or for the duration of the interaction, or pursue a different strategy for problem-solving.

References

American Counseling Association. (ACA, 2014). *ACA code of ethics*. Alexandria, VA: Author. Retrieved from www.counseling.org/resources/aca-code-of-ethics.pdf

American Psychological Association. (2013). *APA guidelines for the undergraduate psychology major*. Washington, DC: Author. Retrieved from www.apa.org/ed/precollege/about/psymajor-guidelines.pdf

Beck, J. S. (1995). *Cognitive therapy: Basics and beyond*. New York, NY: Guilford Press.

Beck, J. S. (2011). *Cognitive therapy: Basics and beyond* (2nd ed.). New York, NY: Guilford Press.

Brooks-Harris, J. E. (2008). *Integrative multitheoretical psychotherapy*. Boston, MA: Houghton Mifflin.

Campbell, E. L. (2013, April). *Key introductory strategies training: Training paraprofessionals in basic helping skills*. Symposium conducted at the annual meeting of the Western Psychological Association, Reno, NV.

Campbell, E. L., Davidson, K., & Davidson, S. M. (2017). Effectiveness of LifeRAFT undergraduate helping skills training model. *Psychology Teaching Review*, *23*(2), 32–41.

Carkhuff, R. R., & Anthony, W. A. (1979). *The skills of helping: An introduction to counseling skills*. Amherst, MA: Human Resources Development.

Corey, G. (2009). *Theory and practice of counseling and psychotherapy* (8th ed.). Belmont, CA: Thomson/Brooks/Cole.

Cowan, E. W., & Presbury, J. H. (2000). Meeting client resistance and reactance with reverence. *Journal of Counseling & Development*, *87*, 411–419.

Egan, G. (2014). *The skilled helper: A problem-management and opportunity development approach to helping* (10th ed.). Belmont, CA: Brooks/Cole.

Erford, B. T. (2014). *Orientation to the counseling profession: Advocacy, ethics, and essential professional foundations* (2nd ed.). Boston, MA: Pearson.
Faiver, C., Eisengart, S., & Colonna, R. (2004). *The counselor intern's handbook* (3rd ed.). Belmont, CA: Cengage.
Franklin, B. (1775). To Joseph Priestley. In *Wilcox, W. B. (1975): The papers of Benjamin Franklin: January 1 through December 31, 1772, 19* (pp. 299–300). New Haven: Yale University Press.
Greenberg, L. S. (2002). *Emotion-focused therapy: Coaching clients to work through feelings*. Washington, DC: American Psychological Association.
Greenberg, L. S., & Watson, J. C. (2005). *Emotion-focused therapy for depression*. Washington, DC: American Psychological Association.
Hackney, H. (1992). Differentiating between counseling theory and practice, *Highlights: An ERIC/CAPS Digest*, Ann Arbor, MI: Counseling and Personnel Services Clearinghouse, University of Michigan.
Halbur, D. A., & Halbur, K. V. (2019). *Developing your theoretical orientation in counseling and psychotherapy* (4th ed.). Boston, MA: Pearson.
Harris, J. E., Kelly, L. J., Campbell, E. L., & Hammond, E. S. (2014). Key strategies training: An introduction to multitheoretical practice. *Journal of Psychotherapy Integration, 24*(2), 138–152. doi:10.1037/a0037056
Hill, C. E. (2014). *Helping skills: Facilitating exploration, insight, and action* (4th ed.). Washington, DC: American Psychological Association.
Ivey, A. E., Ivey, M. B., & Zalaquett, C. P. (2016). *Essentials of intentional interviewing: Counseling in a multicultural world* (3rd ed.). Boston, MA: Cengage Learning.
Martell, C. R., Dimidjian, S., Herman-Dunn, R., & Lewinsohn, P. M. (2010). *Behavioral activation for depression: A clinician's guide*. New York, NY: Guilford Press.
Myers, D. G. (2012). *Exploring psychology* (9th ed.). New York: Worth Publishers.
Prochaska, J. O., Norcross, J. C., & DiClemente, C. C. (2005). Stages of change: Prescriptive guidelines. In G. P. Koocher, J. C. Norcross, & S. S. Hill (Eds.), *Psychologists' desk reference* (2nd ed., pp. 226–231). New York: Oxford University Press.
Walsh, A. (2005). *The tutor in problem-based learning: A novice's guide*. Hamilton: McMaster University.

8 Stage Four

Modifying through Actions

Chapter Goals

This chapter will prepare you to:

- Learn about modifying through the action strategy, the first of three strategies in the fourth stage of the LifeRAFT model.
- Understand the select step for actions through the microskills of listening skills, questions, and focusing.
- Use the assess step for actions by ramping up to the microskills of information and logical consequences.
- Learn the identify step for actions with the addition of the microskills of feedback and confrontation.
- Use the launch step for actions by ramping up to the microskills of reframing and directives.

Introduction

This chapter will concentrate on the modifying stage through the action strategy. Once helpers have joined with a helpee in the support stage, addressed or ruled out any referral needs in the watch stage, surveyed the helpee's concerns in the investigating stage, and determined that a behaviorally based problem-solving approach will be most helpful for the modify stage, they are ready to modify through an actions approach (see Figure 8.1; action). The actions approach consists of a sequence of four action steps based on the theory of Behavioral Activation, which defines presenting concerns in terms of ineffective behaviors or activities in need of change (Martell, Dimidjian, Herman-Dunn, & Lewinsohn, 2010). This chapter will describe the theory of Behavioral Activation and then apply it to the four action steps for problem-solving with helpees.

Description of Modifying through Actions

Theory of Behavioral Activation

Behavioral Activation is a form of Behavior Therapy in professional counseling originally developed to treat depression and is now used to effectively treat a variety of psychological disorders and presenting issues (Martell et al., 2010). Behavioral Therapy is an umbrella term for many different action-based approaches. This method has taken many forms over the last several decades. Incorporating more recent clinical research, Martell et al. (2010) integrated several principles

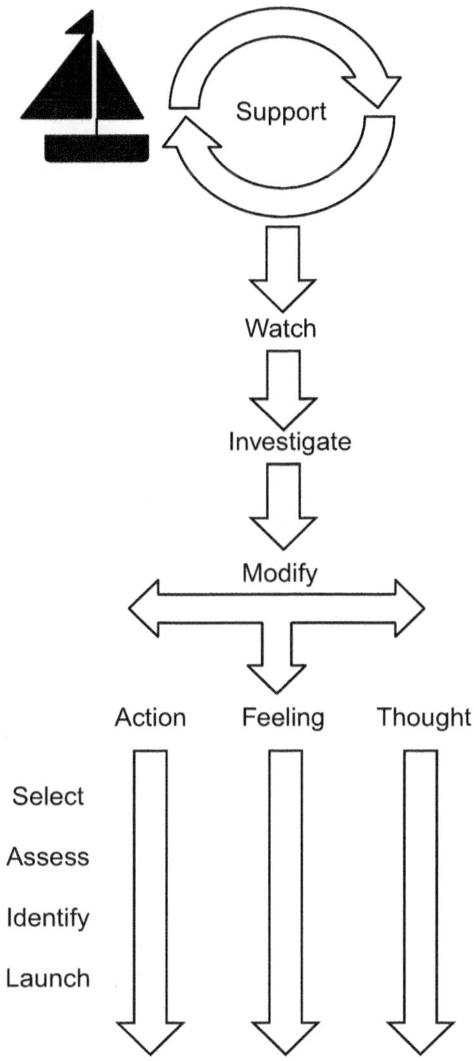

Figure 8.1 LifeRAFT Model

from former behavioral models into practice to develop a revised approach called the "Behavioral Activation Model."

The Behavioral Activation Model operates primarily on the principles of operant conditioning. Operant conditioning is a learning theory developed by B.F. Skinner (1971), which posits that intentional actions are modified by their consequences of reinforcement, either by rewards or punishments. That is to say, behaviors that are rewarded tend to be repeated and strengthened while behaviors that are not rewarded or punished tend to be weakened and discontinued. For example, if you tell a joke and it is rewarded with laughter, you will likely share the joke with others. Yet if the joke fails to land or is met with disapproval, you will likely choose to keep it to yourself next time. The motivation to engage in any activity is based on learning from consequences of previous experiences, resulting in expectations of receiving rewards and escaping punishment. Humans are instinctually driven toward rewards and away from punishment, and they suffer psychologically when exposed to continuous experiences of punishment and lack of reinforcement (Lejuez, Hopko, & Hopko, 2001). Following this premise, Behavioral Activation asserts: "problems in vulnerable individuals' lives reduce their ability to experience positive reward from their environments, leading to the symptoms and behaviors that we classify as depression" (Martell et al., 2010, p. 21). Thus, in operant conditioning approaches, the roots of problems are ultimately traced back to behaviors and their consequences.

Martell et al. (2010) expanded on operant conditioning with the "ABCs of behavior" model, depicted in Figure 8.2. According to this model, psychological problems are defined in terms of antecedents, behaviors, and consequences. They assert that "the key to changing how people feel is helping them change what they do" (p. 22). Behaviors to increase often include those that lead to pleasurable or rewarding consequences, whereas behaviors to decrease are typically escape or avoidance behaviors that interfere with managing one's needs and goals. Certain antecedents or environmental instances increase the likelihood that certain behaviors and consequences will occur. The way that antecedents lead to behaviors and then consequences is illustrated by the horizontal arrows in Figure 8.2.

Consider an example of the ABCs of behavior. If Amor wakes up in the morning to a headache (A), she might choose to stay in bed and sleep in (B). This likely will produce naturally reinforcing consequences of escaping discomfort from the headache and inducing pleasurable feelings of rest (C). This may be effective as a one-time solution; however, the model notes that this kind of avoidant behavior can create long-term problems if overused. If Amor continues to wake up with headaches and use the same behavioral response of staying in bed each time, she may get stuck in an ineffective behavior pattern. Although the headache began as the primary problem, Behavioral Activation asserts that it is actually Amor's behavioral response that ultimately perpetuates problems to keep her stuck. Sleeping in day after day would continue to bring immediate relief but create other adverse consequences of inactivity and avoidance of Amor's job and daily responsibilities. She might start to feel anxious and depressed, resulting in even more headaches, followed by more avoidant behavior of staying in bed. Such actions ultimately reduce pleasure and interfere with Amor's ability to manage her needs and goals. Thus, behavioral responses become secondary problems in and of themselves.

In order to alleviate these problems, Behavioral Activation suggests that helpees "must be assisted in engaging in behavior that they will ultimately find pleasurable or productive, or that will improve their life situations in such a way as to provide greater rewards" (Martell et al., 2010, p. 21). In this way, it tells us to reverse our typical way of responding by living from the outside in rather than the inside out. We typically choose our outward behaviors based on our inward thoughts and feelings. In Amor's example, her behavior of staying in bed was based on her inward thoughts of wanting to stay in bed and her feelings of relief generated by doing so. Thus, we typically act as if thoughts and feelings cause behaviors by originating from the inside to the outside. When this approach no longer produces healthy consequences, Behavioral Activation says we need to engage in the opposite by living from the outside in. This means changing behaviors to healthy ones such as deciding to get up even when thoughts and feelings are telling Amor to stay in bed until healthy thoughts and feelings follow, such as "Now that I'm up, I'm

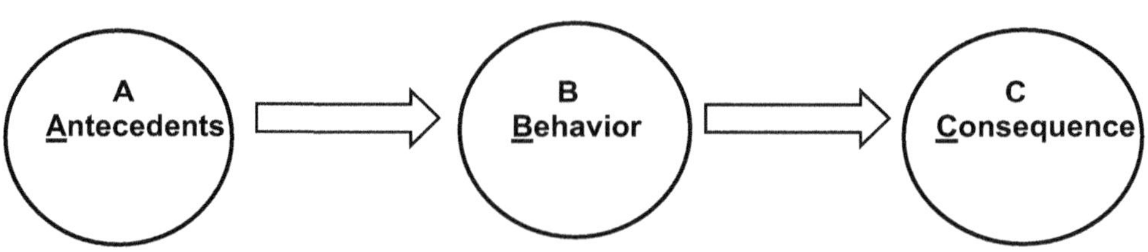

Figure 8.2 ABCs of Behavior Model

glad I got out of bed and want to stay up." Behavioral Activation therefore serves to activate effective behaviors that eventually lead back to psychological health.

Personal Reflection

Consider how behavioral steps apply to your own life. As you reflect on the Behavioral Activation Model, answer the following questions:

- Can you think of a time when an antecedent resulted in consequences that were positive in the short term but problematic in the long term? Write down your recollections of that time, highlighting the activating event and the consequences.
- What were the behaviors you engaged in (or avoided engaging in) that served to mediate the relationship between the event and the consequences?
- Can you think of alternative behaviors that might have resulted in different, more effective consequences? Write down these alternative behaviors.
- Based on these new behaviors, what would be the new consequences?

Actions Steps

The theory of Behavioral Activation is a counseling theory intended for use in professional therapy (Martell et al., 2010). Although initially applied and presented in ways that are inappropriate for use by nonprofessionals, the theoretical premise of Behavioral Activation can be usefully adapted for nonprofessional use. This is accomplished through the use of our SAIL steps of select, assess, identify, and launch. The following sections will integrate the theoretical rationale of Behavioral Activation to each of the steps of the actions approach.

This chapter will describe the four action steps that include selecting and focusing on actions, assessing ineffective actions, identifying potential shifts from ineffective to effective actions, and launching toward effective actions. Recall that these four steps are uniquely applied to the actions approach yet they parallel those used in the other RAFT strategies of feelings and thoughts, which will be described in subsequent chapters (see Table 8.1). The following sections will describe each step, when to use them, how to use them in conjunction with the microskills hierarchy and ramp-up, and their anticipated results. Case examples of the steps in practice will also be provided.

Table 8.1 LifeRAFT Modify Steps

SAIL Steps	*Description*	*Action Steps*	*Feeling Steps*	*Thought Steps*
Select	Select a focal area	Select and focus on actions	Select and focus on feelings	Select and focus on thoughts
Assess	Assess for problem	Assess ineffective actions	Assess maladaptive feelings	Assess dysfunctional thoughts
Identify	Identify potential shifts for improvement over problem	Identify potential shifts from ineffective to effective actions	Identify potential shifts from maladaptive to adaptive feelings	Identify potential shifts from dysfunctional to functional thoughts
Launch	Launch toward improvement of problem	Launch toward effective actions	Launch toward adaptive feelings	Launch toward functional thoughts

Select

Description

The theory of Behavioral Activation assumes that behaviors are key to human functioning and are often the most effective point of intervention to promote psychological well-being. A behavioral approach begins with attending to the specific behaviors the helpee is engaging in and those they are avoiding. According to Martell and colleagues (2010), a therapist's job is "to engage the helpee in a careful and detailed examination of . . . behaviors" (p. 25). In order to apply this to nonprofessional situations, we must use the ABCs of behavior to look closely at behaviors that impact other areas of functioning. To this end, helpers should begin by encouraging helpees to talk about and examine their own behaviors by using action-based language.

When to Select

When helpees do not realize how their problems may be related to their behavior, it can be useful for helpers to focus the attention of their helpees on their actions (Campbell, Davidson, & Davidson, 2017). The helper acts as a coach, guiding the helpee to collaboratively examine actions. As an objective observer, you as the helper may be able to recognize areas of ineffective action that your helpee fails to acknowledge. Explore with the helpee what they are doing in order to gradually and gently bring these actions into focus so that they can see the way their responses to antecedents result in problematic consequences.

How to Select

In the first step of selecting, helpers should redirect the conversation specifically to actions. The essence of selecting is to isolate the specific behaviors that are most closely associated with current distress (Campbell et al., 2017). Helpers should try to understand helpees' behaviors in concrete terms by breaking concerns down into small, manageable action points.

Microskills: Questions, Focusing

Through this stage, helpers should continue to use the microskills of attending, paraphrasing, reflection of feeling, questions, and focusing to encourage helpees to talk specifically about actions related to their concern. Remember to continue employing skills according to the microskills ramp-up (see Figure 8.3).

According to Martell and colleagues (2010), the most basic way to select and focus on actions is to ask questions such as "What happened?" to elicit antecedents and "What did you do in response?" to elicit behaviors when a helpee is reporting a distressing situation (p. 41). Some helpees may engage in a sequence of behaviors rather than an isolated action and might initially share several different behaviors related to a particular situation. Consider continued questioning to discover any subsequent behaviors by asking, "And then what did you do?" or "What did you do after that?"

Result

Selecting and focusing on actions is designed to increase the helpee's awareness of their behaviors, which is necessary before they can do more in-depth behavioral modifications (Campbell et al., 2017). Promoting this type of behavioral awareness allows helpees to gain insight into how their current behaviors may contribute to and perpetuate negative thoughts and feelings.

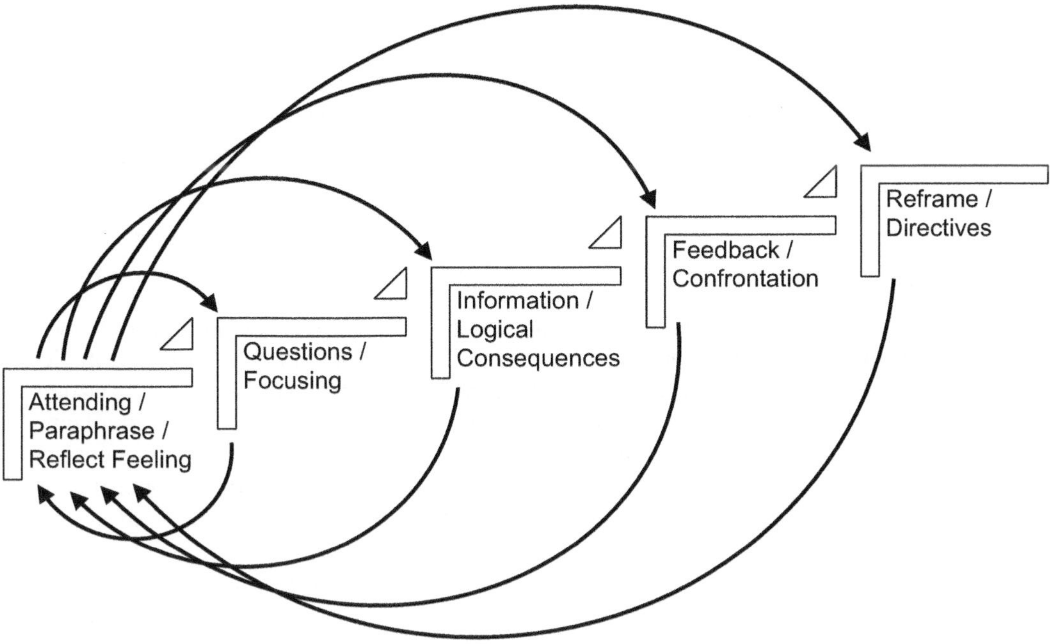

Figure 8.3 Microskills Ramp-Up

Case Example

To show how these behavioral steps can be used in practice, a case example will be used throughout this chapter. This case example shows how a university academic advisor named Lee works with a helpee named Yasmina, a college student in her early twenties who mentioned during an advising meeting that depression is interfering with her classes and schoolwork. Lee offered to help and Yasmina agreed, so they engaged in the supporting, watching, and investigating stages of LifeRAFT. Lee ruled out warning signs of crisis, identified that class attendance was the primary concern, and determined that an actions approach would be most helpful. In this example, Lee decides to select and focus on actions related to Yasmina's presenting concern.

HELPEE: Nothing is going right. I'm doing awful in school. I just want to lie in bed all the time and stay away from everybody. I miss my friends, but it's just too hard.

HELPER: It certainly has been tough. [Empathic reflection]

HELPEE: This isn't me. I'm such a mess and spending all of my time in bed.

HELPER: Sounds like you're feeling so bad that it's making it difficult to do your normal activities. [Paraphrase] I am interested to hear more about a particular time when you stayed in bed this week. [Selecting]

HELPEE: Ok. It happened on Tuesday. My morning alarm went off for class. I felt bad and just continued to hide in my room instead. I never used to skip school.

HELPER: So, what did you do instead? [Open question]

HELPEE: I just hid away in my room and didn't go to class.

HELPER: I can hear your frustration about this. [Empathic response] And then what did you do in your room? [Open question]

HELPEE: I watched some television and went back to sleep for a bit.

HELPER: That's understandable, given what you were feeling in the moment. It might be helpful to look more closely at what is interfering with going to class. [Selecting]
HELPEE: Ok, that sounds good.

As a result of selecting and focusing on actions, Lee helped Yasmina isolate a specific behavior: staying in bed instead of going to class, which is distressing and likely to be contributing to Yasmina's school challenges.

Written Practice

As you learn about each of the action steps, you will be asked to write questions or statements that implement each step to encourage you to think about how you would implement these skills in practice. Throughout this chapter, your written practice will focus on a family member named Zach, who is having trouble returning to driving his car after being in a motor vehicle accident six months prior. He is working with a professional counselor and you attended a session with him to ask his therapist how you could be supportive. As Zach works toward his goal of returning to driving, his therapist encouraged you to support Zach between therapy appointments around his goals. To practice selecting and focusing on actions, imagine that Zach asks to talk the situation through with you and he makes the following statements:

> "I can't stop thinking about the accident. It's really getting in the way. I'm having trouble sleeping through the night."
>
> "I'm so jumpy whenever I'm in the car. Hearing brakes screech or honking is awful. And driving on the freeway? Forget it. It's just city streets for me now."
>
> "I never realized how dangerous driving is and how many threats there are out there. There's so many bad drivers on the road to look out for."

In response to these helpee statements, write down two or three open questions you could ask that would help you select and focus on actions. What could you do to identify specific behaviors that might relate to Zach's symptoms?

Assess

Description

Assessing is the second step of exploring ineffective actions that are holding the helpee back from resolving the presenting issue (Campbell et al., 2017). Behavioral Activation focuses on the way actions influence other areas of functioning and assumes that behaviors are the most effective point of leverage to promote change.

The behavioral approach assumes not only that most problems are associated with ineffective behaviors but also that health is related to effective behaviors. The theory notes that familiar coping methods in response to environmental stressors may result in temporarily positive thoughts and feelings, but overuse of these coping methods can produce a downward spiral that keeps a helpee stuck in psychological distress. Ineffective behaviors disconnect helpees from reinforcements, while effective behaviors reconnect them with these rewards. Thus, it is important to understand connections between behaviors and how to differentiate between effective and ineffective behaviors.

When to Assess

Once helpees are able to intentionally select and focus on actions, the next step is to evaluate which behaviors are ineffective and in need of modification (Campbell et al., 2017). It is helpful to determine which actions are effective or ineffective to begin targeting which behaviors to increase and which to decrease.

How to Assess

With assessing, helpers should focus their conversation on actions to assess, which might be problematic (Campbell et al., 2017). In doing so, it is beneficial to note helpful actions as well. Aim to understand the consequences of the helpee's actions, particularly pertaining to their distress and attempts to cope with it (Martell et al., 2010).

Ineffective actions tend to have similar characteristics and tend to fall into at least one of four categories: overcoping, avoidance, withdrawal, and/or unintentionality (Martell et al., 2010).

Overcoping means using a behavior that was once helpful and soothing and engaging in it excessively until the coping behavior itself becomes the problem. An example of this is eating a cookie to feel better when you feel sad. It might help periodically, but if you constantly try to use more and more cookies to cope with sadness, it could contribute to a host of other issues, such as physical discomfort, health issues, and disordered eating.

Avoidance means attempting to prevent an undesired consequence by evading a situation and is closely related to withdrawal, which involves pulling back from a situation to escape undesired consequences. Someone who is socially anxious might avoid going to a party or they might attend the party but withdraw from conversation when approached.

Unintentionality means acting without conscious purpose. Haphazardly acting without consideration of the consequences can lead to ineffective actions, such as speeding on the drive to work without thinking about the dangers of doing so. As helpees discuss actions and their consequences with you, listen for ineffective actions by looking for instances of overcoping, avoidance, withdrawal, and/or unintentionality.

Microskills: Information, Logical Consequences

Using the microskills ramp-up, helpers add the skills of information and logical consequences to help guide the helpee in assessing their stuck points. This process will take time with multiple different microskill responses. Information and logical consequences are introduced into the conversation using the same ramp-up sequence as before: listening skills first, then ramping up to information and logical consequences as needed to assess ineffective actions, and finally listening skills again before returning to more influencing skills of either questions/focusing or information/logical consequences. Remember the purpose of this sequence is to resist seeming interrogative or judgmental and to continually return to empathy in order to provide the helpee with a safe space to consider change without sparking anger or defensiveness. The microskills ramp-up gives the helpee opportunities to reflect, take ownership, and help themselves as much as possible (Egan, 2014), which ultimately leads to better outcomes (Hill, 2014).

INFORMATION

Information involves sharing specific information with a helpee by providing facts that are true for most people to inspire them to think more deeply about their own actions (Ivey, Ivey, & Zalaquett, 2016). Use information for actions by offering information about possible ineffective actions that might be holding the helpee back. An example would be, "People often find that repeatedly using alcohol to cope in the moment causes problems in the long run. I wonder if this relates at all to your experience." Notice how the example offers information about an ineffective behavior for "people" and invites the helpee to consider the connection with their situation without calling them out or automatically labeling their actions as ineffective.

LOGICAL CONSEQUENCES

Exploring logical consequences is another method of encouraging the helpee to assess potential problems and areas for change without raising defenses. It involves empathically exploring the positive and negative consequences that would logically result from each one with the ultimate purpose of assessing where negative consequences are occurring (Ivey et al., 2016). For example, a helper might say, "What are some positive things that result from drinking alcohol? What are negative things that result?" Another way to ask about logical consequences for actions are, "What are things you do that seem to make problems worse? In what ways do these things make life better?" Notice how both positive and negative consequences are elicited to allow your helpee the opportunity to fully consider the situation and decide which behaviors are problematic for them, rather than you decide for them. Still, helpees may have trouble assessing a full list of positive and negative consequences for a behavior. Give helpees an opportunity to voice the pros and cons they notice and then tentatively suggest other possibilities, such as "Perhaps another negative result of drinking is that you had a headache the next day" or "I'm curious if a positive result of drinking alcohol is that it helps you forget your problems for a while." Do not be afraid to suggest positive or negative consequences, because doing so does not reinforce the behavior but instead prompts nonresistant evaluation of behaviors. Instead, worry more about keeping the list of pros and cons accurate and balanced (Miller & Rollnick, 2002).

Some actions will be associated with desirable consequences, while other actions will have undesirable consequences, and some will result in a combination. Oftentimes, actions have desirable consequences in the short term but undesirable ones in the long term (Martell et al., 2010). For example, someone may decline a party invitation and immediately feel relief but later feel lonely and further withdrawn from social support. Taken together, this information can yield valuable data about effective and ineffective behaviors.

Result

The intended outcome of assessing behaviors is an increase in helpees' awareness of how their actions impact other areas of functioning and how ineffective behaviors may contribute to affective distress and dysfunctional thinking (Campbell et al., 2017). By exploring the impact of actions, helpees will gain insight into why they continue to act in ways that are incongruent with their desired goals and acknowledge secondary gains of which they were previously unaware.

When actions are analyzed, it is expected that helpers and helpees will gain increased awareness into *how* particular actions are impacting helpees. This step may move the helpee to consider making behavioral changes but is unlikely to convince them completely. Instead, it prepares both helpers and helpees for subsequent interventions aimed at increasing effective actions and decreasing ineffective ones (Campbell et al., 2017).

Case Example

Once Lee helped Yasmina isolate a specific behavior of staying in bed instead of going to class, Lee wanted to help assess ineffectiveness by seeing how staying in bed might be impacting other areas of functioning and to determine the consequences of attending class versus staying in bed.

HELPER: This is a challenging situation [empathic reflection]. Sometimes people find that staying in bed helps them feel better in the moment but interferes with their life in much bigger ways. Help me understand how staying in bed impacts your life. [Information]

HELPEE: It's not good. My grades are slipping. My professor and the other students probably think I'm a slacker. It makes me feel awful.

HELPER: Yikes, I bet that does feel bad. [Paraphrase]

HELPEE: I dread having to face the fact that I missed class again. I feel disappointed in myself and I'm embarrassed that I keep doing this.

HELPER: A terrible feeling to experience all that dread, disappointment, and embarrassment. [Reflection of feelings] How does staying in bed during class impact how you think about yourself? [Logical consequences]

HELPEE: Makes me think I'm a lazy loser who can't even get out of bed. I'll bet everyone else is thinking bad things about me too.

HELPER: You think others are judging you for this. [Paraphrase]

HELPEE: Yes, I think everyone thinks I'm a bad student. I sure am acting like one.

HELPER: Ouch. I can hear that staying in bed results in some harsh thoughts about yourself, like it makes you think you're lazy and bad, and that others also see you as bad. [Paraphrase]

HELPEE: Yes, it's awful. I know I need to stop skipping class but it's really hard.

HELPER: Help me understand that better. Even though staying in bed leaves you disappointed and embarrassed and seeing yourself as lazy and bad, it's still happening for a reason. What are some positive things that come from staying in bed? [Logical consequences]

HELPEE: I don't know. I guess I'm scared the students won't like me. I'm not good at meeting new people. I'll make a bad impression and never make friends. I'm so lonely and I don't want to mess this up.

HELPER: I think I see what's happening here. You miss class to avoid being judged negatively by your classmates and getting off on the wrong foot with them. [Paraphrasing]

HELPEE: Yes, exactly. I know it's stupid, but I get so worried about it in the moment, I just stay there.

HELPER: You're scared and trying to cope; that makes sense. [Reflection of feeling/paraphrase] I wonder if another positive result of staying in bed is that it feels good to keep resting. [Closed question]

HELPEE: Not really. Usually staying in bed feels good, but I feel so guilty that I don't get any rest out of it.

HELPER: Thank you for clarifying. So, staying in bed is problematic because it leaves you disappointed and embarrassed and leads to seeing yourself as lazy and bad. It also helps you to avoid the frightening possibility of meeting new classmates. [Paraphrase]

HELPEE: Yes, that's it. This needs to stop but it's really hard.

As a result of assessing behaviors, Yasmina has identified that avoiding class is an ineffective behavior with both positive and negative results that she is having difficulty changing. Lee helped Yasmina articulate the way her actions make her feel disappointed and embarrassed and see herself as lazy and bad and identify how it was rewarding by helping her to avoid a feared situation.

Written Practice

As a result of using selecting and focusing on actions, you and Zach were able to isolate one behavior that seemed to be central to his experience of fear of driving after the vehicle accident: using side streets to avoiding freeway driving. In order to assess this behavior, you will want to help Zach analyze in what ways this avoidance behavior is effective and ineffective. For each of the following areas, write down one or two things you could say to Zach, incorporating the appropriate microskills:

- What could you say to Zach to help him assess whether driving side streets is an effective or ineffective behavior? Incorporate the use of the microskill information in your response.
- What could you say to encourage Zach to discuss what he notices about his behavior that seems to make problems better? Incorporate the use of the microskill logical consequences in your response.
- How could you prompt Zach to explain what he notices about his behavior that seems to make problems worse? Incorporate the use of the microskill logical consequences in your response.

Identify

Description

The third step involves identifying potential shifts from ineffective to effective actions (Campbell et al., 2017). At this point, the helpee understands that they are engaging in an ineffective behavior but feels unable or unwilling to make changes. Identifying is an exercise in which the helper and the helpee explore the pros and cons of changing problematic choices by highlighting inconsistencies and mismatches.

The purpose of identifying is to fully embrace the consequences of behaviors—good, bad, and otherwise—and make an informed choice about problem resolution steps (Egan, 2014). Identifying also serves to soothe helpee resistance by providing them with a safe and nonjudgmental space to wrestle with their choices (Campbell et al., 2017).

In the action approach, Behavioral Activation focuses on the specific ways that life events and stressors can lead to behaviors that yield decreases in positive reinforcement and increases in punishment. Put another way, methods of coping with life sometimes become the problem by producing dysphoria and withdrawal from healthy activities. Martell et al. (2010) suggest that these behaviors may persist despite their adverse outcomes because of reinforcement, saying, "To the extent that the behavior is likely to recur as a result of escape and avoidance, we can then say that it has been negatively reinforced" (p. 116). Discovering these reinforcement patterns of rewards and punishments helps to illuminate why ineffective behavior persists. Challenging helpees to face this fact provides the motivation needed to decrease ineffective behavior and increase effective behavior.

When to Identify

Once ineffective behaviors have been identified, it may be helpful to directly confront ineffective actions. Helpees at this point have identified areas of problems and recognize the need for change but are likely resistant to making changes. With the identify step, helpers challenge helpees to push through resistance and make changes through an evaluation of problematic choices as opposed to nonproblematic choices (Campbell et al, 2017).

How to Identify

Use the information gathered thus far about the helpee's distress, wants, and ineffective actions to note where conflicts might exist. Although the identifying step is about confronting, this refers to challenging the mismatch or dissonance between what a helpee ultimately wants and the results of their current behaviors (Ivey et al., 2016). Do not forget, however, this is carried out with the utmost care, empathy, and respect.

Behaviorist Lejuez and colleagues (2001) noted that behaviors generally occur to either acquire or get something desirable or escape or avoid something undesirable. Thus, both the reasons for wanting to stop an ineffective behavior and the reasons the ineffective behavior continues are likely motivated by wanting something good or escaping something bad. The goal of the identifying step is to highlight the discrepancy so the helpee can grapple with whether they want to change or not.

Microskills: Confrontation, Feedback

Using the microskills ramp-up, helpers use listening skills and then ramp up to the next level of influencing skills to continue moving helpees forward toward change. Helpers add the use of more microskills, including confrontation and feedback, to challenge the helpee to push through resistance and make changes.

CONFRONTATION

Confrontation is defined as supportively challenging your helpee by highlighting their conflicts, mixed messages, and discrepancies (Ivey et al., 2016). An example of confrontation would be, "You say you want to stop drinking because it's causing health problems, and yet you continue to do so because it helps relieve stress in the moment." Another confrontation might be, "I hear you say that alcohol relieves stress in the moment, and yet I'm seeing that overusing alcohol is causing you a lot more stress." This allows the helpee to wrestle directly with the discrepancy between addressing their distress and the challenges of change that are holding them back.

FEEDBACK

Feedback involves the helper transmitting reactions based on their own evaluation of the helpee (Egan, 2014). This is accomplished using the praise and polish method. Recall that the praise and polish method involves offering supportive, genuine, comprehensive, and specific reactions aimed at assisting the helpee to make changes by providing both positive and negative comments (Ivey et al., 2016). An example of praise and polish feedback is,

> I admire how you're prioritizing your wellbeing by considering working on your stress level. I'm also worried because alcohol seems to be adding to your stress by ultimately hurting your health and I'm scared that continuing to use is going to cause a critical health risk.

This once again offers the helpee the opportunity to confront their resistance and consider behavioral change.

Result

The intended outcome of identifying is to motivate helpees to push through resistance and make changes by making potential shifts from ineffective to effective actions (Campbell et al., 2017). By highlighting and challenging mixed messages directly, helpees can view their stuck points in context and see the broader value of change. This step may move the helpee to consider making behavioral changes, but they will likely be tentative and uncertain about their ability to do so. Thus, identifying also offers the opportunity to try on the possibility of changing without committing to it yet. It prepares both helpees and helpers for committing to a specific plan for change (Campbell et al., 2017).

Case example

Earlier, Lee helped Yasmina articulate that avoiding class is an ineffective behavior related to depression, but it continues as a way to avoid potential rejections by classmates. Lee wanted to identify and confront the discrepancies between Yasmina's desire to do well in school and make friends and her avoidance of class.

HELPER: This is quite a predicament. Thank you for helping me understand what this has been like for you. [Encouraging]

HELPEE: I'm scared. I make plans to get out of bed and go to class and then they fall flat and I'm back in bed again. I'm worried about failing my classes.

HELPER: I hear the fear that staying in bed is causing. I also heard earlier about your fears around attending class and not making friends. Both of those seem like real concerns. [Reflection of feelings]

HELPEE: They are. Fear is ruling my life right now and it makes me feel so depressed. I want to stop but I feel incapable of doing it. I just can't.

HELPER: Yasmina, you're so strong for talking this through and finding ways back to class. I'm also concerned when I see you shut down and continue staying in bed. [Feedback]

HELPEE: I know, I need to do something. My grades are bad and skipping class probably doesn't look good to my classmates anyway. I feel backed into a corner about this and I don't know what to do.

HELPER: I can see how scary this is for you as you wring your hands. You're really thinking this through. [Reflecting feelings, paraphrase]

HELPEE: I wish this could all just be fixed for me. It would be nice if I was already doing well in school and already had friends in class that were waiting for me. I'll bet it would be easier to get out of bed then.

HELPER: That would be nice; in this case, it looks like your actions will determine this situation. [Paraphrase] So on the one hand, you say that you want to do well in school and make friends, and on the other hand, you make it impossible for yourself to accomplish your goals by hiding in bed. [Confrontation]

HELPEE: It's true. I'm really sabotaging myself here. I know that staying in bed was a problem because it's hurting my grades, but I didn't really think about how much it's making my problems worse. I'll never do well in school or ever make friends if I keep hiding in bed. At least if I went, I'd be scared but I'd have a chance to do well.

HELPER: Incredible insights, Yasmina. You're doing a great job working with this through. I'm grateful to get to keep talking it through with you. [Encouragement]

As a result of identifying areas for change, Lee helped Yasmina discover the incongruity between her actions and her goals of performing well in school and making friends. Yasmina remains hesitant about how to make changes and following through with them, but she now has increased motivation toward attempting changes.

Written Practice

The purpose of the identifying step is to embrace the consequences of behaviors and soothe helpee resistance about change in preparation for making an informed choice about problem resolution steps. This would be the time to motivate Zach to push through his resistance to making changes through identifying and experimenting with discrepancies involved in his ineffective action of exclusively using side streets and avoiding the freeway. To this end, it may be helpful to note what you see Zach doing well and where he is struggling in this process and to challenge directly how his behaviors are inconsistent with his goals. For each of the following areas, write down one or two things you could say to Zach:

- What could you say to help Zach see both the strengths and the areas for growth in his behavior? Incorporate the use of the microskill feedback in your response.
- What could you say to encourage Zach to consider how his behaviors are inconsistent with his goals? Incorporate the use of the microskill confrontation in your response.

Launch

Description

The fourth and final step in the actions strategy involves launching toward effective actions by generating a helpful and healthy resolution. This most notably involves plans to engage in effective actions. The purpose is for the helpee to end the helping interaction armed with a method for behavioral change.

In the action approach, Behavioral Activation focuses on ensuring change occurs by planning out the behavioral change step-by-step. When a helpee considers possible changes, they need to feel confident in their ability to do so by knowing exactly what to do and how to do it. According to Martell et al. (2010),

> clients also should not be expected to simply rely on willpower to engage in an agreed-upon assignment. The therapist should take time to discuss a plan of implementation with the client. The more specific and detailed the plan, the better!
>
> (p. 33)

Helpees are more likely to get unstuck from ineffective actions if they are provided thorough and concrete support in doing so.

When to Launch

Once helpers have challenged helpees to seriously consider inconsistencies between their behaviors and their goals, it may be helpful to discuss how they could go about generating effective actions instead. Helpees are likely to have increased motivation toward change but remain hesitant and uncertain about their ability to do so. The launch step can help prepare them by further mobilizing their confidence and strategizing with them how to accomplish change (Campbell et al., 2017).

How to Launch

New actions can be difficult to implement, so helpers should guide helpees toward preparing for new behaviors through support, reframing, and planning. To maximize the usefulness of this step, helpers should make certain that agreed-upon behavioral changes are realistic and understandable (Martell et al., 2010). As the helper, you may reflect on the following question: "Does the new behavior we discuss give us both enough information, so it is clear to both of us exactly what the helpee plans to do from here?"

Microskills: Reframing, Directives

Through the microskills ramp-up, helpers move to the highest level, adding the use of the remaining microskills, including reframing and directives, to motivate their helpees toward a new perspective and a healthier direction in an effort to resolve the presenting issue or get unstuck from their current predicament.

REFRAMING

Reframing is defined as providing helpees with a new, more positive perspective on themselves and their concerns. It often involves taking a negative thought and reframing it by generating a more adaptive and balanced response (Ivey et al., 2016). Reframing helps to solidify decisions to change by adding an encouraging angle. For reframing within the actions approach, provide your helpee with a positive viewpoint of the changes they are considering making. For example, a reframe would be,

> I hear your frustration in yourself for alcohol becoming a problematic part of your life. The changes you are considering are so admirable. Change is not easy, and you are making plans to embrace a healthier and happier life for yourself.

This helps motivate helpees to change and focus on the positive aspects about the changes they are making.

DIRECTIVES

Directives are defined as the instructions provided to helpees to follow specific actions (Hill, 2014). In other words, the microskill of directives means giving them advice. This is reserved for the end of the helping interaction and only as needed to support the helpee in making step-by-step plans for change. For example, directives may include "Perhaps this could start by calling your alcoholics anonymous (AA) sponsor today. Can we agree to that?" Notice how you can make every effort to maintain helpee autonomy, even with the highest level of influencing skill, by making tentative suggestions. Also note that ending directives with a question about the helpee's willingness and agreement with the directive puts the power back in their hands to choose whether or not to proceed.

Result

The intended outcome of launching is to motivate helpees to make plans and increase the likelihood that they will follow through with making behavioral changes (Campbell et al., 2017). If used effectively, a shift from an ineffective to an effective behavior is expected to result in a wider repertoire of effective actions. As a helpee gets unstuck from their current distress by doing one good thing for themselves, more good things are likely to follow (Corey, 2009). In our earlier example, a helpee distressed from problematic alcohol use who calls their AA sponsor is more likely to experience other positive consequences toward their goals, such as discontinuing problematic alcohol use. Behavioral Activation teaches us that we can and should start small when it comes to behavioral change (Martell et al., 2010).

Case Example

In the identifying step, Lee helped Yasmina discover the incongruity between her actions and her goals of performing well in school and making friends. Yasmina remains hesitant about how to make changes and following through with them. Lee wanted to launch Yasmina toward change and help her make concrete plans on how to get out of bed and attend class.

HELPEE: I can't believe how I've made my problems so much worse by staying in bed. I'm a mess.

HELPER: I hear that you feel like a mess. I see you very differently. I see you as insightful in making connections and willing to give yourself a chance to succeed by showing up. [Reframing]

HELPEE: I like that idea. Just show up to give myself a chance. But I'm scared I won't be able to do it when the time comes.

HELPER: Seems like the motivation is there and the fear continues to hold you back. [Paraphrase, reflection of feeling]

HELPEE: Exactly. I can say all of this now, but it really comes down to what happens when I wake up on class day.

HELPER: Perhaps we could make some concrete plans and preparations now to make it more likely that you are successful in attending class. Would that be alright? [Directive]

HELPEE: Ok, what were you thinking?

HELPER: I see you considering this possibility, which is great! [Paraphrase, encouragement] What ideas do you have to prepare to get out of bed and go to class? [Open question]

HELPEE: Hmm, let me think. . . . Well, I really liked that idea, "Just show up. Give myself a chance." Maybe I could tell myself that when I wake up.

HELPER: Excellent idea! [Encouragement] So you'll use that as a kind of mantra to motivate yourself. [Paraphrase] Perhaps you could write that down, so you remember it. [Directive]

HELPEE: Yes, and then maybe I could put the card next to my alarm, so I see it right when I wake up.

HELPER: Seeing your mantra right away seems so helpful. [Paraphrase] What else could you do to prepare for success? [Open question]

As a result of launching, Lee helped Yasmina make plans to attend class. Yasmina may remain hesitant and uncertain, but her distress is likely to be reduced, and she has an increased likelihood of getting unstuck and engaging in effective actions as a result of her work with Lee.

Written Practice

The purpose of launching is to raise confidence toward change and make concrete plans for replacing ineffective actions with effective actions. This would be the time to motivate Zach by reframing his actions in positive terms and developing specific plans to reduce driving avoidance and get closer to driving on the freeway again. Remember that starting with small changes is helpful. To this end, it may be helpful to note how you view Zach's progress and explore with him a change he could make toward unrestricted driving. For each of the following areas, write down one or two things you could say to Zach:

- Zach tells you he feels like a "wimp" for being afraid of the freeway. What could you say to help Zach see himself more positively? Incorporate the use of the microskill reframing in your response.

- Zach shares with you that he wants to consider riding as a car passenger on the freeway. What could you say to encourage Zach to consider the concrete steps involved in how this could be accomplished? Incorporate the use of the microskill directive in your response.

Role-Play Practice

The purpose of this exercise is to rehearse the modifying stage for the action strategy. This time you will practice using the entire LifeRAFT SWIM stages of supporting, watching, investigating, and modifying, then choose your RAFT strategy of actions, and finally SAIL steps for actions. For this exercise, find a volunteer helpee to role-play a helping scenario with you and provide feedback afterward. Set a timer and conduct your helping scenario for at least 20 minutes. Attempt to support using listening skills of attending, paraphrasing, and reflecting feelings only and then watch for concerns. Investigate using listening skills, questions, and focusing and finally choose actions as a strategy and engage in modifying using all microskills via the microskills ramp-up. Complete the following:

1. Consider pairing with a fellow helper-in-training and take turns being the helper and the helpee.
2. Video record the scenario. Follow the ethical guidelines discussed in Chapter 1, including consent to video record.
3. Ask your helpee to select a topic to discuss. Consult Chapter 1, "Problem Triggers," for topic ideas. Request that they focus on a behavioral change they would like to make in their life. Helpees should avoid crises or any concerns that would highlight warning signs necessitating the full watch stage.
4. As the helper, attempt to support using listening skills of attending, paraphrasing, and reflecting feelings and then investigate using listening skills, questions, and focusing. Choose the actions strategy and progress through modifying using all needed microskills via the microskills ramp-up.
5. At the end of the role-play, request feedback from your helpee about what you did well and what you could improve on next time. Ask what interventions felt especially empathic and supportive and which ones were awkward or uncomfortable. Write down your helpee's responses.
6. Review the video recording. What do you think you did well and what you could improve on next time as the helper?

Summary

In this chapter we discussed the following:

Description of Modifying through Actions

- Modifying for actions is based on Behavioral Activation and operant conditioning, in which behaviors are based on consequences. Ineffective behaviors develop and are maintained due to their initial desirable outcomes that typically develop into overcoping, avoidance, withdrawal, and/or unintentionality. Problem-solving occurs by converting ineffective behaviors into effective ones.
- Modifying involves choosing actions and guiding the helpee through a basic problem-solving process of four steps: select, assess, identify, and launch.

Select

- The select step uses attending, paraphrasing, reflection of feeling, questions, and focusing to encourage helpees to talk specifically about how actions impact their concern.

Assess

- The assess step involves assessing ineffective actions that are holding the helpee back from resolving the presenting.
- Using the microskills ramp-up, helpers add information and logical consequences to guide helpees to assess their stuck points.

Identify

- The identify step uses feedback and confrontation to challenge helpees to push through resistance and consider behavioral changes through an evaluation of ineffective and effective behaviors.

Launch

- Helpers add the use of remaining microskills, including reframing and directives, to motivate their helpees toward a new perspective and a concrete plan of action in an effort to resolve the presenting issue.

References

Campbell, E. L., Davidson, K., & Davidson, S. M. (2017). Effectiveness of LifeRAFT undergraduate helping skills training model. *Psychology Teaching Review*, *23*(2), 32–41.

Corey, G. (2009). *Theory and practice of counseling and psychotherapy* (8th ed.). Belmont, CA: Thomson/Brooks/Cole.

Egan, G. (2014). *The skilled helper: A problem-management and opportunity development approach to helping* (10th ed.). Belmont, CA: Brooks/Cole.

Hill, C. E. (2014). *Helping skills: Facilitating exploration, insight, and action* (4th ed.). Washington, DC: American Psychological Association.

Ivey, A. E., Ivey, M. B., & Zalaquett, C. P. (2016). *Essentials of intentional interviewing: Counseling in a multicultural world* (3rd ed.). Boston, MA: Cengage Learning.

Lejuez, C. W., Hopko, D. R., & Hopko, S. D. (2001). A brief behavioral activation treatment for depression. *Behavior Modification*, *25*, 255–286.

Martell, C. R., Dimidjian, S., Herman-Dunn, R., & Lewinsohn, P. M. (2010). *Behavioral activation for depression: A clinician's guide*. New York, NY: Guilford Press.

Miller, W. R., & Rollnick, S. (2002). *Motivational interviewing: Preparing people to change* (2nd ed.). New York: Guilford Press.

Skinner, B. F. (1971). *Beyond freedom and dignity*. New York: Knopf.

9 Stage Four

Modifying through Feelings

Chapter Goals

This chapter will prepare you to:

- Learn about modifying through the feelings strategy, the second of three strategies in the fourth stage of the LifeRAFT model.
- Understand the select step for feelings through the microskills of questions and focusing.
- Use the assess step for feelings by ramping up to the microskills of information and logical consequences.
- Learn the identify step for feelings with the addition of the microskills of feedback and confrontation.
- Use the launch step for feelings by ramping up to the microskills of reframing and directives.

Introduction

This chapter continues to guide you in the modifying stage, but this time through the feelings strategy. We use the feelings approach only after we have supported the helpee, watched for and addressed or ruled out any referring needs, investigated the helpee's concerns, and determined modification using an emotion-focused approach will be most helpful (see Figure 9.1; feeling). The feelings approach consists of a sequence of four feelings steps based on the theory of Emotion-Focused Therapy, which defines presenting concerns in terms of maladaptive emotions in need of investigation and validation (Greenberg, 2002). This chapter will describe the theory behind Emotion-Focused Therapy and then apply it to the four action steps for problem-solving with helpees.

Description of Modifying through Feelings

Theory of Emotion-Focused Therapy

Emotion-Focused Therapy (EFT) is a contemporary experiential approach to professional counseling. It integrates elements of attachment theory and humanistic approaches, both of which emphasize the importance of relationship and providing emotional validation as an essential component of treatment. Originally developed by Leslie Greenberg and Sue Johnson (1988) as a treatment in couple therapy, EFT has also been applied to individuals (Greenberg, 2002) and families (Johnson & Lee, 2000). EFT has been extensively researched and is an empirically

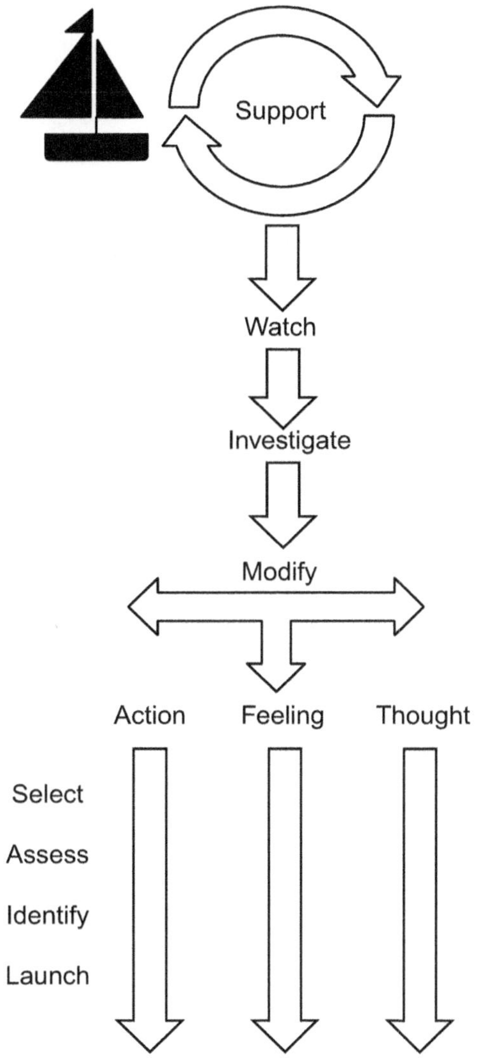

Figure 9.1 LifeRAFT Model

supported therapy for multiple modalities, clients, and presenting concerns (Watson, Gordon, Sermac, Kalogerakos, & Steckley, 2003; Wiebe & Johnson, 2016).

EFT has been manualized for use in professional counseling (Goldman & Greenberg, 2015) with numerous steps and stages that can get complicated. Yet the basic premise of Emotion-Focused Therapy is relatively simple and straightforward for use in nonprofessional helping (Campbell, Davidson, & Davidson, 2017).

The primary purpose of EFT is to "work to enhance clients' emotional intelligence, which involves the recognition and use of their own and others' emotional states to solve problems and regulate behavior" (Greenberg &Watson, 2006, p. 9). Thus, EFT attempts to guide helpees to identify and experiment with their own emotions to better understand and experience their value and express them appropriately. By better understanding, expressing, and accepting their feelings, we expect helpees to embrace adaptive emotions and let go of maladaptive ones

(Brooks-Harris, 2008). Once feelings become more adaptive, effective actions and functional thoughts are also expected to follow.

The features by which this process occurs involve two primary EFT concepts: primary and secondary emotions and emotional signals.

Primary and Secondary Emotions

EFT suggests that people in distress experience emotions as a series of chain reactions or layers. It is rare for a person to experience one emotion in isolation; instead, they have multiple emotional reactions in response to an experience. It is far more common for people in distress to feel multiple negative emotions such as anger, sadness, and fear in response to an unpleasant event (Greenberg, 2002). For example, a person who discovers that their house is infested with termites might feel angry at the cost of repairs, sad that their beloved home is in disrepair, and fearful of the extent of the damage. All of these reactions are legitimate and real for the individual by pertaining to different aspects of the same situation, and all can occupy their experience at the same time. See Figure 9.2 for a visual representation of primary and secondary emotions.

Primary emotions are those initial, genuine responses to a given situation (Greenberg, 2002) that arise instinctually without thought or processing. If a car is speeding toward you, you automatically feel a genuine primary emotion of fear. Primary emotions are also deeply rooted. While one person may feel a primary emotion of gratitude in response to caring from others, another might feel anger at being fussed over. People are not always aware of their primary responses, particularly if their reactions are not considered appropriate or socially acceptable (Greenberg & Johnson, 1988), such as the case with feeling angry when people show care and concern. Primary emotions are sometimes buried and only accessed through exploration, such as in a helping situation. Notice as depicted in Figure 9.2 that primary emotions can include multiple different emotions and are concealed within layers of secondary emotions.

Secondary emotions appear as a reaction to primary emotions, layering over them as a protective and regulatory measure (Greenberg & Watson, 2006). Secondary emotions frequently represent the socially acceptable, dignified, or expected response to a situation, and people are often unaware that might be covering for deeper, less "acceptable" ones. For example, a person may

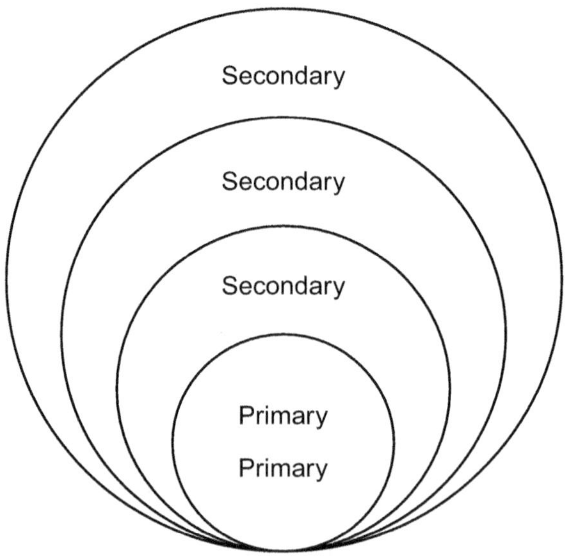

Figure 9.2 Primary and Secondary Emotions

grieve after the death of a loved one as a secondary emotion. While they may legitimately experience grief, they may feel pressure to feel or express it more intensely because it is an expected reaction and may, deep down, feel primary feelings of relief or even gladness that a loved one is no longer suffering. Secondary emotions can also be unrealistically intensified versions of primary emotions. A lottery winner might genuinely feel delighted about the win but secondarily intensified to a frenzy over winnings to satisfy expectations. Lastly, secondary emotions can also represent emotional reactions to primary emotions. Called "metafeelings," these are feelings about feelings. Common expressions of metafeelings are guilt and shame. For example, the lottery winner may feel guilty for feeling only slight excitement and the person who lost a loved one might feel ashamed for feeling relieved about a death. These reactions can lead to additional metafeelings such as anger from getting caught up in a web of guilt or fear that the feelings will not subside.

The theory behind EFT suggests that individuals need to "name it to tame it" (Siegel & Payne Bryson, 2011, p. 27); in other words, each experienced emotion needs to be given attention and understanding before it can subside. Thus, part of the purpose of EFT—and therefore a goal of our LifeRAFT feelings strategy—is to peel back the emotional layers of a helpee's experience so that each emotion has an opportunity to be expressed and validated until the secondary emotions give way to primary emotions (Campbell et al., 2017). In this way, focusing on emotions is like peeling the leaves of an artichoke until you reach the heart.

Emotional Signals

Allowing a helpee to fully express their feelings is a valuable exercise in accessing important emotional signals. EFT suggests that our emotions are valuable parts of the human experience that must be attended to, particularly in times of distress. Emotions exist to provide our bodies with important indicators of our wants and needs. Just as our growling tummies can signal us that we need food or heavy eyes tell us we need rest, our emotions serve to provide valuable data about our needs (Greenberg, 2002).

When emotions appropriately signal us to satisfy needs through our thoughts and actions, our feelings are considered to be adaptive (Greenberg & Paivio, 1997). Adaptive signals for the basic emotions of sadness, anger, and fear are summarized in Table 9.1. Sadness is considered adaptive when it signals disconnection and motivates us to discover what is missing and reconnect. Anger is adaptive when it signals a violation and motivates us to take assertive action. Fear is adaptive when it signals impending threat and mobilizes us to escape or engage in preparations. However, the clutter of multiple emotional responses and layers of secondary emotions can confuse our signaling systems. Thus, EFT and our LifeRAFT feelings strategy seek out and identify adaptive emotional responses for the purpose of guiding the helpee to experience their emotional signaling system to its fullest (Campbell et al., 2017). The expectation is that helping them to reconnect with their own emotions will help them to get unstuck from their distress whirlpool through healthy emotional expression and clarity.

Table 9.1 Emotional Signals

Emotion	*Signal*	*Motivated Response*
Sadness	Disconnection	Discover what is missing Reconnect
Anger	Violation	Take assertive action Protect oneself
Fear	Impending threat	Mobilize escape Engage in preparation

Personal Reflection

Consider how primary and secondary emotions and emotional signals apply to your own life. As you reflect on these features of EFT, answer the following questions:

- Can you think of a time when secondary emotions clouded your awareness and expression of your primary emotions? Write down your recollections of that time, highlighting primary and secondary emotions.
- What do you believe your emotions were signaling and motivating you to do?
- How might talking about these feelings help you access primary emotions and adaptive signals?

Feelings Steps

Although initially applied and presented in ways that are inappropriate for use by nonprofessionals, the theoretical premise of EFT can be adapted for nonprofessional use (Campbell et al., 2017). This is accomplished via our SAIL steps of select, assess, identify, and launch. The following sections will integrate the theoretical rationale of EFT to each of the steps of the feelings approach.

Note how the SAIL steps of select, assess, identify, and launch are the same ones used for the actions approach. Although this problem-solving process is similar, the goal and purpose of the actions and feelings approaches are very different. Recall that the actions approach sought ultimately to produce behavioral changes by generating a concrete plan of action. The goal of the action approach makes particular sense to most helpers because behavioral modifications are how many people define change. However, recall our discussion from earlier chapters about the stages of change (Prochaska, Norcross, & DiClemente, 2005). We know that change is a process that can involve behavioral change but does not necessarily have to. Instead, the process of change involves a great deal of psychological shifts involving awareness and motivational processes.

We must then view helping through this lens and embrace the goal of EFT and the LifeR-AFT feelings strategy. The goal of the feelings approach is not to produce behavioral changes or develop an action plan. Although it is assumed that adaptive feelings will ultimately lead to effective actions and functional thoughts, our objective instead is helping the helpee get unstuck from distress through adaptive feelings (Brooks-Harris, 2008). This entails aiding the helpee to fully experience and accurately express their emotions while accepting them as genuine and valid without judgment or shame. We accomplish this by being encouraging and nonjudgmental, ultimately offering the message that the helpee and their feelings are acceptable and worthy. Unlike actions, the feelings approach is likely to intensify a helpee's emotional experience and you may actually cause them to feel temporarily worse in the moment (Egan, 2014). Helping a person help themselves by reorienting to the signals of their own body may require a temporary increase in discomfort for the sake of better understanding of their needs. Thus, the steps of the feelings approach are used for the primary goal of catharsis through release of trapped emotions.

This chapter will describe the four feelings SAIL steps that include selecting and focusing on feelings, assessing maladaptive feelings, identifying potential shifts from maladaptive to adaptive feelings, and launching toward adaptive feelings. Recall that these four steps are uniquely applied to the feelings approach, yet they parallel those used in the other strategies of actions and thoughts (see Table 9.2). The following sections will describe each step, when to use them, how to use them in conjunction with the microskills hierarchy and ramp-up, and their anticipated results. Case examples of the steps in practice will also be provided.

Table 9.2 LifeRAFT Modify Steps

SAIL Steps	*Description*	*Action Steps*	*Feeling Steps*	*Thought Steps*
Select	Select a focal area	Select and focus on actions	Select and focus on feelings	Select and focus on thoughts
Assess	Assess for problem	Assess ineffective actions	Assess maladaptive feelings	Assess dysfunctional thoughts
Identify	Identify potential shifts for improvement over problem	Identify potential shifts from ineffective to effective actions	Identify potential shifts from maladaptive to adaptive feelings	Identify potential shifts from dysfunctional to functional thoughts
Launch	Launch toward improvement of problem	Launch toward effective actions	Launch toward adaptive feelings	Launch toward functional thoughts

Select

Description

The theoretical basis for EFT suggests that human emotions are connected to basic needs and require attention in order to effect thoughts and actions to produce psychological well-being (Greenberg, 2002). This process begins with tuning in and attending to a helpee's emotions. According to Greenberg and Watson (2006),

> Therapists can help clients become aware of and understand their feelings by attending to the triggers, or situational stimuli, that spark the feelings. Identifying the triggers helps clients and therapists begin to understand how clients construe the events in their lives and react to those events.
>
> (p. 175–176)

In LifeRAFT, a feelings approach begins by inquiring about helpees' feelings and the situations that may have prompted them. In order to accomplish this, helpers should begin by encouraging helpees to talk about and examine their own feelings by using emotional language (Campbell et al., 2017).

When to Select

When helpees fail to realize how their feelings and problems may be related, helpers can select and focus the attention of their helpees on their feelings (Campbell et al., 2017). The helper acts as a caring supporter who invites the helpee to experience and express their emotions as they arise. As a witness to this process, you may be able to recognize emerging feelings that the helpee is not aware of or willing to acknowledge. Gradually and gently bring these emotions into awareness so that the helpee can give them the attention they require.

How to Select

In the first step of selecting, helpers should redirect the conversation to feelings. The purpose of this is to name and experience the feelings most closely associated with the current distress (Campbell et al., 2017). Helpers should try to understand helpees' feelings to the fullest by empathizing and taking time to fully sit with and experience the feelings in the moment before moving to the next emotion.

Microskills: Questions, Focusing

Up to this point of the interaction, helpers continue to use the microskills of attending, paraphrasing, reflection of feeling, questions, and focusing to encourage helpees to talk specifically about feelings related to their concern. Reflecting feelings is the best microskill to use to focus on emotions, because it was created for this purpose (Ivey, Ivey, & Zalaquett, 2016). Consider using this microskill as much as possible when working in the feelings strategy. Remember to continue employing skills according to the microskills ramp-up (see Figure 9.3).

Open-ended questions are another way for the helper to assist the helpee in identifying their feelings, sitting with them, and learning more about each feeling's trigger and context. A helper might ask, "How are you feeling right now?" or "What emotion is coming up as you talk about that?" The helper can then reflect the feelings discussed and follow up with more questions to explore a helpee's feelings (Hill, 2014).

Helpers are encouraged not to stop at simply reflecting a feeling but instead to deepen the helpee's experience and understanding of each feeling. EFT suggests that emotional signals need to be fully expressed to reach full adaptive value (Greenberg, 2002). Stay with a feeling for a time by learning more about it. Ask questions about how the feeling is experienced, such as "What does the sadness feel like for you right now?" and "Where do you feel sadness in your body?" and "What is it like for you to feel sad about this?" As helpees talk about the emotion, they will transition from talking about it to connecting with it fully and experiencing it in the moment (Brooks-Harris, 2008). Note how example questions emphasize focusing on the present using words such as "right now" and present tense of "feel" rather than "felt" to encourage helpees to experience their feelings in the moment. Encourage this further by relying heavily on empathic attending skills and experiencing each emotion for yourself to mirror back to your helpee. In this approach, emotional release, such as through intensified discussion and crying, is welcome and encouraged (Greenberg & Johnson, 1988).

Continue conversation around each emotion through clarifying feelings and questions about their origins, even when answers seem obvious. For example, "In what way did your mother

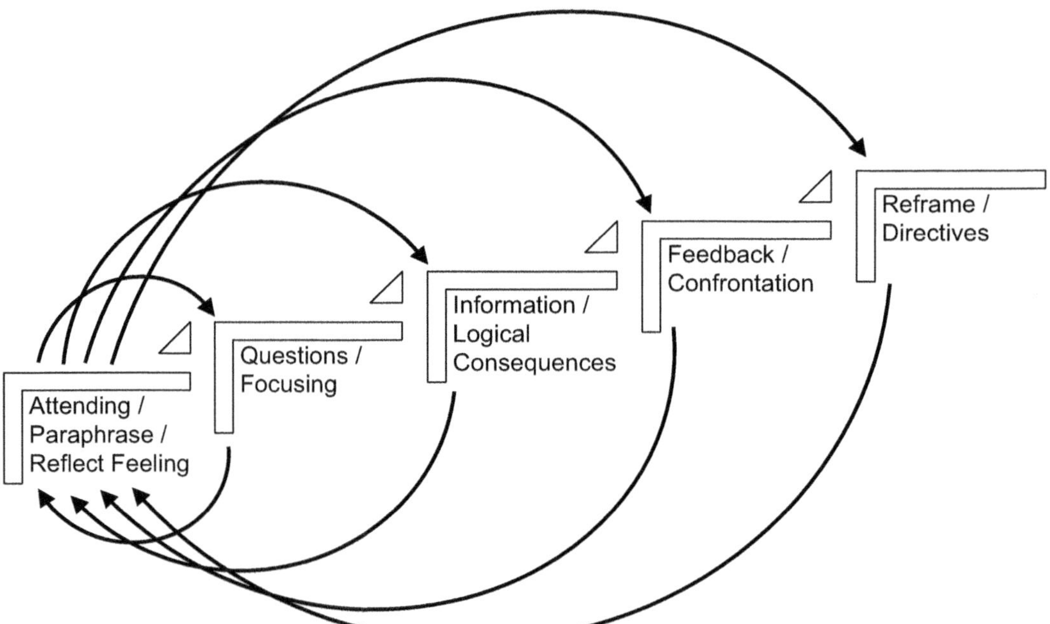

Figure 9.3 Microskills Ramp-Up

yelling at you make you angry?" and "What about dropping a kitchen knife near your foot scared you the most?" The answer may surprise you or lead to new insights and understanding (Ivey et al., 2016). Note how the word "why" is avoided in these questions to avoid perceived judgment. Helpees may also need some coaching to clarify their emotions. They may offer a vague emotional response such as "I feel upset" or replace feelings with thoughts such as "I feel like I don't know what I'm doing." Assist helpees in identifying specific feelings by reflections of feelings like "That sounds to me as if you're feeling apprehensive" or asking clarifying questions such as "When you say that you're upset, what feeling would you use to describe that?"

Result

Selecting and focusing on feelings aid helpees in talking about and becoming more aware of their feelings, which are necessary before they can tune into the emotional signals their body may be expressing to them. This type of emotional expression and awareness allows helpees to gain insight into how their current feelings may connect to the distressing situation that perpetuates negative thoughts and actions (Harris, Kelly, Campbell, & Hammond, 2014).

Case Example

To show how these behavioral steps can be used in practice, a case example will be used throughout this chapter, showing how Amy, a nurse and helper, works with Buffy, a patient visiting her family physician. In this example, Amy selects and focuses on feelings to isolate specific emotions that may be contributing to Buffy's distress regarding her doctor's suggested lifestyle changes.

HELPEE: I'm so disappointed in myself. The doctor said it's become critical for me to cut salt from my diet to lower my blood pressure. It's embarrassing that I've let myself get to this point.

HELPER: Oh, Buffy I feel for you. Sounds like you're feeling a lot of guilt and shame right now. [Reflection of feeling]

HELPEE: I've known my blood pressure was high and that I should address it. Eating low sodium is such a simple change. I'm mortified that the doctor had to lecture me about it.

HELPER: I'm hearing that embarrassment is what you're feeling most. [Reflecting feeling] Help me understand what that feels like for you. [Indirect open question]

HELPEE: It feels like I'm a child who misbehaved and my parent found me out and had to scold me. I'm not a child; I'm a grown adult. This shouldn't be a big deal. I should just do it. I should have done it already.

HELPER: I see. So, you feel guilty that the doctor had to say something to you about it rather than just doing it on your own. [Reflecting feeling]

HELPEE: Sort of. I guess I feel kind of sad that managing my high blood pressure isn't a priority. It's embarrassing for that to be pointed out, but it really brings me down to see myself fail in this way.

HELPER: I watched your face change as you said that. I can see this hurts you. [Reflecting feeling] What hurts the most about this? [Open question]

HELPEE: I'm sad I'm not being the person I want to be. I want to be someone who balances enjoying food with also taking care of health concerns. Lowering my salt intake isn't a big deal. I should just do it already.

As a result of selecting and focusing on feelings, Amy helped Buffy focus on her emotional reactions. She connected with and explored specific feelings of guilt and sadness, which are likely contributing to Buffy's distress regarding lifestyle changes.

Written Practice

As you learn about each of the feelings steps, you will be asked to write questions or statements that implement each step to encourage you to think about how you would implement these skills in practice. Throughout this chapter, your written practice will focus on Casey, a bank customer who is angry about an error applied to his account. He was charged a fee by mistake that has already been removed, but he remains angry about the incident and asked to speak to a supervisor. You are the customer service supervisor who will attempt to help. To practice selecting and focusing on feelings, imagine that Casey makes the following angry statements:

> "This should never have happened! What kind of business are you running here? Why should I keep my money with such a terribly run bank?!"
>
> "Your employee refunded my money, but he was rude, and it took forever. This is not how you treat customers!"
>
> "I give you my business and trust you with my money. I don't feel like this bank cares about its customers at all!"

In response to these helpee statements, write down three reflections of feeling and three open questions you could say for the selecting feelings step. What could you say to further explore Casey's experience and the triggers for his feelings?

Assess

Description

The second step involves assessing maladaptive emotions that might interfere with allowing the helpee to fully express and experience those emotions that may help them resolve the presenting issue (Campbell et al., 2017). According to Greenberg and Watson (2006), "A crucial distinction to be made is between primary emotions that are adaptive, which are accessed for their useful information, and primary emotions that are maladaptive, which need to be transformed" (p. 69). During this step, helpers continue to investigate emotions to look for areas of maladaptation. Maladaptive feelings include emotions that do not match the situation, are disproportional in intensity, or are metafeelings that serve to cover or block primary emotions (Brooks-Harris, 2008).

When to Assess

Once helpees are able to intentionally focus on feelings by using emotional language and experiencing their feelings in the moment, the next step is to assess which emotions are maladaptive and in need of modification (Campbell et al., 2017).

How to Assess

At this point, you want to guide the conversation to assess not only potentially maladaptive feelings but adaptive ones as well (Campbell et al., 2017). Aim to understand the context of each feeling that emerges, including how it is experienced and the triggers for them (Greenberg, 2002). Using information and logical consequences, offer helpees the opportunity to consider alternate emotions, especially potentially adaptive ones.

Microskills: Information, Logical Consequences

Using the microskills ramp-up, helpers add the skills of information and logical consequences to aid the helpee in assessing their stuck points (Campbell et al., 2017). Information and logical consequences are introduced into the conversation using the same ramp-up sequence as before. Listening skills come first, then ramp up to information or logical consequences as needed to assess maladaptive feelings, and finally return to listening skills once more before moving to more influential skills like questions/focusing or information/logical consequences. Remember the purpose of this sequence is to resist seeming interrogative or judgmental and to continually return to empathy in order to provide the helpee with a safe space to consider change without sparking anger or defensiveness. The microskills ramp-up gives the helpee opportunities to reflect, take ownership, and help themselves as much as possible (Egan, 2014), which ultimately leads to better outcomes for the helpee (Hill, 2014).

INFORMATION

Information involves providing facts that are true for most people to inspire the helpee to think more deeply about their own actions (Ivey et al., 2016). One method is to offer information about possible adaptive emotions that might be buried as primary emotions. An example would be, "In addition to feeling scared, some people might also feel angry that someone threw eggs at their house. It's damaging and a mess to clean up. I wonder if you might feel that way, too." Notice how the example offers information about a potentially adaptive primary emotion like anger for "people" and invites the helpee to consider the connection to their situation without forcing them to feel in certain ways or labeling their emotions as "maladaptive."

LOGICAL CONSEQUENCES

Examining logical consequences is another method to encourage the helpee to consider the presence of other, previously unacknowledged emotions and assess potentially maladaptive ones without raising defenses. This means empathically exploring the result of emotions (Ivey et al., 2016). With feelings, logical consequences are conducted somewhat differently than with actions, where we explored positive and negative results. Instead, we ask helpees to consider what it might be like (i.e., the consequences) to welcome the presence of alternate feelings. For example, a helper might say, "If you were to get angry about your house getting egged, what might that be like? What would that look like?" Helpees may discover unacknowledged feelings, genuinely disavow suggested feelings, or defend against buried ones by denying their presence (Greenberg & Watson, 2006). Regardless, it is important to offer possibilities for emotional expansion. Reflect and empathize with what your helpee reports while also monitoring their reactions.

Maladaptive feelings present themselves in the assessing step when adaptive emotions are suggested and helpees deny them, which can manifest itself in a multitude of ways. The primary form is inconsistency in verbal and nonverbal manifestations of emotion (Ivey et al., 2016), such as when one emotion is communicated verbally while another emotion is communicated nonverbally.

Result

The intended outcome of assessing feelings is to increase helpees' awareness of the presence of previously unacknowledged emotions and for them to see where blocks and mismatches to adaptive emotions might exist (Campbell et al., 2017). If helpees continue to freely consider and experience feelings as they emerge and are suggested, they are effectively helping themselves. When helpees remain stuck in maladaptive feelings despite encouragement to consider other more adaptive feelings, continued steps are required.

Case Example

Once Amy helped Buffy select and focus on emotions, she wanted to explore blocks and mismatches that might indicate maladaptive emotions keeping Buffy in distress over reducing her sodium intake.

HELPER: This has brought up some feelings for you [empathic reflection]. It stood out to me that you said a few times that reducing sodium shouldn't be a big deal. [Paraphrase]

HELPEE: It shouldn't! That's a relatively small change to make for my health.

HELPER: For some people, it is a big deal. They can feel frustrated by the daily impact it has on their lives or feel angry at losing something they enjoy. I'm curious if you might be feeling some irritation by this, too. [Information]

HELPEE: I don't think so. I'm fine—a little embarrassed and guilty—but whatever. (clenching fists) It's sad that things have to change. I guess I'm disappointed.

HELPER: Sounds like more sadness is coming up for you now, as well as disappointment. [Reflecting feeling]

HELPEE: I really did want this situation to just resolve itself and it hasn't. I'm bummed.

HELPER: What are you most bummed about?

HELPEE: (Loud sigh) This is going to be a daily—no, multiple times daily—commitment. I like adding salt to my food, especially dinner. It's not the most terrible thing and I can live with it. Still, this sucks! (raised voice)

HELPER: That's a completely understandable reaction. [Empathic statement] What might it be like if you were to feel frustrated about the change? [Logical consequences]

HELPEE: I'd probably feel ridiculous about getting upset like that. It's not that bad. It's fine, I'm just kind of sad.

As a result of using assessing feelings, Amy identified sadness and guilt as secondary emotions, and sadness as a potential maladaptive emotion that was covering up a primary emotion of anger. She offered Buffy the opportunity to consider mild versions of anger such as frustration and irritation, which Buffy verbally denied by saying, "I don't think so. I'm fine . . . just kind of sad," while continuing to display typical nonverbal indicators of anger such as a raised voice, clenched fists, and loud sighs.

Written Practice

As a result of using the selecting step and focusing on feelings, you, a customer service supervisor, and your customer, Casey, were able to focus on Casey's lingering anger about the bank's error in charging a fee to his account after the fee was removed. Next, you will want to help Casey assess maladaptive emotions. While he continues to report only anger, you begin to suspect that he may also feel fear about the bank making more costly mistakes for him and fail to provide supportive service in the future. For each of the following areas, write down two things you could say to Casey:

- What could you say to Casey to help him consider fear regarding future bank mistakes? Incorporate microskills of reflecting feelings and information in your responses.
- What could you say to help discuss potential worries about lack of future support from the bank? Incorporate microskills of reflecting feelings and logical consequences in your responses.

Identify

Description

The third step involves identifying maladaptive versus adaptive feelings (Campbell et al., 2017). At this point, your helpee does not readily acknowledge adaptive feelings but, rather, gives verbal and/or nonverbal signs that the feeling is present. The identify step is an exercise in which you assist helpees in becoming aware of disowned parts of themselves and explore the possibility of embracing greater depth of emotions. According to Greenberg and Watson (2006), "Therapists need to work more specifically on accessing new feelings. Focusing clients' attention on possibilities . . . is one important general principle of accessing new feelings" (p. 251). Helpers should focus on adaptive feelings that match the situation and the helpee's emotional signals in a proportional manner (Brooks-Harris, 2008).

When to Identify

Once maladaptive emotions have been identified by the helper and confirmed through discussion with the helpee, it may be helpful to directly confront them with your helpee (Campbell et al., 2017). At this point, helpees may have some conscious knowledge of unexpressed feelings but likely feel resistance to fully owning and expressing them. In the identify step, helpers challenge helpees to push through resistance and embrace adaptive emotions through an evaluation of maladaptive and adaptive emotional signals.

How to Identify

Use the information gathered thus far about the helpee's verbal and nonverbal expressions of emotions to note where blocks and mismatches might exist. This refers to challenging the mismatch or dissonance between what a helpee is admitting to feeling and what their body seems to be communicating that they are feeling (Ivey et al, 2016) and is carried out with the utmost empathy, care, and respect.

As a starting point, the basic feelings you can consider for the helpee to try on are the six basic emotions: sadness, anger, disgust, fear, surprise, and happiness (Ekman & Cordaro, 2011). Search for verbal cues and nonverbal signs of these emotions and then present them through the microskills of confrontation and feedback. As the helpee tries on different emotions, they should find the feeling that best fits their entire experience and the situation.

Microskills: Confrontation, Feedback

Using the microskills ramp-up, helpers use listening skills and then ramp up to the next level of influencing skills, including confrontation and feedback, to challenge the helpee to push through resistance and make changes (Campbell et al., 2017).

CONFRONTATION

Confrontation is defined as supportively challenging your helpee by highlighting their conflicts, mixed messages, and discrepancies (Ivey et al., 2016). An example of emotional confrontation would be, "I hear you say that you're happy, and I also see that you're crying," while another confrontation might be, "Your facial expression and words tell me that you're angry and your legs and feet tell a different story. They're shaking, as if you're also afraid." Note how confrontations reflect that both expressions are valid and true and avoid negating words such as "but," "yet," and "however." Thus, we say, "you're happy *and* crying," or "angry . . . *also* afraid," because "but" can suggest that one is true while the other is not (Corey, 2009). Instead, hold both as true while noting them in one response to highlight the discrepancy. This allows the helpee to wrestle directly with inconsistencies between their emotional experience and resistances holding them back (Ivey et al., 2016).

FEEDBACK

Feedback involves the helper transmitting reactions based on their own evaluation of the helpee (Egan, 2014). This is accomplished using the praise and polish method. Recall that the praise and polish method involves offering supportive, genuine, comprehensive, and specific reactions aimed at assisting the helpee to make changes by providing both positive and negative comments. An example of emotional praise and polish feedback is,

> I appreciate that you're sharing your sadness and concerns about your friend's injury. I'm also concerned because it seems like there's more emotion inside that you're not sharing. I see the look of shock and disgust on your face when you talk about seeing the wound site. I imagine bottling that up will continue to interfere with getting all of your feelings out.

This once again offers the helpee the opportunity to confront their resistance and consider owning feelings not previously experienced.

Result

The intended outcome of identifying feelings is to motivate helpees to push through resistance to identify and experiment with discrepancies involved in maladaptive emotions (Campbell et al., 2017). By highlighting and challenging the mixed messages directly, helpees can view their stuck points in context and see the broader value of experiencing all feelings. This step may move the helpee to consider embracing additional emotions and allowing them to be fully expressed (Harris et al., 2014). This shift occurs when helpees begin to emote in the new emotional direction, such as expressing disgust directly as in the example above. Yet helpees will likely be tentative and uncertain about their ability to do so. Certain emotions were buried for a reason, and bringing them out may unearth additional metaemotions, particularly guilt and shame. An example would be expressing disgust and then feeling ashamed for doing so. Thus, the identify step offers the opportunity to "try on" the possibility of embracing emotions without fully committing to them just yet (Campbell et al., 2017).

Case Example

We saw nurse Amy assess feelings and uncover nonverbal indications from Buffy that, in addition to feeling sadness and embarrassment, she may also feel angry about her doctor's directive to lower her sodium intake for her blood pressure. Buffy is not aware of and/or acknowledging any such anger, although her mannerisms suggest the emotion is there. Amy now wants to identify and confront the dissonance between Buffy's verbal and nonverbal expression of emotions.

HELPER: Yes, as you said: it will be fine, and it's also sad. [Paraphrase; reflecting feeling]

HELPEE: Thanks. I'll figure it out. I just really like making a fun meal for myself and flavoring it just the way I like it. Food can be fun. Part of that fun is being taken away. Ugh, so dumb!

HELPER: What's dumb about it, Buffy?

HELPEE: The whole thing. It's just food, but I don't like that I have to choose between taking care of my health and eating something I like. Other people don't have to make that choice. One of my friends has low blood pressure and actually has to eat extra salt sometimes. Why can't I have that problem? [Shaking fists]

HELPER: It seems so unfair. [Paraphrase]

HELPEE: [raising voice] Yes! It's just sad. Argh!

HELPER: Buffy, I hear you saying that you're sad. I also hear you raising your voice, expressions of, "Argh!" and shaking your fists over this, suggesting some anger, too.

HELPEE: I guess maybe that's how I express my sadness.

HELPER: Perhaps. I definitely have heard that this is a sad realization for you. And I also sense your body is trying to express other feelings. [Reflecting feeling]

HELPEE: I don't know. I just don't really ever get angry.

HELPER: Thank you for helping me understand. This is a big change and I respect how you're feeling your way through it. I'm also concerned that if you don't have an opportunity to experience all the reactions you're having about this, perhaps including some anger, it will continue to hold you back from embracing making needed changes for your health. [Feedback]

HELPEE: I really don't like the idea of not salting things. Even if it's silly and not a big deal, I am kind of upset about it. It's irritating and unfair.

HELPER: Certainly. You're doing a great job of sorting out your feelings, Buffy. [Encouragement]

As a result of identifying maladaptive feelings, Amy helped Buffy address the dissonance between Buffy's verbal and nonverbal expression of emotions. Buffy remains hesitant about embracing feelings of anger but appears to be processing through the possibility.

Written Practice

The purpose of identifying feelings is to motivate helpees to identify and experiment with discrepancies involved in maladaptive emotions. This step offers the opportunity to motivate our helpee, Casey, to push through his resistance to discussing other emotions through identifying discrepancies involved in his verbal and nonverbal emotional communications. Specifically, he readily discusses feelings of anger while displaying clear signs of fear about continued errors by the bank through continually referencing the potential for future errors, raised and shaking voice, and wringing hands. To this end, it may be helpful to praise Casey's general expression of his feelings to you and note the potentially blocked fear and to challenge directly how his behaviors communicate discrepant emotional messages. For each of the following areas, write down two things you could say to Casey:

- What could you say to Casey to offer praise and suggestion for additional emotion? Incorporate the use of the microskill feedback in your response.
- What could you say to encourage Casey to consider how his verbal report of feelings is different than his nonverbal expression? Incorporate the use of the microskill confrontation in your response.

Launch

Description

The fourth and final step of the feelings strategy involves launching toward helpful and healthy emotional expression. This most notably involves acknowledging and beginning to experience adaptive emotions once again (Greenberg, 2002). The purpose is for the helpee to end the helping interaction with a more comprehensive experience and understanding of their emotional signals.

With EFT, returning to adaptive emotion means returning to an ongoing and free-flowing process of emotional self-discovery. According to Greenberg and Paivio (1997), "The natural process of feeling can be depicted as a set of phases, those of emergence, awareness, owning, expressive action, and completion, followed again by the emergence of new feelings, thereby beginning the cycle again" (p. 27). In LifeRAFT, the identifying step implements this concept in a way that encourages awareness and expression of feelings so the helpee can embrace adaptive emotions and let go of maladaptive feelings (Campbell et al., 2017).

When to Launch

Once helpers have challenged helpees to seriously consider discrepancies between their verbal and nonverbal expression of emotions, it may be helpful to encourage them to verbalize and emote adaptive feelings. Helpees are likely to have increased motivation toward doing so but remain hesitant and uncertain about their ability to connect. The launch step can help boost their confidence through support and validation of their feelings (Campbell et al., 2017).

How to Launch

The key ingredient to launching toward adaptive feelings is the helper focusing on maintaining an honest and caring relationship with their helpee (Campbell, 2013). Although this is important throughout every helping scenario, it is essential for the feelings strategy and this final step in particular. Helpees learn to feel safe and supported in their feelings and how to openly accept and communicate their feelings to themselves and others. Helpers accomplish this through reframing helpees' apprehension by telling them that their feelings are important and valid and encouraging them through the use of directives to invite emotions into their experience (Brooks-Harris, 2008). Attending skills and empathic expression should remain the primary focus of the launch step.

Microskills: Reframing, Directives

Through the microskills ramp-up, helpers ramp up their microskills to the highest level, adding the remaining microskills, reframing and directives, to motivate their helpees toward a healthier emotional connection in an effort to resolve the presenting issue and get unstuck from their current distress (Campbell et al., 2017).

REFRAMING

Reframing is defined as providing helpees with a new, more positive perspective on themselves and their concerns. It often involves taking a negative thought and reframing it by generating a more adaptive and balanced response (Ivey et al., 2016). Reframing helps to solidify decisions to change by adding a positive angle. For the feelings approach, it is natural at this point for a helpee to experience negative reactions in response to confronting previously unacknowledged feelings (Greenberg, 2002); they were unacknowledged for a reason and resistance or additional metafeelings such as guilt and shame will likely emerge. For example, a helpee might say, "I'm a terrible person for feeling angry about this" or "I shouldn't be scared."

Your role as a helper is to encourage helpees to accept their feelings without judgment (Greenberg & Watson, 2006). Help them understand that feelings are not good or bad; they just are. Resisting them will only make problems worse and serve to block important signals. Regardless of what emotional reaction emerges, it is acceptable, and they are still an acceptable and worthwhile person. Use reframing to provide your helpee with a positive viewpoint of emerging emotions. For example, a reframe would be,

> I hear you shaming yourself for feeling anger. It may not feel good and so I can understand why you might not want to let that in. Anger is also an important signal that our bodies use to tell us when they are feeling violated. When you let yourself experience anger and all the emotions that come up in turn, you are working the problem through. That's a good thing.

This helps motivate helpees to let go of blocks and barriers to fully engage with and understand their feelings.

DIRECTIVES

Directives are the instructions provided to helpees to follow specific actions (Hill, 2014). In other words, directives means giving helpees advice. This is reserved for the end of the helping interaction and only as needed to support the helpee in facilitating change. For example, directives may include, "You are safe here. It is okay to feel angry right now." Another example would be, "Could we try connecting with that worry I see expressed in your foot shaking? Perhaps you could begin by sharing with me what is going on inside related to that." Notice how you can make every effort to maintain helpee autonomy, even with the highest level of influencing skill, by tentatively suggesting directives such as the wording "could we try" and "perhaps you could begin by." Also note that ending directives with a question about their willingness and agreement with the directive puts the power back in their hands to choose whether or not to proceed. For example, you could end with, "Would you like to try that?"

Result

The intended outcome of launching is to motivate helpees to verbalize and emote adaptive feelings. Helpees are likely to have increased confidence to do so through helper support and validation of their feelings. When helpers create an environment where helpees can openly communicate their feelings, it is more likely that helpees will learn to express their feelings in a positive manner to themselves and other people. Through reconnection with adaptive feelings, helpees are better equipped to continue working through distress by listening to the signals their bodies provide (Brooks-Harris, 2008).

Case Example

Previously, Amy helped Buffy discover the discrepancy between her stated feeling of sadness and her nonverbal expression of anger. Buffy remains hesitant about owning and expressing angry feelings. Amy wanted to launch Buffy toward accepting her feelings and to provide direction and resolution toward concerns with the lifestyle changes required by Buffy's doctor.

HELPEE: I feel embarrassed again. This is a stupid thing to get angry about. It's no one's fault but my own. It's not a big deal but I can hear it in my voice that I'm upset.

HELPER: Seems like there's uncertainty in your voice, as if you feel like your anger is unjustified. It is completely justified, as are all of your feelings. Emotions are not good or bad; what we do with them is what's important. It is honorable that you are listening to those emotional signals to help you sort this out and move forward. [Reframing]

HELPEE: I never thought about it that way. I guess I always saw getting angry as someone yelling and scaring everyone, which is not okay. Between you and me, I don't want to change how I eat. I like making my food flavorful and it feels unfair that it is getting taken away. I'm unhappy about it.

HELPER: Excellent insights, Buffy. Change is difficult. [Paraphrase]

HELPEE: I don't really let myself get angry. This is uncomfortable.

HELPER: Certainly. Perhaps I could help? (Helpee shakes her head yes) Anger usually is a signal of feeling violated. Let's try learning more about that. Maybe try clenching your fists again. What might that communicate right now? [Directive]

HELPEE: I do feel kind of irritated. I don't like being told that I have to stop something I like. Enjoyable food is being taken from me and other people get to enjoy food. I don't want to lose that! Argh!

HELPER: That's excellent, Buffy. I really hear the anger coming through about how frustrating this is. [Reflecting feeling]

HELPEE: I hate that things have to change. I really hate it!

HELPER: What are you most angry with about this situation? [Open question]

HELPEE: I'm angry that I feel as if I have no say in this. I was told it had to happen. I feel like I'm being given no choice but to give up my love of cooking and eating the way I want.

HELPER: This anger has given us valuable insight. Seems like you're saying you don't want this to take away your ability to make choices and enjoy your food. [Reflecting feeling; paraphrase]

HELPEE: Exactly. I want to take care of my body and have cooking and mealtime still be fun. I think I need explore how to do this my way. Not just take away salt but look into my own alternatives to keep things flavorful.

HELPER: Wonderful ideas. Your demeanor switched as you talked about doing this your way. Seems as if you're feeling more hopeful about this situation now. [Reflecting feeling]

As a result of launching, Amy helped Buffy experience new adaptive feelings. Buffy may remain hesitant and uncertain yet her distress is likely to reduce, and she has an increased likelihood of getting unstuck and accepting a broader range of adaptive emotions as a result of talking with Amy.

Written Practice

The purpose of launching is to motivate helpees to verbalize and emote adaptive feelings. This would be the opportunity to support and validate Casey's unacknowledged feelings of fear about the bank making future mistakes and providing inadequate support in the future while also respecting the fact that this is a customer service relationship.

To this end, it may be helpful to carefully and respectfully note how you view Casey's willingness to share his concerns with you and explore with him the possibility of directly expressing his fears about his ongoing relationship with the bank. For each of the following areas, write down one or two things you could say to Casey:

- Casey tells you that most customer service representatives "blow [him] off" and "refuse to listen." You begin to understand why Casey has held back from sharing his fears about future situations with the bank. As a representative of the company you work for, you want to support Casey and let him know the bank does care. What could you say to help Casey see the value of sharing his fears? Incorporate the use of the microskill reframing in your response.
- Casey tells you he is hesitant to share his worries because some are unrelated to the original bank error. You are interested in making the best experience possible for your customers, so you want him to elaborate anyway. You also want to show Casey that he is cared about and will be supported. What could you say to encourage Casey to share specific concerns? Incorporate the use of the microskill directive in your response.

- You likely noticed that this assignment required you to use different wording in a customer service situation than you might with a family member, friend, or more traditional helping situation. Discuss what you learned about how to modify your language to better fit this situation.

Role-Play Practice

The purpose of this exercise is to rehearse the modifying stage for the feelings strategy. This time you will practice using the entire LifeRAFT sequence of supporting, watching, investigating, and modifying. For this exercise, find a volunteer helpee to role-play a helping scenario with you and provide feedback afterward. Set a timer and conduct a helping scenario for at least 20 minutes. Attempt to support using listening skills of attending, paraphrasing, and reflecting feelings only and then watch for warning signs for referring. Investigate using listening skills, questions, and focusing, and finally choose feelings as a strategy and engage in modifying using all microskills via the microskills ramp-up. Complete the following:

1. Consider pairing with a fellow helper-in-training and take turns being the helper and helpee.
2. Video record the scenario. Follow ethical guidelines, including permission to video record.
3. Ask your helpee to select a topic to discuss. Consult Chapter 1, "Problem Triggers," for topic ideas. Request that they avoid crisis issues warranting the watch stage and to initially keep emotions simple to focus on expanding their emotional awareness throughout the helping scenario.
4. As the helper, attempt to support using listening skills of attending, paraphrasing, and reflecting feelings and then investigate using listening skills, questions, and focusing. Choose the feelings strategy and progress through modifying using all needed microskills via the microskills ramp-up.
5. At the end of the role-play, request feedback from your helpee about what you did well and what you could improve on next time. Ask what interventions felt especially empathic and supportive and which ones were awkward or uncomfortable. Write down your helpee's responses.
6. Review the video. What do you think you did well and what you could improve on next time as the helper?

Summary

In this chapter we discussed the following:

Description of Modifying for Feelings

- Modifying for feelings is based on Emotion-Focused Therapy (EFT), which asserts that emotions serve as signals of basic needs. Emotions are comprised of primary emotions, which are initial genuine responses to a given situation, and secondary emotions, which are reactions to primary emotions and serve a protective and regulatory function to block and hide primary emotions when they are deemed unacceptable. Problem-solving occurs by expanding emotional awareness and expression from maladaptive emotions to adaptive emotions by creating safety around exploring secondary emotions to uncover primary emotions.

- Modifying involves choosing feelings as a strategy and guiding the helpee through a basic problem-solving process of four steps: select, assess, identify, and launch.

Select

- The select step uses attending, paraphrasing, reflection of feeling, questions, and focusing to encourage helpees to talk specifically about how feelings impact their concern.

Assess

- The assess step involves assessing maladaptive feelings that are holding the helpee back from resolving the presenting concern.
- Using the microskills ramp-up, helpers add information and logical consequences to assess helpees' emotional blocks and mismatches.

Identify

- The identify step uses feedback and confrontation to challenge helpees to push through resistance and consider accepting unacknowledged emotions through an evaluation of maladaptive and adaptive emotions.

Launch

- Helpers add the two remaining microskills, reframing and directives, to motivate their helpees to verbalize and emote adaptive feelings in an effort to resolve the presenting issue.

References

Brooks-Harris, J. E. (2008). *Integrative multitheoretical psychotherapy*. Boston, MA: Houghton Mifflin.

Campbell, E. L. (2013, April). *Key introductory strategies training: Training paraprofessionals in basic helping skills*. Symposium conducted at the annual meeting of the Western Psychological Association, Reno, NV.

Campbell, E. L., Davidson, K., & Davidson, S. M. (2017). Effectiveness of LifeRAFT undergraduate helping skills training model. *Psychology Teaching Review*, *23*(2), 32–41.

Corey, G. (2009). *Theory and practice of counseling and psychotherapy* (8th ed.). Belmont, CA: Thomson/Brooks/Cole.

Egan, G. (2014). *The skilled helper: A problem-management and opportunity development approach to helping* (10th ed.). Belmont, CA: Brooks/Cole.

Ekman, P., & Cordaro, D. (2011). What is meant by calling emotions basic. *Emotion Review*, *3*(4), 364–370.

Goldman, R. N., & Greenberg, L. S. (2015). *Case formulation in emotion-focused therapy: Co-creating clinical maps for change*. Washington, DC: American Psychological Association.

Greenberg, L. S. (2002). *Emotion-focused therapy: Coaching clients to work through feelings*. Washington, DC: American Psychological Association.

Greenberg, L. S., & Johnson, S. M. (1988). *Emotionally focused therapy for couples*. New York: Guilford Press.

Greenberg, L. S., & Paivio, S. C. (1997). Working with emotions in psychotherapy. In *The practicing professional*. New York: Guildford Press.

Greenberg, L. S., & Watson, J. C. (2006). *Emotion-focused therapy for depression*. Washington, DC: American Psychological Association.

Harris, J. E., Kelly, L. J., Campbell, E. L., & Hammond, E. S. (2014). Key strategies training: An introduction to multitheoretical practice. *Journal of Psychotherapy Integration, 24*(2), 138–152. doi:10.1037/a0037056

Hill, C. E. (2014). *Helping skills: Facilitating exploration, insight, and action* (4th ed.). Washington, DC: American Psychological Association.

Ivey, A. E., Ivey, M. B., & Zalaquett, C. P. (2016). *Essentials of intentional interviewing: Counseling in a multicultural world* (3rd ed.). Boston, MA: Cengage Learning.

Johnson, S. M., & Lee, A. C. (2000). Emotionally focused family therapy: Restructuring attachment. In *Children in therapy: Using the family as a resource* (pp. 112–136). New York: Norton and Company.

Prochaska, J. O., Norcross, J. C., & DiClemente, C. C. (2005). Stages of change: Prescriptive guidelines. In G. P. Koocher, J. C. Norcross, & S. S. Hill (Eds.), *Psychologists' desk reference* (2nd ed., pp. 226–231). New York: Oxford University Press.

Siegel, D. J., & Payne Bryson, T. (2011). *The whole-brain child: 12 revolutionary strategies to nurture your child's developing mind.* New York: Bantam Books.

Watson, J. C., Gordon, L. B., Sermac, L., Kalogerakos, F., & Steckley, P. (2003). Comparing the effectiveness of process-experiential with cognitive-behavioral psychotherapy in the treatment of depression. *Journal of Consulting and Clinical Psychology, 74*(4), 773–781.

Wiebe, S. A., & Johnson, S. M. (2016). A review of the research in emotionally focused therapy for couples. *Family Process, 55*(3), 390–407.

10 Stage Four

Modifying through Thoughts

Chapter Goals

This chapter will prepare you to:

- Learn about modifying through the thoughts strategy, the third of three strategies in the fourth stage of the LifeRAFT model, through the use of the microskills hierarchy and ramp-up.
- Understand the select step for thoughts through the microskills of questions and focusing.
- Use the assess step for thoughts by ramping up to the microskills of information and logical consequences.
- Learn the identify step for thoughts with the addition of the microskills of feedback and confrontation.
- Use the launch step for thoughts by ramping up to the microskills of reframing and directives.

Introduction

This chapter continues to guide you in the modifying stage, this time for the thoughts strategy. After helpers have supported a helpee, watched for and addressed any crisis referrals, investigated the helpee's concerns, and determined that modifying using a cognitively based approach will be most helpful, the thoughts strategy follows (see Figure 10.1; thought). Like the other two strategies, the thoughts approach consists of a sequence of four steps implemented based on the theory of Cognitive Therapy, which defines presenting concerns in terms of dysfunctional thoughts in need of restructuring (Beck, 1995). This chapter will describe the theory behind Cognitive Therapy, and then apply it to the four SAIL steps for problem-solving with helpees.

Description of Modifying through Thoughts

Theory of Cognitive Therapy

Cognitive-Behavioral Therapy (CBT) is a group of professional counseling theories which share the assumption that behavioral and emotional dysfunction are mediated by unhealthy thoughts that can be modified to promote health. Aaron Beck's Cognitive Therapy is a popular CBT approach that was originally developed to treat depressive disorders and has since been successfully used to treat a number of other disorders and presenting issues (Beck & Weishaar, 2000).

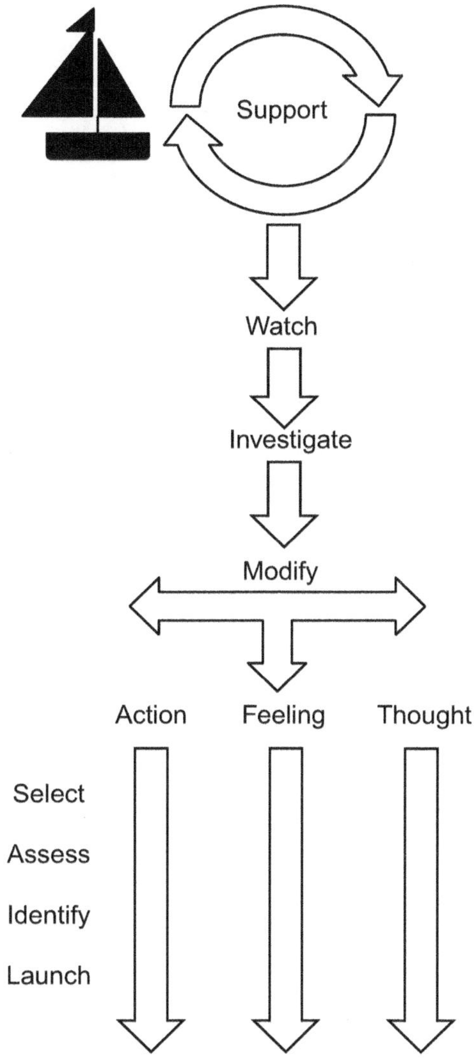

Figure 10.1 LifeRAFT Model

Cognitive Therapy has been established for use in professional counseling (Beck, 2011); yet the basic premise of Cognitive Therapy is adaptable for use in nonprofessional counseling (Campbell, Davidson, & Davidson, 2017). Cognitive Therapy is based on the relationship of thoughts as a mediator to situational responses, as depicted in Figure 10.2.

Situations in life seem to automatically produce emotional and behavioral responses. For example, when a situation arises where you see a spider, it may seem as if you automatically feel afraid and jump away in response. However, according to Cognitive Therapy, automatic thoughts mediate the relationship between situations and responses. For example, the thought "This spider will harm me" produces a fear response, while the thought "This spider is harmless" would produce indifference and perhaps no behavioral response. A positive automatic thought such as "This spider is beautiful and interesting" might generate delight and the behavioral response of leaping toward the creature instead. Cognitive Therapy asserts that it is how a person perceives a situation that determines their emotional and behavioral responses. Thus, when distress and

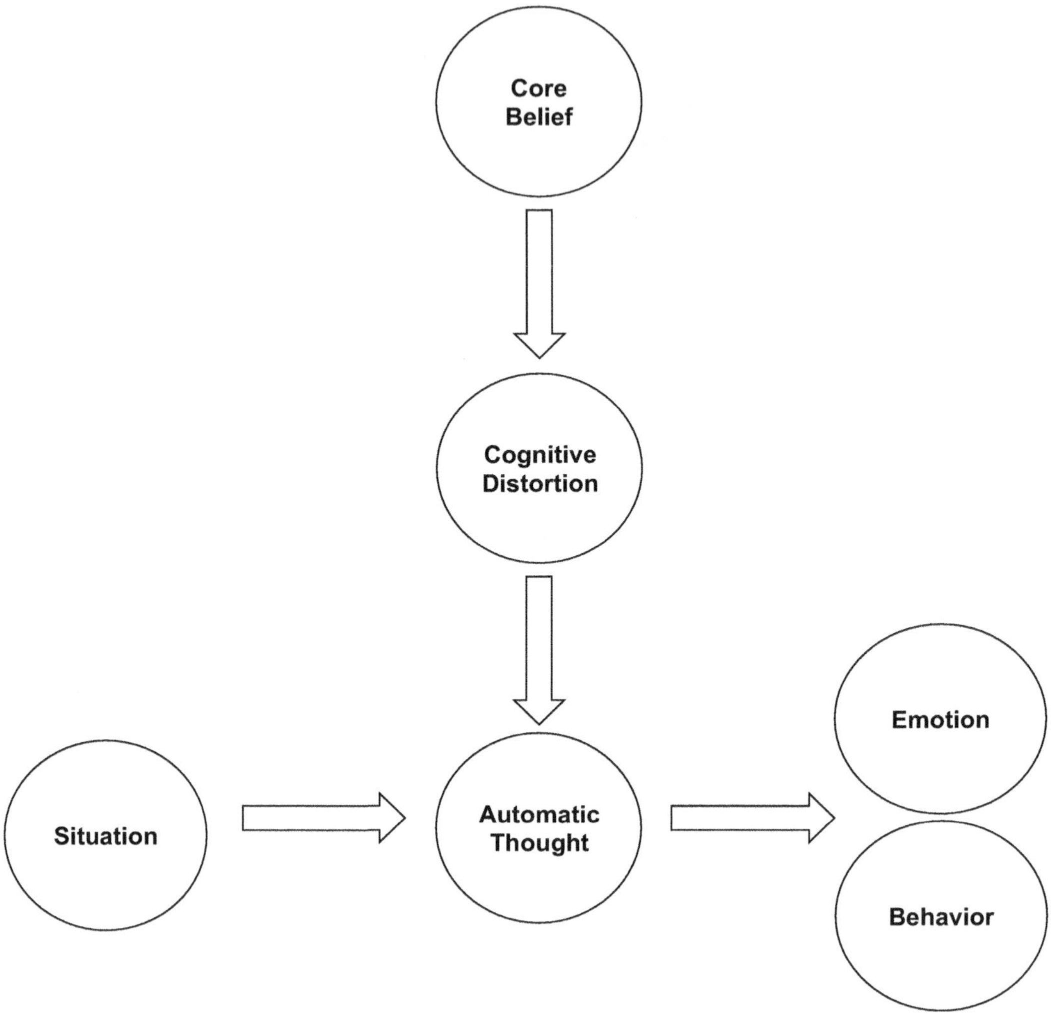

Figure 10.2 Relationship of Thoughts

dysfunction arise, the goal is to change how a person perceives the situation to improve how they act and feel in response (Beck, 2011).

Automatic thoughts are called automatic because we are rarely aware of them and simply act on them as if they were true, only noting the response that emerges from them (Beck, 2011). In the aforementioned example, a person would likely be aware of feeling afraid of a spider but not the thought process in which their brain determined a threat was present. Automatic thoughts are believed to emerge spontaneously from situations based on core beliefs, which are broad beliefs that have been formed by experiences throughout our lives. What we believe is then triggered in a situational moment to produce an automatic thought. For example, the automatic thought "This spider will harm me" likely connects to a broader core belief "Spiders are dangerous," perhaps learned from warnings from parents, knowledge gained about poisonous spiders, or perhaps a past experience with a dangerous spider bite.

Like thoughts, core beliefs can be either functional or dysfunctional (Corey, 2009). Functional core beliefs tend to be balanced, flexible, and realistic ideas about oneself and the world that help people to effectively navigate their lives, such as "I have some gifts and talents and some areas for growth" and "The world can be safe and unsafe at times." Dysfunctional core beliefs tend to focus on rigid and extremely negative perceptions of oneself and the world, such as "I am worthless" and "The world is unsafe." They are often related to perceiving oneself as helpless, unlovable, or worthless. These core beliefs may be expressed through thoughts such as "I'm incompetent/I can't do anything right," "I'm unattractive/not good enough to be loved by others," or "I'm bad/dangerous" (Beck, 2011, p. 233). Dysfunctional beliefs may also be about other people or the world, such as "Other people will hurt me" or "The world is unfair" (Beck, 2011, p. 229). When triggered, dysfunctional core beliefs typically give rise to situational automatic thoughts that are negative and cause distress.

Dysfunctional core beliefs tend to produce negative automatic thoughts through cognitive distortions or systematic biases in cognitions (Corey, 2009). Beck (2011) identified several cognitive distortions. See Table 10.1 for descriptions and examples of common cognitive distortions. Common distortions include (1) arbitrary inference, meaning drawing conclusions without corroborative evidence, (2) overgeneralization, which is drawing general conclusions on the basis of a single event, (3) selective abstraction, meaning attending to detail and ignoring the context, (4) personalization, which is incorrectly attributing external events to oneself, (5) labeling, meaning ascribing fixed and global labels to oneself and others, and (6) dichotomous thinking, meaning thinking in polarized, "either/or" ways. Although everyone is guilty of cognitive distortions at times, they become problematic when they produce automatic thoughts that are not challenged and keep us in distress.

Table 10.1 Common Cognitive Distortions

Cognitive Distortion	*Description*	*Example*
Arbitrary inference	Drawing conclusions without corroborative evidence	"I just have a feeling that person hates me."
Overgeneralization	Making general conclusions based on a single event	"I had a setback so I obviously can't do it."
Selective abstraction	Attending to detail and ignoring the context	"She said the project was good but there was a flaw that ruined it."
Personalization	Incorrectly attributing external events to oneself	"Everything bad that happens is my fault."
Labeling	Ascribing fixed, global labels	"I'm a loser."
Dichotomous thinking	Thinking in polarized, "either/or" ways	"Either I'm a total success or I'm a total failure."

Personal Reflection

Consider how automatic thoughts and cognitive distortions apply to your own life. As you reflect on these features of Cognitive Therapy, answer the following questions:

- Consider a recent distressing change or problem you experienced in the context of the relationship of thoughts as depicted in Figure 10.2. Briefly describe the situation and your emotional and behavioral reactions.
- Now consider the mediating role of thoughts. What were two automatic thoughts you had during that time to produce your emotional and behavioral reactions?
- Compare your automatic thoughts to the common cognitive distortions in Table 10.1. Do you see evidence of cognitive distortions in your automatic thoughts? Why or why not?
- How might identifying thoughts and distorted thinking help you during distressing experiences?

Thoughts Steps

The theory of Cognitive Therapy is a counseling theory intended for use in professional therapy (Beck, 2011). Although initially applied and presented in ways that are inappropriate for use by nonprofessionals, the theoretical premise of the approach can be usefully adapted for nonprofessional use. This is accomplished through the use of our SAIL steps of select, assess, identify, and launch. The following sections integrate the theoretical rationale of Cognitive Therapy to each of the steps of the thoughts approach.

Note while the SAIL steps are the same ones used for the actions and feelings approaches, the goal and purpose of the actions and feelings approaches are very different. Recall that the actions approach sought to produce behavioral changes ultimately through generating a concrete plan of action whereas the feelings approach aimed at expanding emotional awareness and expression to unblock signals. For the thoughts strategy, we must once again shift our perspective as helpers to embrace the goal of Cognitive Therapy and the LifeRAFT thoughts strategy.

Although it is assumed that functional thoughts will ultimately lead to effective actions and adaptive feelings, attention resides with changing thoughts only. The goal of the thoughts strategy is to change dysfunctional thoughts to functional ones, as they pertain to a distressing situation (Campbell et al., 2017). Dysfunctional thoughts are negative and rigid automatic thoughts that represent cognitive distortions and are likely connected to dysfunctional core beliefs. Conversely, functional thoughts are more balanced and realistic and disconnected from dysfunctional core beliefs. The idea is that if a helpee is guided to see a situation in a more logical and accurate way, their perspective will shift to a more balanced and hopeful perspective, thereby giving them the motivation to move forward on their own. We accomplish this by helping them to identify and evaluate the accuracy and usefulness of their thinking (Brooks-Harris, 2008).

This chapter will describe the four thoughts steps that include selecting and focusing on thoughts, assessing dysfunctional thoughts, identifying potential shifts from dysfunctional to functional thoughts, and launching toward functional thoughts. Recall that these four steps are uniquely applied to the thoughts strategy, yet they parallel those used in the other strategies of actions and feelings (see Table 10.2). The following sections will describe each step, when to use them, how to use them in conjunction with the microskills hierarchy and ramp-up, and their anticipated results. Case examples of the steps in practice will also be provided.

Select

Description

Cognitive Therapy suggests that psychological distress stems from commonplace but faulty cognitive processes that negatively impact resulting emotional and behavioral responses (Greenberger &

Table 10.2 LifeRAFT Modify Steps

SAIL Steps	*Description*	*Action Steps*	*Feeling Steps*	*Thought Steps*
Select	Select a focal area	Select and focus on actions	Select and focus on feelings	Select and focus on thoughts
Assess	Assess for problem	Assess ineffective actions	Assess maladaptive feelings	Assess dysfunctional thoughts
Identify	Identify potential shifts for improvement over problem	Identify potential shifts from ineffective to effective actions	Identify potential shifts from maladaptive to adaptive feelings	Identify potential shifts from dysfunctional to functional thoughts
Launch	Launch toward improvement of problem	Launch toward effective actions	Launch toward adaptive feelings	Launch toward functional thoughts

Padesky, 1995). Cognitions require attention in order to correct them and produce psychological well-being. This process begins with attending to a helpee's automatic thoughts, self-talk, and situational interpretations (Beck, 1995). In LifeRAFT, a thoughts approach begins by inquiring about helpees' thoughts and the situations that may have prompted them. In order to accomplish this, helpers should begin by encouraging helpees to talk about and examine their own thoughts by using cognitive language (Campbell et al., 2017).

When to Select

When helpees do not realize how their thoughts may be related to problems, it can be useful for helpers to focus the attention of their helpees on thoughts (Campbell et al., 2017). The helper acts as a curious and empathic coach who guides the helpee to collaboratively investigate thinking patterns. As an objective observer, you may be able to recognize areas of dysfunctional thinking that helpees leave unexamined and assume to be true. It will be helpful for you to gradually and gently bring these thoughts into focus so that your helpee can see the way their thinking may be flawed and result in distressful emotions and problematic behavioral consequences.

How to Select

In the first step of selecting, helpers should redirect the conversation to thoughts. The essence of selecting and focusing on thoughts is to isolate the specific thoughts that are associated with current distress (Campbell et al., 2017). Try to understand helpees' thoughts in specific terms by generating a mental list of automatic thoughts pertaining to the distressing situation.

Microskills: Questions, Focusing

Up to this point of the interaction, continue to use the microskills of attending, paraphrasing, reflection of feeling, questions, and focusing to encourage helpees to talk specifically about thoughts related to their concern. Remember to continue employing skills according to the microskills ramp-up (see Figure 10.3).

Guide your helpee to talk about their thoughts on the presenting issue. Thoughts tend to be the most difficult strategy for some beginning helpers to elicit because they are so different from what we ask in casual conversation (Campbell, 2013). Beck (2011) suggests that the most basic way to focus on thoughts is to use open-ended questions such as "What is going through your mind right now?" (p. 22). Also ask about beliefs the presenting issue elicited about self and the world, with questions such as "With that in mind, what does that make you think about yourself?" or "What is your conclusion?" It can also be helpful to ask about feelings before focusing on thoughts more directly (Beck, 2011). Reflect feelings and then use open questions to elicit the thought connected to the resulting emotion, such as "Sounds as if you are scared. What are you scared of?" Note that helpees will often express automatic thoughts tentatively or pose them as questions; for example, a helpee might say, "I'm scared because part of me is worried that maybe I can't do this. What if I'm not good enough?" Paraphrase the automatic thought back to the helpee to check on the accuracy, such as "It sounds like part of you is worried by thoughts of 'I can't do this. I'm not good enough.'"

Result

Selecting and focusing on thoughts attempts to guide helpees to talk directly about their automatic thoughts. They will become more aware of their thinking and begin to identify the stream of automatic thoughts, which is necessary before helpees can identify which ones are most distressing and dysfunctional. Promoting this type of cognitive awareness allows

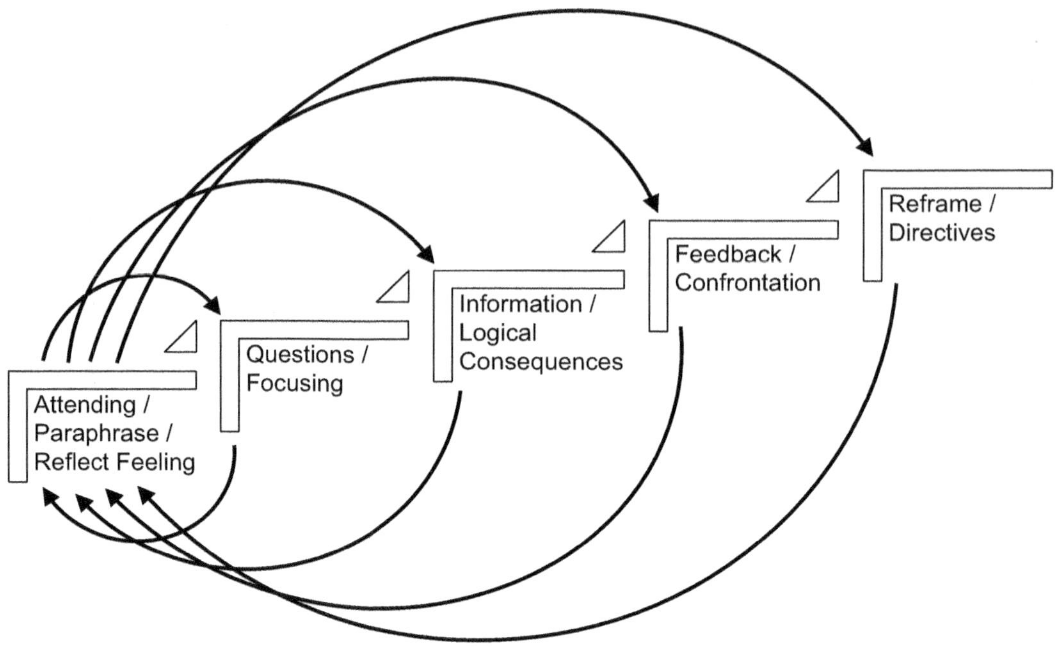

Figure 10.3 Microskills Ramp-Up

helpees to gain insight into how their thoughts may connect to the distressing situation that perpetuates a chain of negative emotional and behavioral reactions (Harris, Kelly, Campbell, & Hammond, 2014).

Case Example

To show how the LifeRAFT thought steps can be used in practice, a case example will be used throughout this chapter. This case example shows how Don, a probation officer and helper, works with Irvin, a parolee who is currently looking for work. Don and Irvin have been working together to find jobs for Irvin, despite Irvin's concerns about his criminal record preventing him from finding a job. Irvin is distressed after being turned down for his first job application. In this example, Don selects and focuses on thoughts to isolate specific thoughts that may be contributing to Irvin's distress regarding the job rejection.

HELPEE: This is exactly what I was worried about. I was so upset when I got the rejection letter. They don't want to hire me because of my record.

HELPER: I hear how disappointed you are that you didn't get this job. [Reflection of feeling]

HELPEE: It confirmed exactly what I worried might happen, and now that it has, it's even worse than I imagined.

HELPEE: What did it confirm for you? [Open question]

HELPEE: People only see my criminal record. What if I never find a job?

HELPER: You're worried that having a record will be the thing that blocks you from ever getting hired. [Paraphrase]

HELPEE: I don't know. Part of me feels like that. I'm just worried.

HELPER: I can hear your worry and I want to help you work through it. What are you most worried about?

HELPEE: I'm scared that this one mistake will ruin the rest of my life. People won't trust me. I'll never get a job.

HELPER: Sounds like a lot of concerns are coming up. I hear thoughts running through your mind of, 'My life is ruined. I won't be trusted. I'll never get hired.' [Paraphrase]

HELPEE: It's brought up all of those things, constantly. Since I got the letter, I keep thinking about what this means for me now.

HELPER: What else is running through your mind when you think about the letter?

HELPEE: I think about how they didn't like me and how they see me as just a criminal. I'm not that guy.

HELPER: Pretty discouraging to see others as labeling you as a criminal and discounting your many qualifications. [Reflecting feeling]

As a result, Don helped Irvin select and focus on his automatic thoughts related to the job rejection. They identified several automatic thoughts that were likely contributing to Irvin's distress, including "I will never get hired," "My life is ruined," "I won't be trusted," and "People only see me as a criminal."

Written Practice

As you learn about each of the thought steps, you will be asked to write questions or statements that implement each step to encourage you to think about how you would implement these skills in practice. Throughout this chapter, your written practice will focus on a friend named Hope, who is feeling lonely and dismissed by her other friends after she discovers they attended a party without inviting her. To practice selecting and focusing on thoughts, imagine that Hope asks to talk the situation through with you and she makes the following statements:

> "My friends have stopped inviting me places. It hurts my feelings so much."
>
> "I feel alone all the time. Even when they do call, it's only for a brief time and they say they have to get off the phone."
>
> "I think it's something with me that pushed them away. They tell me they still like me and they're glad we're friends, but they're probably just trying to be nice."

In response to these helpee statements, write two open questions you could ask. What could you do to identify specific automatic thoughts that might be connected to Hope's loneliness?

Assess

Description

The second step of assessing involves recognizing dysfunctional automatic thoughts that might interfere with the helpee's ability to view the situation from a realistic and healthy perspective (Campbell et al., 2017). According to Beck (1995), "The cognitive therapist is concerned with identifying those thoughts that are dysfunctional, that is, those that distort reality, that are emotionally distressing and/or interfere with the patient's ability to reach her goals" (p. 76). In LifeRAFT, helpers continue to investigate thoughts to look for dysfunction (Campbell et al., 2017). Dysfunctional thoughts include those that are irrational or inaccurate and appear to relate to a cognitive distortion (Brooks-Harris, 2008) and can be further identified by discovering the dysfunctional core beliefs connected to the automatic thought (Beck, 1995).

When to Assess

Once helpees are able to intentionally focus on thoughts by discussing them and freely identifying their automatic thoughts regarding the distress, the next step is to evaluate which thoughts are most distressing and in need of modification (Campbell et al., 2017). It is helpful to isolate and assess one specific thought that appears to be the most distressing before assessing the connecting dysfunctional core belief.

How to Assess

In the second step of assessing, helpers should guide the conversation specifically to assessing dysfunctional automatic thoughts (Campbell et al., 2017). The goal is to assess the single most distressing automatic thought, the core belief it is connected to, and the cognitive distortion involved in the connection. Use information and logical consequences to discover the connection between their distressing automatic thought, core belief, and cognitive distortion.

Microskills: Information, Logical Consequences

Using the microskills ramp-up, helpers add the skills of information and logical consequences to help guide the helpee in assessing their stuck points (Campbell et al., 2017). Information and logical consequences are introduced into the conversation using the same ramp-up sequence as before, of listening skills first and interspersed with influencing skills. However, the ramp-up sequence for thoughts is more prescribed than it is for actions or feelings. This time use listening skills first, then ramp up specifically to information only, and finally return to listening skills again before ramping up to logical consequences. From there, you will continue to ramp up and down between listening skills and logical consequences several times before returning to the less structured format. In this sequence, the microskill of information is used to introduce the helpee to an intervention, and logical consequences are used repeatedly for what Cognitive Therapy calls the "downward arrow" technique.

Remember the purpose of this sequence is to resist overusing influencing skills and seeming interrogative or judgmental and to continually return to empathy in order to provide the helpee with a safe space to consider change without sparking anger or defensiveness. The microskills ramp-up gives the helpee opportunities to reflect, take ownership, and help themselves as much as possible (Egan, 2014), which ultimately leads to better outcomes for the helpee (Hill, 2014).

INFORMATION

The microskill of information involves sharing specific information with a helpee (Ivey, Ivey, & Zalaquett, 2016), such as facts that are true for most people to inspire them to think more deeply about their own thoughts. Use information as a way to introduce the downward arrow technique by explaining that what you are about to ask them is helpful for most people and then ask if they would be willing to try as well (Burns, 1980). An example is, "When people have distressing thoughts about a specific situation like you are, they often find it helpful to understand the deeper meaning behind those thoughts. I wonder if you might be interested in that as well." Notice how the example offers information about what "other people . . . often find helpful" and invites the helpee to consider it as well. This exploratory method serves to highlight potential dysfunction without raising defenses.

LOGICAL CONSEQUENCES

Exploring logical consequences is another method to encourage the helpee to assess potential problems and areas for change without raising defenses. It means empathically exploring results that likely follow an experience. The ultimate purpose is to assess where negative consequences are occurring (Ivey et al., 2016).

Unlike logical consequences for actions and feelings, which involves using it only once, logical consequences are used in the thoughts approach by repeating the intervention multiple times to produce the desired effect. This repetitive process is the downward arrow technique (Burns, 1980). Helpees are asked what consequence they can draw based on their automatic thought, assuming the automatic thought were true. The helper repeatedly asks about consequences to each emerging thought until a core belief is uncovered. Helpers phrase the question in the following way: "If that belief were true, then what would that mean about you?" They then repeat the question to continue to elicit consequences: "And if that were true (and I'm not saying it is, but if it were true), then what would that mean?" Continue to ask for consequences until the helpee states a core belief, such as "It means I am unlovable." Core beliefs typically represent the final consequence to their thoughts, so if you are uncertain whether you have reached the core belief, ask the question one more time. When a core belief is reached, helpees will typically repeat the same belief again in confirmation, such as "It shows just how unlovable I am."

You may be tempted to immediately respond by reassuring your helpee that their core belief is untrue but hold off. (Continue reading later steps to understand why this approach is faulty). Instead, use this opportunity to thank your helpee for sharing a deeply personal and likely painful belief. You may also validate their beliefs while also quickly offering praise and then return to validation again. This might take the form of "I hear that you feel unlovable. I want you to know that I see you as loveable *and* see that you aren't feeling that way." Notice how validation is offered as a paraphrase first, then a brief self-disclosing praise, and then another validation with a paraphrase. Also note the emphasis on the word "and" rather than "but" between the praise and final paraphrase so as to validate both statements equally.

Result

The intended outcome of assessing dysfunctional thoughts is to increase helpees' awareness of their most distressing automatic thought, its connected core belief, and the cognitive distortions linking the two together (Campbell et al., 2017). At this point, helpees will be able to articulate their negative automatic thought and core belief. If helpees recognize that their thinking is negative and extreme, and they shift their thinking accordingly, they are effectively helping themselves. However, when helpees remain stuck in dysfunctional thinking, continued steps are required.

Case Example

Once Don helped Irvin select and focus on automatic thoughts related to his distress from being turned down for a job, he wanted to explore the most distressing thought and the connection to a core belief that might keep Irvin in distress over the job rejection.

HELPEE: This is really disheartening. I've lost my motivation to even try for another job.

HELPER: I know this has brought up several negative thoughts about yourself and job prospects. [Paraphrase]

HELPEE: Can you blame me? There is so much stacked against me to fail and my mind is spinning about it.

HELPER: Irvin, of all the thoughts you're having about this rejection, which one is most upsetting? [Closed question]

HELPEE: They are all pretty upsetting. I guess if I had to choose, it would be that I'll never get a job.

HELPER: That is a frightening prospect. I hear that you're feeling hopeless about your chances. [Reflecting feeling]

HELPEE: My chances don't look good. This letter confirms it.

HELPER: Negative thoughts like that could really hold you back. Some people find that in order to move past them, they need to understand more of what's behind them. I wonder if you might be interested in that as well. [Information]

HELPEE: I guess we could try.

HELPER: That's excellent. This isn't easy and you're doing great. [Empathic statement] In order to understand more deeply, let's assume for a moment that your thought is true: you will never get a job. What would that mean about you?

HELPEE: It would mean I can't take care of myself or my family.

HELPER: A worrisome possibility. [Reflecting feeling] And if that were true, that you couldn't take care of yourself and your family, then what would that mean?

HELPEE: That would be awful.

HELPER: You'd be really upset. What would be the worst part about it?

HELPEE: It would mean I'm a failure as a person. I really am a screw-up for life.

HELPER: A harsh thought. If that were true that you were a failure, what would that mean about you?

HELPEE: It means I'm no good. Totally worthless. [Core belief—worthlessness]

HELPER: I think I understand now—you're feeling worthless.

HELPEE: Yeah, I guess so.

HELPER: I want you to know I see you as a person of worth and value. I also hear that *you* are in a place where you feel worthless right now. [Validation, praise, validation]

As a result of assessing for dysfunctional thoughts, Don helped Irvin assess his most distressing dysfunctional thought: "I'll never get a job." Don then implemented the downward arrow technique to uncover the connected core belief of "I'm worthless." It is now clear that the original situation, receiving the job rejection letter, resulted in worry and disappointment because it prompted the automatic thought "I'll never get a job," which triggered the broader assumption "I'm worthless."

Written Practice

As a result of selecting and focusing on thoughts, you and Hope were able to focus on her thoughts connected to feeling lonely. You also helped her isolate one most distressing thought: "My friends don't want to spend time with me." In order to continue, you will want to help Hope to explore the connection between her most distressing automatic thought and her core beliefs. For each of the following areas, write down what you could say to Hope:

- What could you say to Hope to *introduce* the downward arrow technique? Write two different ways you could word it to her. Incorporate the use of the microskill information in each response.
- What could you say to *implement* the downward arrow technique with Hope? Incorporate the use of the microskill logical consequences in your response. Write out a transcript of what you could say and also what she might say in response for the entire downward arrow technique, including her reveal of a core belief of "I am unlovable."

Identify

Description

The third SAIL step for thoughts involves identifying dysfunctional versus functional thoughts (Campbell et al., 2017). At this point, the helpee has gained awareness of their negative automatic thought and the dysfunctional core belief it is connected to, but they do not fully acknowledge the cognitive distortion involved. Identifying offers the opportunity for helpees to understand the cognitive distortion made by their automatic thought. According to Cognitive Therapy, "Automatic thoughts can be evaluated according to their *validity* and their *utility*. The most common type of automatic thought is distorted in some way and occurs despite evidence to the contrary" (Beck, 1995, p. 77).

During the identify step, helpers should focus on challenging the distortion and automatic thoughts only (Brooks-Harris, 2008). Although core beliefs tend to be highly distressing and helpers may be tempted to challenge the core belief directly, for example, by saying "No, you're not bad," this is ill-advised. Core beliefs are strongly held assumptions usually based on years of mental hardwiring (Beck, 1995). Changing core beliefs requires professional counseling and is outside a nonprofessional's scope of competence (Young, Klosko, & Weishaar, 2003). Attempting to challenge the core belief directly is unlikely to be successful and will more likely result in the helpee feeling invalidated, much like you might feel if someone discounted a negative but strongly held belief you hold. For example, when you are having a bad day, someone telling you "No, you're having a good day" does not change your mind about the day but instead leaves you feeling invalidated and annoyed. You may have had such an experience like that before. If so, use it as motivation not to discount your helpees' core beliefs.

Instead, a better option is to attend to the current situation at hand, because this is within a nonprofessional helper's scope of competence and is readily changeable through support and validation. Instead of attacking the core belief, the goal of the identify step is to sever the connection between the automatic thought and the core belief by exposing and neutralizing the cognitive distortion connecting them. Although both continue to exist independently, the automatic thought is isolated to reduce immediate distress. What's more, while this isn't our immediate goal, repeatedly severing connections between automatic thoughts and core beliefs ultimately serves to shrink and negate core beliefs (Beck, 1995). See Figure 10.4 for a visual representation of the goal of the identifying step.

When to Identify

Once the most distressing negative automatic thought and its connected dysfunctional core belief have been identified, it may be helpful to directly confront the cognitive distortion connecting the two (Beck, 1995). At this point, helpees may have some conscious knowledge of the illogical nature of their thoughts but likely feel resistance to changing them completely. In the identify step, helpers challenge helpees to push through resistance and embrace more functional thinking through an evaluation of dysfunctional versus functional thoughts.

How to Use

Use the information gathered thus far about the helpee's automatic thought and core belief to determine what cognitive distortion (or distortions) might connect the two. Review the list of common cognitive distortions listed in Table 10.1. The distortions overlap and often present in combination, so use your best judgment on which one you think best applies. You will use this information to confront the irrationality of the helpee's automatic thought with the utmost care, empathy, and respect (Beck, 2011).

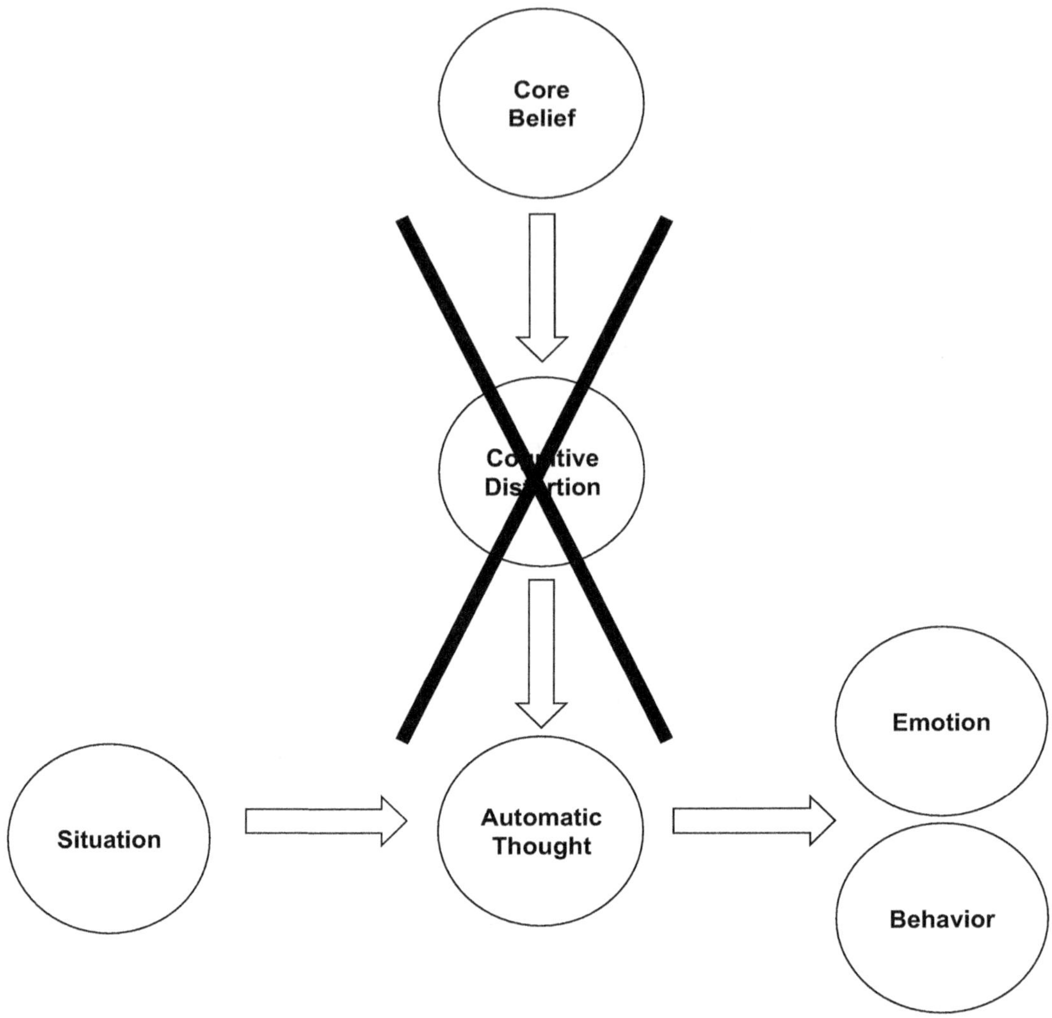

Figure 10.4 Goal of Identifying

Microskills: Confrontation, Feedback

Using the microskills ramp-up, helpers use listening skills and then ramp up to the next level of influencing skills to continue to move helpees forward toward modification. Helpers add the use of more microskills, including confrontation and feedback, to challenge the helpee to push through resistance and make changes (Campbell et al., 2017).

CONFRONTATION

Confrontation is defined as supportively challenging your helpee by highlighting their conflicts and discrepancies (Ivey et al., 2016). With thoughts, confrontation is used to highlight the logical discrepancy between the triggering situation and the core belief so as to weaken the automatic thought. Thus, confrontations occur between two verbal statements the helpee has made that do not seem to match each other. An example of confrontation for thoughts would be, "On the one hand, you're saying you burned dinner. On the other hand, you're saying this means you're a terrible father. I'm having a hard time making the leap of how one burned dinner means you're terrible." Another confrontation would be, "So you're saying that one low grade means you're stupid?" Notice how the situation is presented first and then the core belief is stated. This allows the helpee to wrestle directly with their distorted thinking to address their distress that is holding them back.

FEEDBACK

Feedback involves the helper transmitting reactions based on their own evaluation of the helpee (Egan, 2014). This is accomplished using the praise and polish method. Recall that the praise and polish method involves offering supportive, genuine, comprehensive, and specific reactions aimed at assisting the helpee to make changes by providing both positive and negative comments.

With feedback for thoughts, begin by praising your helpee for sharing their thoughts and then offer polish by explaining the cognitive distortion you see them making and how this can result in distress. An example of feedback with thoughts is,

> I appreciate that you're sharing what this means to you. I'm also concerned because it seems like polarized thinking might be clouding your judgment. Everyone makes mistakes so it seems unrealistic to view situations in black and white terms that they either confirm you're completely smart or else completely stupid.

In this example, praise was offered first, followed by a polish of describing the cognitive distortion, and then how it results in distress.

With confrontation and feedback for thoughts, keep in mind that the primary target of resistance is with the person's thought processes. As you read the above examples, you may read them as particularly provocative or even antagonistic. If not, try reading aloud in your most judgmental voice the following: "So you're saying that one low grade means you're stupid?" Presented that way, the words can sound downright insulting. With this in mind, recall the importance of implementing this step with strong and consistent attending skills. Empathic presence, facial expressions, and caring vocal tones are necessary to soften the challenging nature of confrontation (Ivey et al., 2016). Once again, try reading aloud the following using your most caring, empathic, and nonjudgmental attending skills: "So you're saying that one low grade means you're stupid?" Notice the difference? With confronting thoughts as in all helping interactions, attending skills are most important (Rogers, 1961).

Result

The intended outcome of identifying dysfunctional thoughts is to motivate helpees to push through resistance to identify and experiment with distortions involved in their dysfunctional thoughts (Campbell et al., 2017). By highlighting and challenging the distorted nature of their thoughts directly, helpees can view their stuck points in context and see the illogical connection between their core belief and the situation at hand. This step may shift the helpee to more functional thinking, which occurs when helpees begin to consider alternative explanations for the situation. Yet they will likely be tentative and uncertain about abandoning their negative automatic thought. Thus, identifying prepares both helpees and helpers for considering alternative thoughts about the situation (Campbell et al., 2017).

Case Example

We observed how Don uncovered Irvin's most distressing automatic thought, "I'll never get a job," and how it was connected to a core belief, "I'm worthless." Don now wants to identify

Irvin's dysfunctional thoughts to confront the cognitive distortion occurring from the originating situation of receiving the job rejection letter triggered by the core belief of worthlessness.

HELPEE: I appreciate that you see me as having value, but I really don't feel like that right now.
HELPER: Seems like you're in a dark place over this. [Paraphrase]
HELPEE: I knew this would happen. I'm sunk. This is pointless.
HELPER: So Irvin, you're telling me that because you receive one rejection letter for the first job you apply for, that means you're completely worthless? [Confrontation]
HELPEE: Well no, it's not just the letter. It's a lot of things but I really need a job to support myself and my family. I was worried I wouldn't be able to get one with my record and then I didn't get one.
HELPER: How incredibly frustrating to have what you were most worried about happen. Of course that's rattling your confidence. [Reflecting feeling]
HELPEE: My confidence wasn't good to start with. I'm trying to rebuild myself and this shows that I'm not going to be given a chance.
HELPER: I respect you for exploring how all of this has impacted your attitude, especially about yourself. I also fear that you are overgeneralizing one experience and jumping to conclusions about the rest of your life. That seems extreme and self-sabotaging when job rejections are a part of a normal job search. [Feedback]
HELPEE: I know. We talked about how some rejections would be expected. I just was so hopeful about this first one and now I'm really disappointed.
HELPER: That's completely understandable. It's a letdown to want something and have it not come through. [Paraphrase]

As a result of identifying dysfunctional thoughts, Don helped Irvin confront the cognitive distortion occurring from the originating situation of receiving the job rejection letter triggered by the core belief "I'm worthless." Don noted Irvin was overgeneralizing based on a single job rejection. Irvin remains hesitant about changing his perspective but appears to be considering the possibility.

Written Practice

The purpose of identifying dysfunctional thoughts is to motivate helpees to push through resistance to identify and experiment with distortions involved in their dysfunctional thoughts. This is accomplished through severing the connection between the automatic thought and the core belief by exposing and neutralizing the cognitive distortion connecting them.

This step offers the opportunity to motivate your friend Hope to push through her resistance by exposing cognitive distortions between her friends not inviting her to a party and her core belief, "I am unlovable." To this end, it may be helpful to confront the logical dissonance and offer feedback about the distortion. For each of the following areas, write down two things you could say to Hope:

- What could you say to encourage Hope to consider how it is illogical to leap from the distressing situation to confirming her core belief? Incorporate the use of the microskill confrontation in your response.
- What could you say to Hope to offer praise and feedback about a cognitive distortion? Label the distortion and explain it in a way Hope would understand. Incorporate the use of the microskill feedback in your response.
- What would you do to ensure your responses remained caring and empathic?

Launch

Description

The fourth and final step of the thoughts strategy involves generating functional thoughts (Campbell et al., 2017). The purpose is for the helpee to end the helping interaction with a perspective shift to more realistic and balanced thinking about a situation in order to motivate more adaptive emotional and behavioral responses.

According to Beck (1995), "beliefs that are dysfunctional can be unlearned and new beliefs that are more reality based and functional can be developed and learned through therapy" (p. 16). This same goal can be achieved for a specific helping scenario through the LifeRAFT launch step by encouraging helpees to let go of distorted thoughts and replace them with functional ones (Campbell et al., 2017).

When to Launch

Once helpers have challenged helpees to consider cognitive distortions in their thinking, it may be helpful to encourage them to replace dysfunctional thoughts with functional ones. Helpees are likely to have increased motivation toward doing so but remain hesitant and uncertain about their ability to produce new thoughts. The launch step can help mobilize their confidence through support and encouragement of alternate perspectives (Harris et al., 2014).

How to Launch

Forming functional thoughts involves guiding helpees to consider other ways of looking at the situation (Harris et al., 2014). Because offering a new perspective is the very definition of one of our microskills, reframing emerges as the key ingredient to the launch step for thoughts.

Microskills: Directives, Reframing

Through the microskills ramp-up, helpers ramp up to the highest level of microskills, adding reframing and directives. The goal is to motivate helpees toward generating functional thoughts to resolve the presenting issue and free them from their current distress (Campbell et al., 2017). Because we use these microskills differently within the thoughts approach, it is best this time to begin with directives and follow with reframing.

DIRECTIVES

Using directives means providing helpees with instructions to follow specific acts (Hill, 2014). In other words, the microskill of directives means giving them advice. This is reserved for the end of the helping interaction and, even then, only as needed to support our helpee in facilitating change.

When dealing with thoughts, first direct helpees to discontinue negative self-talk. Negative self-talk, or making critical statements about yourself, worsens mood and is counterproductive toward goals (Greenberger & Padesky, 1995). Can you imagine making self-statements such as "I'm stupid, worthless, and unlovable" to someone else? Or imagine saying to a friend, "You are stupid, have no value, and no one loves you." When said to others, the awfulness of these statements becomes clear, because they are toxic, relationship-ending criticisms (Gottman & Silver, 1999). With this in mind, offer your helpee a directive to stop negative self-talk. An example of this directive is, "Telling yourself that you are a bad person is cruel and damaging. When you find yourself criticizing yourself like that, you might try reminding yourself not to talk to anyone like that, including yourself, anymore."

Another way to use directives is to encourage helpees to consider alternative conclusions or explanations for the initial distressing situation. One way to phrase this includes:

> One explanation you had for burning dinner was that you're a bad father, which was extreme and made you feel really bad. Let's work on coming up with realistic alternative statements to tell yourself. How could we explain the burned dinner differently?

Another example of this approach is, "What if a friend told you that they got a low grade and concluded from that they were stupid. What would you tell them?" Notice how these examples directly state or imply a directive to consider functional automatic thoughts such as "Let's work on coming up with realistic alternative statements to tell yourself." Follow this directive by giving your helpee an opportunity to generate alternative thoughts and then adding your own suggestions or offering changes to theirs.

REFRAMING

Reframing is defined as providing helpees with a new, more positive perspective on themselves and their concerns. It often involves taking a negative thought and generating a more adaptive and balanced response (Ivey et al., 2016). Reframing helps to solidify decisions to change by adding a positive angle.

For the thoughts approach, this involves solidifying more functional thoughts for the situation. This can serve as a summary of alternative explanations discussed by using directives. For example, a reframe would be,

> When you burned dinner, you jumped to the conclusion that you're a bad father. Yet parents of all types and quality burn dinner—the two aren't linked. It's normal to burn dinner sometimes. You're a dad who is trying and learning how to cook; who is doing a good job and doesn't have to be perfect.

Result

The intended outcome of launching toward functional thoughts is to motivate helpees to form more accurate thoughts and thus embrace more functional ways of thinking that will also have a positive impact on actions and feelings (Brooks-Harris, 2008). Of these, feelings typically emerge first, often in the form of an expression of relief or improved mood state (Beck, 1995). Through reconnection with functional thinking, helpees are better equipped to continue working distress and concerns through themselves through a realistic assessment of the situation (Brooks-Harris, 2008).

Case Example

By identifying dysfunctional thoughts, Don helped Irvin confront the cognitive distortion occurring between the job rejection letter and the conclusion that he was worthless. Don noted Irvin was overgeneralizing based on a single job rejection. Irvin remains hesitant about changing his perspective but appears to be considering the possibility. Don now wants to boost Irvin's confidence toward accepting alternative explanations for the job rejection.

HELPEE: The letter really got to me. I feel like a worthless waste of space.

HELPER: Ugh, that's a really unkind way to talk to yourself. I'd imagine saying those things makes you feel even worse. You might consider not permitting yourself to say such critical things about yourself anymore. [Directive]

HELPEE: I guess that is a pretty rude thing to say. I just got so used to telling myself that.

HELPER: Yes, I agree. I would be insulted and angry if someone called me worthless. [Reflecting feeling]

HELPEE: Me too. I probably would be better off not telling myself those things.

HELPER: Perhaps we could consider some other things to tell yourself instead? What are other ways we could frame this job rejection? [Directive]

HELPEE: I guess we talked about how it is rare to get the first job you apply for and rejections are usually part of the process.

HELPER: Excellent, Irvin, that's a great start! Finding a job usually takes multiple tries. Job rejections are normal in job searches. [Paraphrase]

HELPEE: I'm still disappointed about this one, though.

HELPER: Of course, you are. Job rejections are discouraging. [Reflecting feeling] If we switched places and I was in your shoes, what would you tell me? [Open question]

HELPEE: Hmm. I guess I'd tell you that other people with criminal records have told me they've found good jobs. It sometimes takes extra time and effort, but you should stick with it and it'll happen.

HELPER: Kind and helpful advice. People, even when they've made past mistakes, find employers who will give them a chance. Persistence pays off. [Paraphrase]

HELPEE: [sigh] I'm realizing this probably isn't going to happen as quickly as I hoped it would.

HELPER: As you said, job rejections are normal and expected, and many people in your position still get good jobs. It can be frustrating and difficult, but you have the determination to make it happen. [Reframing]

HELPEE: I do. This is going to continue to be a hard road ahead, but I am determined to get a job for myself and my family.

HELPER: That seems like a healthy way of approaching this challenge. I have a lot of respect for you, Irvin. [Empathic statement]

Written Practice

The purpose of launching toward functional thoughts is to motivate helpees to form more accurate thoughts. Now would be the time to direct your friend Hope to discontinue negative self-talk and consider alternate, more functional explanations for being excluded from the party with her friends. It would also be your opportunity to reframe the situation for Hope in a way that moved her toward functional thinking to also have a positive impact on actions and feelings. For each of the following areas, write down two things you could say to Hope:

- Hope has shared her core belief of unlovability with you. Explain to her why negative self-talk is damaging and encourage her to discontinue it. Incorporate the use of the microskill directive in your response.
- Hope explained that her friends went to a party without inviting her, which made her feel lonely and triggered her core belief. What could you say to Hope to encourage her to think of other, more functional reasons why she was not invited to the party with her friends? Incorporate the use of the microskill directive in your response. What alternative explanations might you suggest in addition to the ones she generates?

- Using the alternative explanations, you generated, what could you say to Hope to encourage her to see the situation differently? Incorporate the use of the microskill reframing in your response.

Role-Play Practice

The purpose of this exercise is to rehearse the modifying stage for the thoughts strategy. This time you will practice using the entire LifeRAFT sequence of supporting, watching, investigating, and modifying. For this exercise, find a volunteer helpee to role-play a helping scenario with you and provide feedback afterward. Set a timer and conduct a helping scenario for at least 20 minutes. Attempt to support using listening skills of attending, paraphrasing, and reflecting feelings only. Watch for warning signs that referral is necessary. Then investigate using listening skills, questions, and focusing, before finally engaging in modifying by choosing thoughts as a strategy and using all microskills via the microskills ramp-up. Complete the following:

1. Consider pairing with a fellow helper-in-training and take turns being the helper and helpee.
2. Record the scenario, following the ethical guidelines discussed in Chapter 1, including permission to video record.
3. Ask your helpee to select a topic to discuss. Consult Chapter 1, "Problem Triggers," for topic ideas. Request that they avoid crisis issues warranting the watch stage. Also request that they initially keep thoughts, particularly about themselves, negative to focus on helping them become more functional throughout the helping scenario.
4. Attempt to support using listening skills of attending, paraphrasing, and reflecting feelings and then investigate using listening skills, questions, and focusing. Choose thoughts as the strategy and progress through modifying using all needed microskills via the microskills ramp-up.
5. At the end of the role-play, request feedback from your helpee about what you did well and what you could improve on next time. Ask what interventions felt especially empathic and supportive and which ones were awkward or uncomfortable. Write down your helpee's responses.
6. Review the video recording. What do you think you did well and what you could improve on next time as the helper?

Summary

In this chapter we discussed the following:

Description of Modifying through Thoughts

- Modifying for thoughts is based on Cognitive Therapy, in which cognitive interpretations to situations are responsible for resulting emotions and behaviors. Dysfunctional thoughts are negative automatic thoughts triggered by negative core beliefs. Problem-solving occurs by converting dysfunctional thoughts into functional ones.

- Modifying involves choosing thoughts and guiding the helpee through a basic problem-solving process of SAIL steps: select, assess, identify, and launch.

Select

- The select step uses attending, paraphrasing, reflection of feeling, questions, and focusing to encourage helpees to talk specifically about how thoughts impact their concern.

Assess

- The assess step involves assessing dysfunctional thoughts and connected negative core beliefs that are holding the helpee back from resolving the presenting issue.
- Using the microskills ramp-up, helpers add information and logical consequences to guide helpees to assess their stuck points.

Identify

- The identify step uses feedback and confrontation to challenge helpees to push through resistance and recognize cognitive distortions through an evaluation of dysfunctional versus functional thoughts.

Launch

- Helpers add the remaining microskills, including reframing and directives, to motivate their helpees toward alternative interpretations of the situation and a new perspective in an effort to resolve the presenting issue.

References

Beck, A. T., & Weishaar, M. E. (2000). Cognitive therapy. In R. J. Corsini & D. Wedding (Eds.), *Current psychotherapies*. Itasca, IL: F. E. Peacock Publishers.

Beck, J. S. (1995). *Cognitive therapy: Basics and beyond*. New York, NY: Guilford Press.

Beck, J. S. (2011). *Cognitive therapy: Basics and beyond* (2nd ed.). New York, NY: Guilford Press.

Brooks-Harris, J. E. (2008). *Integrative multitheoretical psychotherapy*. Boston, MA: Houghton Mifflin.

Burns, D. D. (1980). *Feeling good: The new mood therapy*. New York: Signet.

Campbell, E. L. (2013, April). *Key introductory strategies training: Training paraprofessionals in basic helping skills*. Symposium conducted at the annual meeting of the Western Psychological Association, Reno, NV.

Campbell, E. L., Davidson, K., & Davidson, S. M. (2017). Effectiveness of LifeRAFT undergraduate helping skills training model. *Psychology Teaching Review*, *23*(2), 32–41.

Corey, G. (2009). *Theory and practice of counseling and psychotherapy* (8th ed.). Belmont, CA: Thomson/Brooks/Cole.

Egan, G. (2014). *The skilled helper: A problem-management and opportunity development approach to helping* (10th ed.). Belmont, CA: Brooks/Cole.

Gottman, J. M., & Silver, N. (1999). *The seven principles for making marriage work*. New York: Crown Publishing.

Greenberger, D., & Padesky, C. A. (1995). *Mind over mood: Change how you feeling by changing the way you think*. New York: Guildford Press.

Harris, J. E., Kelly, L. J., Campbell, E. L., & Hammond, E. S. (2014). Key strategies training: An introduction to multitheoretical practice. *Journal of Psychotherapy Integration*, *24*(2), 138–152. doi:10.1037/a0037056

Hill, C. E. (2014). *Helping skills: Facilitating exploration, insight, and action* (4th ed.). Washington, DC: American Psychological Association.

Ivey, A. E., Ivey, M. B., & Zalaquett, C. P. (2016). *Essentials of intentional interviewing: Counseling in a multicultural world* (3rd ed.). Boston, MA: Cengage Learning.

Rogers, C. (1961). *On becoming a person*. Boston: Houghton Mifflin.

Young, J. E., Klosko, J. S., & Weishaar, M. E. (2003). *Schema therapy: A practitioner's guide*. New York: Guildford Press.

11 LifeRAFT Integration

Chapter Goals

This chapter will prepare you to:

- Learn how to end a helping interview.
- Gain an understanding of common challenges encountered during helping scenarios and how to address them.
- Reflect on the LifeRAFT model in full, including all SWIM stages, RAFT strategies, and SAIL steps.

Introduction

Congratulations on learning all of the components of the LifeRAFT model! This chapter consolidates and concludes everything you have learned. After you complete the modifying stage by way of the actions, thoughts, or feelings strategies, helpees will hopefully become unstuck from their distress and once more be capable of continuing on their path. In this chapter, we will discuss how to end the helping scenario and also troubleshoot some common challenges that emerge during helping scenarios. Lastly, we will review the LifeRAFT model in its entirety and offer final thoughts with using the model.

Ending Helping

Description

The end of helping refers to the point at which an interaction between a helper and helpee is discontinued or the conversation pivots to another purpose or topic, thereby removing the roles of helper and helpee. Helpers can intentionally end a helping scenario using some basic interventions, similar to those used by professional counselors (Campbell, 2013).

In professional counseling, the end of helping is called "termination" and generally refers to ending an ongoing therapeutic relationship (Faiver, Eisengart, & Colonna, 2004). Although more complex and involved than a single nonprofessional helping scenario, professional counseling termination provides useful considerations for ending a helping session. As summarized by Hill (2014), the three steps for effective termination in professional therapy include looking back, looking forward, and saying goodbye (Dewald, 1971; Marx & Gelso, 1987; Ward, 1984).

The same three steps can be applied to ending nonprofessional helping scenarios (Campbell, 2013). When looking back, helpees review what they got from the helping scenario. This is beneficial for both the helper and the helpee because it reinforces the gains made by the helpee and also offers feedback for the helper about the process. By looking forward, helpees consider their next steps and plans for the future, including how they might use what they got from the scenario. This might include reminders about referrals and making further modifications with actions, feelings, and thoughts. Finally, in saying goodbye, the helper and the helpee express thanks for the interaction and, if exiting the conversation, say their farewells.

When to End the Helping Scenario

When a helping situation reaches the end of the modifying stage and immediate distress has been addressed, it may be helpful to initiate ending the helping scenario (Campbell, Davidson, & Davidson, 2017). The helper acts as a caring and empathic support who guides the helpee to transition out of the helpee role. A helpee may or may not want to end the helping situation or may be unaware that it is naturally drawing to a close. As the helper, it is valuable to provide clear signals and direct guidance to end the helping situation in an effort to maintain appropriate boundaries and encourage helpee autonomy once again.

How to End the Helping Scenario

Briefly address each of Hill's (2014) three steps to end the helping situation through the use of listening skills, questions, and focusing. It is generally no longer recommended to continue the use of other influencing skills at this point because it is counter to the goal of restoring the helpee back to full autonomy.

Microskills: Listening Skills, Questions, Focusing

Return to previously used microskills of attending, paraphrasing, reflection of feeling, questions, and focusing. Remember to continue employing skills according to the microskills ramp-up (see Figure 11.1). The manner in which these are employed is slightly adjusted.

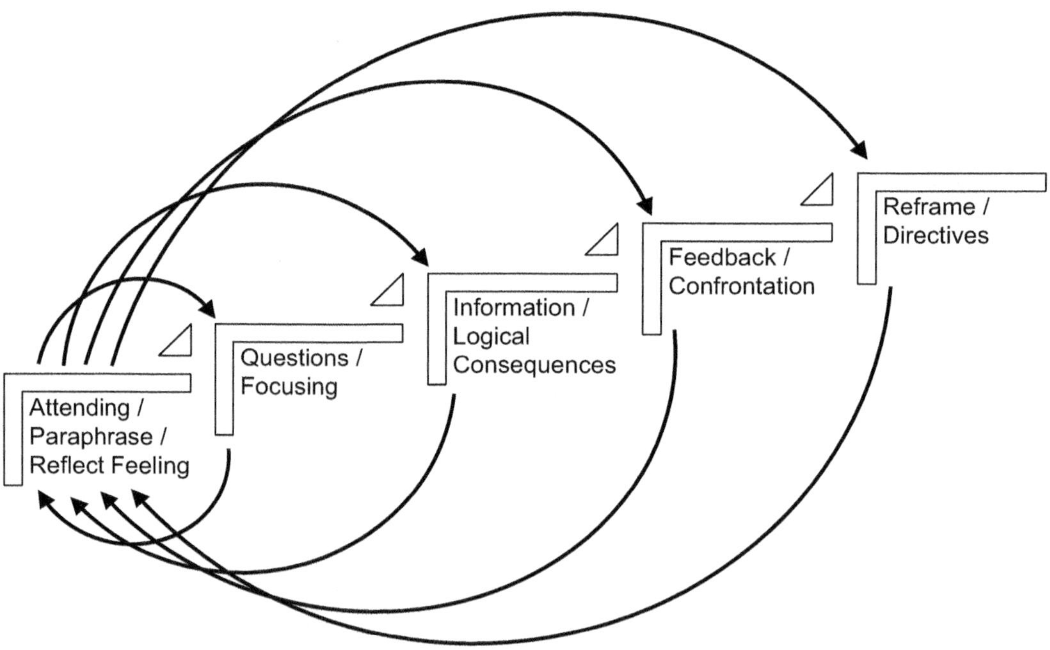

Figure 11.1 Microskills Ramp-Up

Attending, Paraphrasing, and Reflecting Feeling

At the end of the helping situation, reduce the empathic intensity of listening skills. Recall that listening skills of attending, paraphrasing, and reflecting feeling serve to encourage the helpee to continue to talk in greater detail (Ivey, Ivey, & Zalaquett, 2016). At the end of the situation, we want to encourage helpees to reduce and end their disclosures and to transition out of focusing on distress.

Begin to subtly send this message by maintaining an empathic body posture and vocal quality while reducing the empathic intensity of responses. Incorporate subtle non-attention behaviors such as leaning back slightly, reducing length of eye contact, and decreasing head nodding. Shift your vocal tone to a slightly higher and quicker pace that progressively approaches your normal speaking voice. Paraphrases and reflections of feeling should continue, but keep them brief and hopeful, as appropriate. For example, a helpee might say, "I'm feeling bad about forgetting my friend's birthday." At the beginning of a helping situation, an appropriate response might be, "I hear your remorse coming through about forgetting her birthday. Sounds like this mistake hurts you to think about." At the end of a helping situation, a similar response might shift to "You remain remorseful and you've made solid plans to address it." In the second example, notice how the response still briefly acknowledges the helpee's experience, while also reflecting the hopeful and constructive problem-solving that has taken place during the conversation. Work to balance between both an empathic and an increasingly upbeat response to subtly transition out of the helping situation.

Questions and Focusing

Use questions and focusing to guide your helpee to discuss looking back, looking forward, and saying goodbye (Hill, 2014). Address each area in order before moving to the next.

LOOKING BACK

Lead your helpee to look back by reviewing what was just discussed, specifically the problem-solving they just engaged in (Hill, 2014). Paraphrase and reflect feelings as a summarization of what they discussed. For example, "It's great how you've shifted from believing this situation was completely hopeless to recognizing ways you can make change." Another example is, "I'm honored to have walked through this with you as you've expanded your experience from feeling blocked from your feelings to then fully acknowledging a healthy range of reactions of fear, sadness, and anger." Direct and indirect open questions can also help your helpee elicit their own review, such as "What did you get from our talk?" and "I'm curious the ways this conversation was most helpful for you." Be sure to reinforce insights by reflecting their responses back through paraphrases and reflecting feelings.

LOOKING FORWARD

Guide your helpee to look forward by emphasizing the ongoing process of maintaining or building on changes they have made (Hill, 2014). Paraphrase and reflect feelings as a summarization of what occurred during the launch step, emphasizing its continuation into the future. For example, "You started making plans to apologize to your friend tomorrow, and I hope that conversation goes well. I can see you're hopeful for that, too." Direct and indirect open questions can also elicit the helpee's own remarks about the future, such as "What will you do with what we talked about today?" and "I wonder how this might help you moving forward."

Helpers may be tempted to involve themselves in future plans, but they should generally resist the urge to do so (Campbell et al., 2017). They often want to provide additional aid by asking questions such as "How can I help you follow through with those plans?" or "Can we check in about this again tomorrow?" Remember that the hallmark of ethical nonprofessional counseling is to assess and assist a helpee to manage their immediate life concerns more effectively. Professional counselors work with managing ongoing issues while nonprofessionals should focus on immediate concerns. If you find yourself wanting to follow-up on issues or remain involved in a distressing situation, check that you are not crossing an ethical boundary. There are instances when nonprofessional helping may involve multiple occasions of helping over time, such as following up on referrals, particularly in crisis situations. Otherwise, it is generally recommended to avoid making plans to stay involved in ongoing distress management. That said, you are welcome to invite the helpee to request to talk to you in the future. For example, "Please let me know if there's something I can help you with again in the future."

SAYING GOODBYE

Finally, use focusing to shift the attention to saying farewell or ending the helping situation. At this point, open questions are not recommended because they encourage the helpee to open the conversation back up. Instead, thank your helpee for talking with you, offer brief pleasantries, and then say farewell. For example, "Thank you, it means a lot to me that you would talk to me about this. I hope the rest of your day goes better. Goodbye."

In situations where the conversation continues but the helping situation has reached an end, goodbye can be replaced with a direct or indirect closed question to explicitly shift the conversation. For example, "Thank you for talking with me. Can we transition to a story I wanted to tell you?" Another example is, "Thank you for this time and I hope it was helpful. I was wondering if now I could have some time to get your input on something." Notice how the closed question is worded explicitly to indicate a shift so the helpee knows the helping situation is over.

Result

At this point, our intended outcome is to discontinue the helping interaction and/or pivot the conversation to another purpose or topic, thereby removing the roles of helper and helpee. Ending a helping scenario smoothly and gracefully can be tricky, so it is important to be intentional (Hill, 2014). Helpers can make the mistake of assuming that the conversation will naturally draw to a close or that helpees will initiate when they are ready for the situation to be over. Sometimes they will; however, it should not be expected. Keep in mind that the microskills you use are specifically designed to encourage a helpee to continue talking (Ivey et al., 2016). Clients in professional counseling also struggle with this issue. Ending can be awkward or unclear if managed poorly and even undo the valuable work accomplished previously (Wachtel, 2002). Once a helpee feels comfortable to open up and be vulnerable, it can be challenging to close that off again and gracefully stop (Neukrug, 2007). Thus, it is the responsibility of the helper to send clear signals to the helpee when the situation is over. Doing so in a kind and clear way can preserve the relationship as well as reinforce the important work accomplished during the helping session (Hill, 2014).

Helping Challenges

No helping situation will be flawless or follow the LifeRAFT model exactly, and challenges of one kind or another are expected. Remember that a training model is just a "deliberately simplified and usually idealized and imaginary representation of a phenomenon" (Colman, 2015); so too the LifeRAFT model is deliberately simplified and idealized, meaning that it contains a basic set of prescribed steps to explain the helping process and train helpers. A prescribed set of specific steps requires a highly controlled exchange, and so the model is presented more simply and stepwise than helping situations actually occur. When a helpee presents genuine distress in real life, the direction of the conversation cannot be perfectly predicted; thus, helpers rarely follow LifeRAFT exactly to the letter. The value of the LifeRAFT model comes from being not a precise set of steps but rather a set of guidelines of what leads to good practice. You may drift away from some of the details, but if you can remember the basic progression of the model to understand how helping works, you will be miles ahead of untrained helpers (Campbell et al., 2017). Thus, a reasonable goal for helpers is to learn common areas of challenge you encounter, understand how and why they occur, and attend to remediating them.

Common Challenges

Although your growth as a helper will be unique to you, we will explore here some of the most common challenges helpers experience. Our purpose is to understand and resolve frequently encountered problems, as well as use these principles to generalize other problems we might encounter. Some common challenges helpers experience include resistant helpees, LifeRAFT model navigation issues, and lack of helping success.

Resistant Helpees

Throughout the helping scenario, helpees may express resistance in a variety of ways. Resistance may present covertly through subtle reluctance to move forward, such as expressing uncertainty or nervousness about problem-solving or accepting suggestions (Young, 2001), or overtly, such as active opposition by refusing to answer questions or changing subjects (Egan, 2014).

If this is an issue in your helping scenarios, begin by thinking about helpee resistance differently. Recognize that resistance of all kinds is normal and expected and will emerge in nearly every helping situation. In fact, the SAIL steps in the modifying stage are built on the goal of working through helpee resistance to problem-solve. Be empathic and do your best to understand that vulnerability and change are difficult, and we all have at least some resistance to them; if we didn't, we likely would not get stuck or need help from others (Egan, 2014). Embrace this as a primary reason we exist as helpers and join with your helpee by accepting their resistance with empathy, understanding, and non-judgment.

Actions to address resistance in helping scenarios depend on the nature of the resistance. Subtle reluctance can be responded to with increased empathy and attending skills. Work directly with resistance by using listening skills to draw attention and explore it. For example, you can reflect feelings around resistance by saying things like "Seems like the prospect of trying this is scary" or paraphrases such as "I'm hearing you say that you don't believe you are capable to try this." Active opposition from a helpee, such as angrily shifting the conversation, might warrant additional skills such as questions. For example, responding with reflecting feelings and an open question might be helpful: "I noticed a shift and it seems like you might feel irritated. What just happened?" Remember to keep using your microskills ramp-up to intersperse questions with listening skills so the helpee continues to feel supported. If resistance is constant and unrelenting, the helpee may be communicating to you that they do not want to engage in problem-solving of any kind. Even when helpees request help in making a change, such as explicitly stating "Help me figure out what to do," sometimes they want nothing more than to simply be listened to (Young, 2001). In cases such as these, it is always appropriate to return to the LifeRAFT supporting stage and stay there for the duration of the helping situation. A helpful approach to this issue, and many issues that emerge in helping situations, is to return to the support stage and using only listening skills to reorient to the helpee and their needs. In the LifeRAFT model, it is always permissible to back up and revisit an earlier stage.

LifeRAFT Model Navigation Issues

Although the LifeRAFT model was designed to provide simplified steps for helping, it remains a complex model with several components. In a helping situation, a helper can easily get lost in the process or have difficulty navigating from one step to the next, especially in the exact order presented in the model. Difficulties commonly emerge during the modification stage because the goals of each SAIL step become more involved and additional microskills are added. In the real world, helpees tend not to be aware of the helping model you are working from so they do not follow the same line of thinking and may divert into other topics. Helpees may also at any point exit the model completely by resolving their own concerns prior to the completion of LifeRAFT stages. It can be challenging to navigate these issues within the framework with which you were trained.

Address this concern by reorienting your perspective of the LifeRAFT model. Recognize that the model is an idealized version and real-world helping will not follow the exact steps provided. Instead, consider LifeRAFT as a model that provides general guidelines to be adapted and applied for real-world helping. For example, the general sequence of SWIM stages of supporting, watching, investigating, and modifying may not always be used, but they help us remember general guidelines such as offering support and watching for emergencies before problem-solving. Also, strive for the microskills ramp-up goal of listening skills first and most often and intersperse influencing skills later. In this way, addressing issues such as “I forgot to support my helpee first” or “I stopped using listening skills after I started asking questions” is warranted. However, if you find yourself constantly scrutinizing detailed stepwise “errors” in your process, such as “I used reframing before logical consequences” or “My assessing and identifying blended together,” you are being too literal with your use of the model. Furthermore, remember that the full LifeRAFT model should only be followed as far as needed for helpee change. In this way, the goal is not necessarily to complete all the steps but instead to help the helpee to resolve their concern. This can occur at any time, including prior to moving through all of the steps, even perhaps in the supporting stage alone. This should be viewed as a helping success rather than an issue with properly navigating the model.

Addressing LifeRAFT model navigation issues include studying and practice. Effective helping takes time and effort to learn, and you will not memorize LifeRAFT immediately. When you find yourself repeatedly getting lost or having difficulty with the same part of the model, go back and review those components. Role-play that section of the model specifically and have notes available for reminders. When reflecting on helping situations and identifying areas for growth, be intentional about asking yourself whether deviations from the model represent appropriate departures or significant navigation issues that need to be changed. Consult role-play partners for additional perspective.

Lack of Helping Success

Despite your best efforts, sometimes helping is not successful and the helpee will not receive constructive assistance (Egan, 2014). You may reach the end of the LifeRAFT stages and distress is still present or unresolved. Numerous causes for lack of success are possible. Some problems or helpees are not at a point where interpersonal helping is effective. For example, some people need to sort through problems on their own before they are able to articulate them aloud (Connor-Smith & Flachsbart, 2007); attempting to seek help prematurely may result in an unhelpful session. The combination of helper and helpee dynamics may also be mismatched, which negatively impact rapport and the helping relationship, a key ingredient to helping effectiveness (Rogers, 1961). This can be disheartening for both helper and helpee, because both members want the scenario to be effective.

Change your perspective to recognize that feeling unhelpful at times is a normal and expected experience (Egan, 2014). Tell yourself that not every person and every problem can be helped. You cannot be the ideal match for every helpee, and factors beyond your control, such as timing and fit, are bound to interfere sometimes. When helping situations fall flat, recognize that you did what you could. Lastly, maintain hope for your helpee. Because the ultimate goal is for helpees to help themselves, perhaps they got something from the interaction that is not readily apparent. Even insight into the fact that they are not ready to deal with their issue can be valuable. So, the effects of your help may not be immediately obvious, but hope can always be maintained for continued helpee growth.

In response to lack of helping success, there is value in temporarily continuing to try to help. For example, when you reach the end of the LifeRAFT sequence, consider if the helpee might benefit from a different strategy and try the modifying stage again, if you both are willing. For example, you may work through the feelings strategy with no change but then back up and repeat the modifying stage with actions to achieve success. It may also become clear at this point that a return to the watch stage might be warranted to refer to a professional if the situation is more complex than originally perceived.

You can attempt to shift your approach, but also be ready to stop when it is time to quit trying. If nothing is working, gently end the helping interaction. Thank them for talking with you. If it fits your style, you can offer a brief apology that the conversation did not go as hoped. Offer pleasantries and then wish them farewell. For example, you might say, "Thank you for talking with me. I'm sorry we weren't able to help you move forward. I care about you and am hoping for the best. See you tomorrow."

If you find that there is a lack of helping success with several different people, examine the quality of your interventions and reconsider your approach. Although it is unlikely to achieve success with everyone, it is also unlikely to fail to achieve success with everyone (Egan, 2014). Your approach may be in need of revision. Review your helping training, practice with role-play partners, and ask for feedback. Remain open to suggestions and try new approaches. Remember that the art and science of helping is challenging and takes time and effort to learn to do so effectively.

LifeRAFT Model Integration

Now that you have learned each individual component of the LifeRAFT model in detail and understand how to use each one, we can solidify our understanding by putting the components together to briefly review and summarize the entire approach, beginning with the LifeRAFT SWIM stages.

Supporting

Supporting, the first stage of the LifeRAFT helping skills model, involves connecting and strengthening your relationship with your helpee by providing a foundation of nonjudgmental and affirming, emotion-focused helping. The purpose of supporting is to establish and build rapport, earn the right for increasing intervention, and provide a nonjudgmental space for the helpee to help themselves. To support, begin by agreeing to help and reviewing informed consent. Use the microskill listening skills of attending, paraphrasing, and reflecting feelings. The helpee will begin to feel heard and understood and rapport will be established.

Watching

The second stage of watching is meant to assess and facilitate referrals to professional help if needed. To engage in watching, add the microskill of questions. Ask about potential crisis issues such as suicidality, homicidality, and impaired mental status, as well as issues beyond your scope of competence. Should these be present, guide the helpee to appropriate professional help. Through the watch stage, crises will be discovered and appropriate referrals will be made to professionals for ongoing treatment and safety.

Investigating

The third stage of investigating is meant to assess the helpee's concerns, determine what is changeable and what a helper can effectively provide, and decide how to move forward with a problem-solving process. It is about exploring and assessing the situation on two different levels: the helpee's circumstances and counseling strategies. The helpee's circumstances include the person, present, and problem, while counseling strategies include the helpee's actions, feelings, and thoughts. To begin investigating, add the microskill of focusing. An initial understanding of the helper's distress will be gained, and both the helper and the helpee are poised to begin problem-solving.

Modifying

The fourth stage of modifying involves deciding how to move forward with a problem-solving process and then doing so. Helpers choose a RAFT strategy to pursue actions, feelings, or thoughts and then guide the helpee through a basic problem-solving process of four SAIL steps: select, assess, identify, and launch.

Select

The select step uses all previously employed microskills of attending, paraphrasing, reflecting feeling, questions, and focusing to encourage helpees to talk specifically about how the chosen strategy impacts their concern.

Assess

The assess step involves assessing potential ineffective actions, maladaptive feelings, or dysfunctional thoughts that are holding the helpee back from resolving the presenting issue. Using the microskills ramp-up, helpers add information and logical consequences to guide helpees to assess their stuck points.

Identify

The identify step uses feedback and confrontation to challenge helpees to push through resistance and make changes through an evaluation of problematic choices as opposed to nonproblematic choices. Using the microskills ramp-up, helpers add confrontation and feedback to guide helpees to identify solutions.

Launch

The launch step aims to guide helpees toward a helpful and healthy resolution of their presenting concern. Helpers add the use of remaining microskills, including reframing and directives, to motivate their helpees toward a new perspective and a healthier direction in an effort to resolve the presenting issue.

Although the process is similar for each strategy of the modifying stage, the approach differs somewhat depending on the chosen RAFT strategy of actions, feelings, or thoughts.

Actions

Modifying for actions is based on Behavioral Activation and operant conditioning, in which behaviors are based on consequences. Ineffective behaviors develop and are maintained due to their initial desirable outcomes that develop into overcoping, avoidance, withdrawal, and unintentionality. Problem-solving occurs by converting ineffective behaviors into effective ones (Martell, Dimidjian, Herman-Dunn, & Lewinsohn, 2010).

Feelings

Modifying for feelings is based on Emotion-Focused Therapy, which asserts that emotions serve as signals of basic needs. Emotions are comprised of primary emotions, which are initial genuine responses to a given situation, and secondary emotions, which are reactions to primary emotions and serve a protective and regulatory function to block and hide primary emotions when they are deemed unacceptable. Problem-solving occurs by expanding emotional awareness and expression from maladaptive emotions to adaptive emotions by creating safety around exploring secondary emotions to uncover primary emotions (Greenberg, 2002).

Thoughts

Modifying for thoughts is based on Cognitive Therapy, in which cognitive interpretations to situations are responsible for resulting emotions and behaviors. Dysfunctional thoughts are negative automatic thoughts triggered by negative core beliefs. Problem-solving occurs by converting dysfunctional thoughts into functional ones (Beck, 2011).

As a result of the LifeRAFT modifying stage and SAIL steps, it is hoped that the helpee's distress will be reduced and they will become unstuck to resume their functioning or have a plan for how to do so. Helping then can come to an end by reviewing gains made, summarizing plans for future growth, and offering thanks and farewells.

Make LifeRAFT Your Own

Your Style

Becoming a trained helper who follows a research-based approach and established skills is important (Egan, 2014). Yet if you stop there, you will inhibit your potential effectiveness in truly connecting with helpees in a way that only you can (Corey, 2009). Now that you have LifeRAFT to plot your course, you get to decide what that looks like in a way that is authentic for you. There is no one correct way to implement LifeRAFT. Now that you have learned your skills, it is time to start being creative and personalize your implementation. Just as every helpee and helping situation has unique needs and characteristics, so too does each helper have their own style (Ivey et al., 2016). Learn to be flexible and adapt your approach to fit your style.

Begin to discover your style by observing your mentors, helpers, and other models (Halbur & Halbur, 2019). Any time you are in conversation with another person, and particularly in cases where you are being helped or watching someone else helping, take notice of the helper's style. Note their tendencies and what things you would like to emulate. You can also return to the case examples throughout this book and note interventions and wording choices that you particularly like, then mimic these examples and practice doing them yourself, experimenting with how to incorporate them in a way that works for you. For example, one of my signature gestures is to lean forward and put a hand on my heart when I feel close to a helpee and clasp both hands over my heart when I want to express a greater intensity of closeness. It is my way of giving my helpee a visual "hug" without invading their personal space, and it is unique to my personality and helping style. While many of my helping trainees have adopted it as their own, others found it to be a poor fit for their approach. Your style needs to work for you. Other examples are gestures and wording choices I have adopted from my trainees, such as using sighs and verbal utterances of "oh" and "mmm" to communicate empathy, talking more with my hands to help emphasize points, and incorporating humor where appropriate. One trainee's allegorical reference to dysfunctional thoughts as "hobgoblins of fear" has been adopted into my thoughts strategy repertoire; another trainee's signature motivational phrase, "you got this," has become a frequent addition to my reframes.

Your Preferences

In addition to finding your own style, it is also valuable to consider your preferences. Recall that each LifeRAFT strategy of actions, feelings, and thoughts represents an established professional counseling theoretical orientation that has empirical support for being effective in treating a wide range of clients and presenting issues (Beck, 1995; Greenberg, 2002; Martell et al., 2010). Similarly, the strategies of actions, feelings, and thoughts can all effectively provide help to a variety of helpees and distressing situations (Campbell et al., 2017).

LifeRAFT taught you to be proficient in each of these three methods, yet most helping trainees report a preference for one approach (Campbell, 2013). Hopefully you have gained an appreciation and proficiency with all three approaches, but most students can still rank which strategies they most enjoy and feel most competent in. Understanding your reactions to each of these theories can help you identify your preferred helper orientation, and even foretell your emerging theoretical orientation, should you choose to pursue professional counselor training in the future.

Helper preferences

Helpers tend to have a preference for which approach they most prefer to work from when helping another person, typically reflecting their own strengths and beliefs about change and how change occurs (Halbur & Halbur, 2019). By considering your preferences, you can learn more about your approach to helping and identify your strengths. When choosing a strategy to pursue, consider your strategy preference, in addition to the needs of the helpee and the problem type, in order to provide the best helping possible.

Helpee preferences

Helpees also have a preference for which approach they most prefer when receiving help from another person. In other words, during LifeRAFT training, helpers can gain insight into how they like to be assisted when they are the helpee. This may be similar to your preferred strategy as a helper, or it may be different, but it typically reflects ways that you feel cared about and supported when stressed (Connor-Smith & Flachsbart, 2007). LifeRAFT not only offers skills training but also awareness of the entire process of helping, illuminating the journey as both a helper and a helpee. You can learn more about yourself and how you most like to receive help by reflecting on which approach of actions, feelings, or thoughts that you most enjoy being led through. In times of distress, before you reach out for help, you will have a better understanding of the different types of help available to know what to ask for.

With this information, you can begin asking more specifically for what you need from others. Although not everyone is trained in LifeRAFT, the basic strategies can be used to conceptualize your concerns and accurately request what you want from someone else. A general "Can you help me?" may or may not result in the kind of help you were hoping for. Instead, use the basic LifeRAFT principles to consider whether you want actions-, feelings-, or thoughts-based assistance and then ask more specifically for it. For actions-based help, ask, "I have a problem and I'm trying to figure out what to do about it. Can you help me come up with what to do next?" For feelings-based help, ask, "I have a problem and it would help to have the space to talk it through and experience my feelings. Can you help me by listening and offering support?" For thoughts-based help, ask, "I have a problem and I'm stuck in a negative head space about it. Can you help me shift my perspective on this?" Using LifeRAFT even when you are the helpee offers the ability to identify and communicate your needs, increasing your chances of receiving the kind of help you seek.

Personal Reflection

Now that you have learned the LifeRAFT model, it is valuable to identify your preferences and compare them with your earlier predictions. Understanding your reactions to the strategies can strengthen your connection to these approaches, identify your preferred helper orientation, and foretell your emerging theoretical orientation. As you reflect on the strategies of actions, feelings, and thoughts, answer the following questions:

- As a *helper*, how do you rank your preferences for using actions, feelings, or thoughts to provide help? Explain your answer.
- As a *helpee*, how do you rank your preferences for receiving help based on actions, feelings, or thoughts to provide help? Explain your answer.
- Compare your predictions from Chapter 6 regarding what strategies you thought you would most and least prefer. What was similar and different from what you expected? How do you explain the reason that your preferences differed or stayed the same?

Self-Help

LifeRAFT can not only help you identify how you would like to be helped by someone else, it can also be used to help yourself (Campbell, 2013). Now that you have an understanding of how to help others and can identify your own preferences for receiving help from others, you can combine this information to become your own helper and helpee. There is still tremendous value in receiving help from others in the context of a caring helping relationship (Rogers, 1961), but there are times when help from others is not available or warranted. Being able to provide self-help is a powerful self-care tool, and now that you are trained in LifeRAFT, you can use it on yourself as well.

When you are in distress, work through the LifeRAFT model on your own. Take time in the supporting stage to understand your distress, show self-compassion, and validate the reactions that emerge. In watching, question yourself about crisis and whether you are safe and engage in immediate intervention by finding someone or going to the hospital, if needed. With investigating, consider your actions, feelings, and thoughts. In modifying, choose one of the strategies and engage in your own problem-solving process.

LifeRAFT represents the basic components to helping and problem-solving, whether it be interpersonal or intrapersonal (Campbell et al., 2017). It provides the opportunity for the process to be more intentional and overt so you can provide yourself with the best help possible.

Role-Play Practice

The time has come for your full and final LifeRAFT role-play practice. Congratulations! The purpose of this exercise is to rehearse the complete LifeRAFT model. This time you will practice using the full LifeRAFT sequence of SWIM stages of supporting, watching, investigating, and modifying. For this exercise, find a volunteer helpee to role-play a helping scenario with you and provide feedback afterward. Set a timer and for at least 20 minutes. Attempt to support using listening skills of attending, paraphrasing, and reflecting feelings only. After this, watch for warning signs and concerns for referring and then investigate using listening skills, questions, and focusing. Finally, choose a RAFT strategy and engage in modifying using the SAIL steps and all microskills via the microskills ramp-up. Complete the following:

1. Consider pairing with a fellow helper-in-training and take turns being the helper and helpee.
2. Video record the scenario. Follow the ethical guidelines discussed in Chapter 1, including obtaining permission to video record your helpee.
3. Ask your helpee to select a topic to discuss. Consult Chapter 1, "Problem Triggers," for topic ideas. Request that they do not share with you anything about the problem in advance or attempt to guide the conversation toward a particular strategy. Ask the helpee to keep their request for help as natural and free-flowing as possible to allow you the chance to help as needed.
4. As the helper, attempt to support using listening skills of attending, paraphrasing, and reflecting feelings and then investigate using listening skills, questions, and focusing. Choose a RAFT strategy of actions, feelings, or thoughts and progress through modifying using all needed microskills via the microskills ramp-up. Do not plan your approach in advance; choose the strategy based on the helpee, problem, and your preferences as they emerge during the role-play. Incorporate and experiment with your own style as you are able.
5. At the end of the role-play, request feedback from your helpee about what you did well and what you could improve on next time. Ask what interventions felt especially empathic and supportive and which ones were awkward or uncomfortable. Write down your helpee's responses.
6. Review the video. Note your balance between gathering all needed information and remaining empathic and conversational. What do you think you did well, and what you could improve on next time as the helper?
7. Compare your role-play with previous ones, particularly your first role-play. In what ways have you improved in your skills and grown as a helper?

Summary

In this chapter we discussed the following:

Ending Helping

- Ending helping is the point at which an interaction between a helper and a helpee is discontinued or the conversation pivots to another purpose or topic, thereby removing the roles of helper and helpee.
- Helpers initiate ending by guiding the helpee to look back, look forward, and say goodbye. Microskills include attending, paraphrasing, reflecting feeling, questions, and focusing.

Helping Challenges

- Challenges often occur in helping situations. Common challenges include resistant helpees, LifeRAFT model navigation issues, and lack of helping success. Manage challenges by changing your perspective to recognize these issues as normal and expected and engage in actions to manage and reduce their impact.

LifeRAFT Model Integration

- Now that each LifeRAFT model component has been learned, it can be integrated as a full model.
- The LifeRAFT model includes:
    - Supporting, using listening skills of attending, paraphrasing, and reflecting feelings.
    - Watching, by exploring potential crises, safety concerns, and referral needs using listening skills and questions.
    - Investigating, by understanding helpees' actions, feelings, and thoughts using listening skills, questions, and focusing.
    - Modifying, by choosing a RAFT strategy of actions, feelings, or thoughts and progressing through a problem-solving approach of SAIL steps using all needed microskills via the microskills ramp-up.

Make LifeRAFT Your Own

- Incorporate your own style preferences into LifeRAFT as a helper and helpee to make your helping your own and to ask for the specific kind of helping you want from others.
- Use LifeRAFT not only as a model to help others but also incorporate it into your self-help practices.

References

Beck, J. S. (1995). *Cognitive therapy: Basics and beyond.* New York, NY: Guilford Press.

Beck, J. S. (2011). *Cognitive therapy: Basics and beyond* (2nd ed.). New York, NY: Guilford Press.

Campbell, E. L. (2013, April). *Key introductory strategies training: Training paraprofessionals in basic helping skills.* Symposium conducted at the annual meeting of the Western Psychological Association, Reno, NV.

Campbell, E. L., Davidson, K., & Davidson, S. M. (2017). Effectiveness of LifeRAFT undergraduate helping skills training model. *Psychology Teaching Review, 23*(2), 32–41.

Colman, A. M. (2015). *A dictionary of psychology* (4th ed.). Oxford: Oxford University Press.

Connor-Smith, J. K., & Flachsbart, C. (2007). Relations between personality and coping: A meta-analysis. *Journal of Personality and Social Psychology, 93,* 1080–1107. doi:10.1037/0022-3514.93.6.1080

Corey, G. (2009). *Theory and practice of counseling and psychotherapy* (8th ed.). Belmont, CA: Thomson/Brooks/Cole.

Dewald, P. A. (1971). *Psychotherapy: A dynamic approach.* New York: Basic Books.

Egan, G. (2014). *The skilled helper: A problem-management and opportunity development approach to helping* (10th ed.). Belmont, CA: Brooks/Cole.
Faiver, C., Eisengart, S., & Colonna, R. (2004). *The counselor intern's handbook* (3rd ed.). Belmont, CA: Cengage.
Greenberg, L. S. (2002). *Emotion-focused therapy: Coaching clients to work through feelings*. Washington, DC: American Psychological Association.
Halbur, D. A., & Halbur, K. V. (2019). *Developing your theoretical orientation in counseling and psychotherapy* (4th ed.). Boston, MA: Pearson.
Hill, C. E. (2014). *Helping skills: Facilitating exploration, insight, and action* (4th ed.). Washington, DC: American Psychological Association.
Ivey, A. E., Ivey, M. B., & Zalaquett, C. P. (2016). *Essentials of intentional interviewing: Counseling in a multicultural world* (3rd ed.). Boston, MA: Cengage Learning.
Martell, C. R., Dimidjian, S., Herman-Dunn, R., & Lewinsohn, P. M. (2010). *Behavioral activation for depression: A clinician's guide*. New York, NY: Guilford Press.
Marx, J. A., & Gelso, C. J. (1987). Termination of individual counseling in a university counseling center. *Journal of Counseling Psychology*, *34*, 3–9.
Neukrug, E. (2007). *The world of the counselor: An introduction to the counseling profession* (3rd ed.). Belmont, CA: Thomson Higher Education.
Rogers, C. (1961). *On becoming a person*. Boston: Houghton Mifflin.
Wachtel, P. L. (2002). Termination of therapy: An effort at integration. *Journal of Psychotherapy Integration*, *12*(3), 373–383.
Ward, D. E. (1984). Termination of individual counseling: Concepts and strategies. *Journal of Counseling and Development*, *63*, 21–25.
Young, M. E. (2001). *Learning the art of helping: Building blocks and techniques*. Upper Saddle River, NJ: Prentice-Hall.

12 Your Future as a Nonprofessional Counselor

Chapter Goals

This chapter will prepare you to:

- Explore ways you can use your new helping training in the future.
- Consider everyday helping with friends and family members.
- Learn about nonprofessional counseling jobs and options to pursue them, including resources for more information.
- Gain an understanding of professional counseling, options for future training, and resources to learn more.

Introduction

You have learned LifeRAFT and how to be a nonprofessional helper. Congratulations! Now what? It is time to put your training and skills to good use by being a helper. The next question to ask yourself is, "What kind of helper do I want to be?" During your nonprofessional helping skills training, you may have gained new insights regarding your future goals. For most, the process reaffirms a desire to continue helping as an everyday person with family and friends or use helping skills in a job outside of mental health. Some aspire to continue or to pursue nonprofessional counseling as a job. Others desire to continue training to become a professional counselor. All of these options are wonderful and needed in our society. Regardless of your personal path, educate yourself and others about the nonprofessional and professional helping fields to better understand what help is available for yourself and for referrals. To assist you toward your particular helping goals, the following sections offer information and resources for pursuing everyday helping, nonprofessional counseling jobs, and professional counseling education.

Everyday Helping

People in any kind of informal relationship or contact—such as family, friends, coworkers, classmates, and even strangers—are considered everyday people. It is everyday people who are most often called upon as helpers. People often attempt to provide aid when they can (Myers, 2010). Unfortunately, everyday people are rarely trained in helping skills, and the effectiveness of their natural instincts in these scenarios is variable (Egan, 2014). Training is what makes a high-quality helper (Campbell, Davidson, & Davidson, 2017). Thankfully now that you have completed LifeRAFT training, you can provide those you choose to help with effective and verified techniques.

As an everyday helper, it is particularly important that you continue to incorporate your own style in a way that reinforces your role. Unlike nonprofessional and professional counseling jobs where helping is offered within the structure of a defined role, you need to be especially sensitive to the dynamics of informal conversation and relationships. For example, you might be a helper to your best friend, someone who knows you and has talked with you for years using casual language. Using formal language such as "I'd like to guide you through a thought exercise" would be awkward and inauthentic to your relationship. Instead, keep it real. Use the skills and techniques you have learned in a way that works for your relationship. For example, you might change your wording to "This sucks so bad. I want to understand more about what you're thinking so I can help." Adapt your implementation of the LifeRAFT model to fit your life and relationships.

Casual helpers are also encouraged to give the gift of helping away. We all can benefit from a more caring and informed society that is knowledgeable about effective helping techniques. Share what you have learned about helping with everyone, including family and friends. Explain relevant details as they emerge or share the full LifeRAFT model with others. Family and friends will be better equipped to help you the next time you are in distress, and you can inspire others to become trained and effective helpers themselves. Just as basic water-rescue techniques have been adopted by average people to make support more readily available, imagine the difference we could make through more people knowing how to effectively offer LifeRAFT and mental health first aid.

Nonprofessional Counseling Jobs

Nonprofessional counseling jobs are those held by noncredentialed mental health workers. They are people who work in mental health for an occupation but are not considered professional mental health providers. They are *noncredentialed* because their positions do not generally require specific degrees or certifications to perform their job duties or require a professional license to practice.

Helpers in these positions are typically responsible for caring for individuals with mental or emotional conditions, under the instructions and supervision of professional mental health practitioners. They often assist with basic living tasks and self-care. Monitoring and reinforcing behavioral management plans and providing companionship is also common. Concerning mental health help, providers typically interview their clients about concerns and provide supportive counseling and refer to professional practitioners when appropriate. Because noncredentialed mental health workers are most often the people responsible for the day-to-day functioning of people in distress, their primary role is to provide ongoing nonprofessional help by addressing immediate concerns as they arise. Job titles for nonprofessional counseling jobs vary widely and include behavioral health technicians, mental health assistants, life/skills coaches, residential aides, spiritual advisors, and social/human service volunteers. They typically work in offices, clinics, hospitals, group homes, and shelters (O*NET, 2018).

With the knowledge and skills you have gained from LifeRAFT, you may already be equipped to obtain a nonprofessional counseling job. Nonprofessional counseling is considered entry-level work and typically requires a high school diploma, associate degree, or bachelor's degree with little to no prior experience (Bureau of Labor Statistics, 2018), though applicants will need to successfully complete a background check.

To explore nonprofessional counseling jobs, visit an online job exploration site such as the Occupational Outlook Handbook (OOH; Bureau of Labor Statistics, 2018). The OOH is provided by the US Government's Bureau of Labor Statistics as a career guide that provides information on a wide range of occupations. Information for each job includes what workers do on the job, working conditions, required training and education, earnings, and expected job prospects. To browse nonprofessional counseling jobs, choose from the occupation groups "Community and Social Service" and then "Social and Human Service Assistants." These describe typical non-professional counseling positions. From there, read the information provided to further explore and identify your specific interests. Explore "Similar Occupations," which provides a table of additional jobs with similar duties. Note that occupations that list a master's degree as required entry-level education typically fall in professional counseling, which will be discussed next.

Professional Counseling

Professional counselors advise people who suffer from ongoing mental and behavioral problems and/or want to develop strategies for life change and growth (Ivey, Ivey, & Zalaquett, 2016). The approach and goals to helping are similar to nonprofessionals, and even the introductory skills and training share many similarities. Yet unlike nonprofessional counseling, professional counseling goes beyond immediate concerns and focuses on continuing, chronic, and deep-seated difficulties or characteristics targeted for change. Search "Mental Health Counselor" on OOH to learn more (Bureau of Labor Statistics, 2018).

If you love being a helper and want to take your training and capabilities to the next level, professional counseling may be for you. Most professional counseling jobs also require a graduate degree with internship experience and a license to practice (Bureau of Labor Statistics, 2018), and applicants will still need to successfully complete a background check.

Professional Counseling Degree

A master's or doctoral degree in a counseling-related field and a supervised internship experience is typically required for professional counseling. Most professional counselors have master's degrees (Bureau of Labor Statistics, 2018). Master's degrees generally prepare helpers to acquire the knowledge, skills, and experience required for professional counseling; they also provide extra training and credentials to enter a doctoral program (APA, 2018b). There are several different kinds of counseling master's programs, and some of the most common include Master of Arts (MA) or Master of Science (MS) in mental health counseling and school counseling, marriage and family therapy (MFT), and Master of Social Work (MSW). MA or MS degrees denote whether the degree's originating university categorized the program with arts and humanities (MA) or with natural science (MS; Oxford, 2018). The differences between mental health counseling, school counseling, MFT, and MSW will be discussed in more detail below.

Some professional counselors also have doctoral degrees (Bureau of Labor Statistics, 2018). Doctoral degrees prepare helpers with a greater depth of knowledge, skills, and experience in a specialized subfield of psychology. They include Doctor of Philosophy (PhD) or Doctor of Psychology (PsyD). The PhD is a research degree that prepares helpers for research and teaching in an academic setting in addition to applied work in counseling. The PsyD is a professional degree that focuses exclusively on applied work in counseling only (APA, 2018b). Types of professional counseling PhD and PsyD degrees include counseling psychology, clinical psychology, and school psychology, which will be discussed in more detail below.

Pursuing these degrees through traditional education for professional counseling is recommended (APA, 2018c). Traditional education refers to training that is offered in a physical classroom setting as opposed to distance learning through online or other technology-based platforms.

Although online degrees offer flexibility and are sometimes more cost-effective, the relational nature of training for professional counseling is difficult to achieve online. For this reason, the American Psychological Association's (APA) Commission on Accreditation warns that requirements may be "difficult to meet" in online programs and online training techniques "are not considered appropriate for this instructional method" (2018c, p. 1). Learning how to navigate a highly relational profession such as counseling is enhanced by face-to-face training.

Lastly, it is generally recommended to obtain your professional counseling degree from an accredited, traditional education program (APA, 2018a). Accreditation can mean a lot of things within education and training programs. For our purposes, accreditation refers to the specific degree programs, not to universities or individuals. Accreditation is a system for recognizing training quality by indicating that a program has met set standards for competent preparation. Some states require graduation from an accredited program to achieve licensure, and some organizations and federal agencies only hire graduates from accredited programs. Check with the licensing body of the state you intend to practice for guidance and specific requirements. In general, seeking an accredited program may be most advantageous (APA, 2018a). The difficulty is that there is not one accreditation for all professional counseling programs; instead, some states and agencies only recognize accreditation from a specific source specific for each degree. Commonly accepted accreditation sources and resources to find them are provided in the descriptions for each degree type below.

License to Practice

In addition to a graduate degree, professional counseling requires a license to practice. To engage in professional counseling in a state, province, or territory of the United States, a therapist must be licensed according to the laws and regulations of that area's governing entity. Although licenses are generally required, requirements for obtaining a license to practice vary across states. Some place restrictions on certain master's degrees, others require successful completion of an accredited program, and most specify additional requirements, such as competency exams, ethics tests, postgraduate experience, and continuing education (APA, 2018a). Similar to accreditation, the type of license for which therapists are eligible varies by state and degree type. For example, the credential offered by some states is called a "licensed professional clinical counselor" (LPCC; e.g., Board of Behavioral Sciences, 2018) while other states call it a "licensed mental health counselor" (LMHC; e.g., Department of Health, 2018b). Other degree types have still other licenses, such as a licensed marriage and family therapist credential for MFTs (LMFT; e.g., Board of Behavioral Sciences, 2018; Department of Health, 2018b). The variety can make your head spin. More information is provided with specific degree types below. Check with the licensing body of the state you intend to practice for guidance and specific requirements.

Professional Counseling Types

Due to the high amount of variability within the professional counseling career field, we must understand each one in turn. Remember that additional research is needed beyond the following brief descriptions for informed decision-making and career planning, most notably consulting individual state requirements. Also keep in mind that this list of options is not exhaustive. Additional related degrees exist for professional counseling-related careers such as occupational therapy, applied behavior analysis, and chemical dependency counseling (O*NET, 2018). The following provides introductory information about some common types of professional counseling degrees, accreditation sources, licenses, and resources to learn more.

Mental Health Counselor

Mental health counselors are general practitioners who work with individuals and groups with a variety of presenting issues and in a variety of settings to promote psychological and behavioral health (O*NET, 2018). Mental health counselors possess an MA or MS degree from programs with a diverse range of program names. Some examples include clinical mental health counseling, community counseling, and counselor education (CACREP, 2018). Due to the variety of program titles, mental health counseling programs can be difficult to distinguish from subject related, nonclinical master's programs that do not prepare you to be a licensed therapist. For example, some community psychology master's programs train professional therapists to earn licensure while others exclusively focus on the science and theory behind the field with no option for applied work.

State licenses for mental health counselors also vary in their titles. Some examples of the variety of credential names offered by states include licensed professional clinical counselor (LPCC; e.g., Board of Behavioral Sciences, 2018), licensed professional counselor (LPC; e.g., Texas Department of State Health Services, 2018), and licensed mental health counselor (LMHC; e.g., Department of Health, 2018b). The field of mental health counseling is broad and encompasses a wide variety of program titles and licenses, making it challenging to determine exactly what preparatory programs qualify in this category.

Accreditation is particularly helpful for distinguishing mental health counseling programs. The accreditation for this type of degree is offered by the Council for Accreditation of Counseling and Related Educational Programs (CACREP, 2018). Accreditation does not guarantee licensure or a job after graduation, but it does provide recognition that the appropriate knowledge and skill areas meet the standards set by the mental health counseling profession and that you are, in fact, attending a legitimate mental health counseling program.

Learn more about the field of mental health counseling by visiting the CACREP website at www.cacrep.org (CACREP, 2018). Search for accredited mental health counseling programs by searching under "Students" and clicking "Finding a CACREP Program." A search directory is provided to browse CACREP-accredited programs with links to each school to learn more. Verify with your state licensing board that the program you are interested in meets the qualifications necessary to become a licensed therapist in your state.

School Counselor

School counselors work with students in schools to promote the academic and social skills needed to succeed in school (Bureau of Labor Statistics, 2018). Jobs typically focus on mental health as well as academic and career advising. School counselors possess an MA, MS, or Master of Education (MEd) degree in school counseling.

Once again, requirements regarding licenses vary from state to state. Although some states require school counselors to also obtain a general license to practice mental health counseling such as an LPC, the standard credential for school counselors is a state certification (ASCA, 2018).

Accreditation for school counselors is also offered by CACREP (2018). For this reason, a general browse through accredited programs can be confusing to distinguish general mental health counseling programs from school counseling, especially because there are overlap and hybrid degrees.

Learn more about the field of school counseling by visiting the American School Counselor Association (ASCA) website at www.schoolcounselor.org. Search for accredited school counseling programs by visiting the CACREP website at www.cacrep.org. (CACREP, 2018). Under "Students," click "Finding a CACREP Program." A search directory is provided for CACREP-accredited programs. Type "school counseling" in the keywords to search school counseling programs only. Links to each school are provided to learn more. Verify that the program you are interested in is a state-approved program leading to certification for the school counselor role.

Marriage and Family Therapist (MFT)

MFTs possess a master's degree in marriage and family therapy. They work with individuals, couples, and families to address a variety of presenting issues in diverse settings. Whether working with individuals or groups, they approach treatment from a family-centered perspective called "family systems" in which they treat clients' relationships rather than just the clients themselves (Bureau of Labor Statistics, 2018).

State requirements for MFTs are typically a licensed MFT credential (LMFT). Accreditation for MFTs is offered by the American Association for Marriage and Family Therapy (AAMFT) via the Commission on Accreditation for Marriage and Family Therapy Education (COAMFTE, 2019).

Learn more about the MFT field by visiting the AAMFT website at www.aamft.org. Search for accredited MFT programs by clicking "Accredited MFT Programs." A COAMFTE search directory is provided to COAMFTE-accredited programs with links to each school to learn more (COAMFTE, 2019). Verify with your state licensing board that the program you are interested in meets the qualifications necessary to become an LMFT in your state.

Master of Social Work (MSW)

MSWs possess a master's degree in social work. They work with individuals to address problems of daily living in a variety of settings from a community-oriented perspective. The field of social work is broad and often overlaps between nonprofessional and professional counseling. Some social workers provide daily living assistance through coordinating resources such as food and housing. Advocacy, fundraising, and spreading awareness at the local, state, and national levels are also part of the profession. Clinical social workers focus more specifically on psychological and behavioral health by treating client issues within the context of community support and resources (O*NET, 2018).

State requirements for MSWs are typically a licensed clinical social worker (LCSW) to distinguish "clinical" social workers from general bachelor's- and master's-level social workers without a counseling focus (Bureau of Labor Statistics, 2018). Accreditation for clinical MSWs is offered by the Council on Social Work Education (CSWE).

Learn more about the MSW field by visiting the CSWE website at www.cswe.org. Search for accredited clinical MSW programs by clicking "Accreditation" and then "Directory of Accredited Programs." A search directory is provided to browse CSWE-accredited programs with links to each school to learn more (CSWE, 2018). Pay special attention to program websites and ensure they focus on clinical training, not just general social work. Also verify with your state licensing board that the program you are interested in meets the qualifications necessary to become an LCSW in your state.

Counseling and Clinical Psychology

Counseling and clinical psychologists work with individuals, couples, families, and groups to address a variety of presenting issues in diverse settings. There is a significant amount of overlap between counseling and clinical psychologists. Training, licensing parameters, and job activities tend to be similar, but they differ in their primary emphases. Counseling psychologists tend to work with higher functioning populations to address mental health concerns within normative life experiences such as family functioning, aging and life transitions, sports, and career and vocational development. Clinical psychologists tend to work with populations with severe mental illness to address mental health concerns within inpatient, medical, military, and government settings (Bureau of Labor Statistics, 2018; Sayette & Norcross, 2018). Counseling and clinical psychologists possess a PhD degree for counseling, research, and teaching or a PsyD degree for counseling (APA, 2018a).

State requirements for counseling and clinical psychologists typically consist of a licensed psychologist credential (LP). Accreditation for counseling and clinical psychologists is offered by the APA via the APA Commission on Accreditation (APA-CoA, 2018).

Because counseling and clinical psychology doctoral degrees prepare therapists to specialize in a subfield of counseling, it is recommended not to begin with a general search of all possible programs. Instead, begin by learning more about the degree and possible areas of specialization prior to looking for accredited programs. Sayette and Norcross' (2018) book *Insider's Guide to Graduate Programs in Clinical and Counseling Psychology* is published annually to reflect the latest information, and I highly recommend it as a helpful place to start.

Search for accredited counseling and clinical psychology programs by visiting the APA-CoA website at www.apa.org/accreditation. Click "Search Accredited Programs." An APA-CoA search directory is provided to browse APA-CoA-accredited programs. Choose clinical or counseling psychology from the "Substantive Area." Links to each school are provided to learn more (APA-CoA, 2018). Verify with your state licensing board that the program you are interested in meets the qualifications necessary to become an LP in your state.

School Psychology

School psychologists work with students, teachers, and administrators in schools to assess and develop treatment plans for social and academic needs in the school setting. They specialize in student learning, behavioral problems, and designing performance and evaluation plans (Bureau of Labor Statistics, 2018). Similar to other psychologists, school psychologists possess a PhD degree for counseling, research, and teaching or a PsyD degree for counseling, though their degree may also be a Doctor of Education (EdD; NASP, 2018).

State requirements for school psychologists are typically an LP. In addition, most states require a state certification or endorsement (NASP, 2018). Accreditation for school psychologists is offered by the APA via the APA Commission on Accreditation (APA-CoA, 2018).

Learn more about the school psychology field by visiting the National Association of School Psychologists website at www.nasponline.org. Search for accredited school psychology programs by visiting the APA-CoA website at www.apa.org/accreditation. Click "Search Accredited Programs." The APA-CoA search directory is provided to browse APA-CoA-accredited programs. Choose school psychology from the "Substantive Area." Links to each school are provided to learn more (APA-CoA, 2018). Verify with your state licensing board that the program you are interested in meets the qualifications necessary to become a credentialed school psychologist in your state.

Conclusion

Whether you plan to continue helping casually in everyday life, obtain a job as a nonprofessional helper, or continue training to be a professional counselor, LifeRAFT has provided you a solid foundation. Thank you for letting me and LifeRAFT be part of your journey! I hope that you have found this information helpful along the way and I wish you and your helpees all the best. Thank you for using what you have learned to help heal the hurt and brokenness in our world. Together, we can use our love to make waves of change in the lives of many.

Summary

In this chapter we discussed the following:

Help Casually

- LifeRAFT training has equipped you with the ability to provide the people you encounter in everyday life with effective and verified helping techniques.

Nonprofessional Counseling Jobs

- LifeRAFT training has prepared you to obtain a nonprofessional counseling job caring for individuals with mental or emotional conditions, under the instruction and supervision of professional mental health practitioners.

Professional Counseling

- LifeRAFT training may have inspired you to pursue additional training, degree, and licensure to become a professional counselor.
- Several options for professional counseling exist at the master's and doctoral levels, including Mental Health Counseling, School Counseling, Marriage and Family Therapy, Clinical Social Work, Counseling Psychology, Clinical Psychology, and School Psychology.

References

American Psychological Association. (APA, 2018a). Choosing a program. *American Psychological Association*. Retrieved from www.apa.org/ed/accreditation/about/program-choice.aspx

American Psychological Association. (APA, 2018b). Frequently asked questions about graduate school. *American Psychological Association*. Retrieved from www.apa.org/education/grad/faqs.aspx

American Psychological Association. (APA, 2018c). Online education: Graduate programs. *American Psychological Association*. Retrieved from www.apa.org/education/grad/online-programs

American Psychological Association Commission on Accreditation. (APA-CoA, 2018). Office of program consultation and accreditation. *American Psychological Association*. Retrieved from www.apa.org/ed/accreditation/index.aspx

American School Counselor Association. (ASCA; 2018). State certification requirements. *American School Counselor Association*. Retrieved from www.schoolcounselor.org/school-counselors-members/careers-roles/state-certification-requirements

Board of Behavioral Sciences. (2018). General info and requirements. *State of California Board of Behavioral Sciences*. Retrieved from www.bbs.ca.gov/consumers/info.html

Bureau of Labor Statistics, U.S. Department of Labor. (2018). *Occupational outlook handbook*. Retrieved from www.bls.gov/ooh

Campbell, E. L., Davidson, K., & Davidson, S. M. (2017). Effectiveness of LifeRAFT undergraduate helping skills training model. *Psychology Teaching Review*, *23*(2), 32–41.

Commission on Accreditation for Marriage and Family Therapy Education. (COAMFTE, 2019). Directory of COAMFTE accredited programs. *Commission on Accreditation for Marriage and Family Therapy Education*. Retrieved from www.coamfte.org/COAMFTE/Directory_of_Accredited_Programs/MFT_Training_Programs.aspx

Council for Accreditation of Counseling and Related Educational Programs. (CACREP, 2018). Finding a CACREP program. *Council for Accreditation of Counseling and Related Educational Programs*. Retrieved from www.cacrep.org/directory/

Council on Social Work Education (CSWE, 2018). Directory of accredited programs. *Council on Social Work Education*. Retrieved from https://cswe.org/Accreditation/Directory-of-Accredited-Programs.aspx

Department of Health. (2018b). Mental health counselor. *Washington State Department of Health*. Retrieved from www.doh.wa.gov/LicensesPermitsandCertificates/ProfessionsNewReneworUpdate/MentalHealthCounselor

Egan, G. (2014). *The skilled helper: A problem-management and opportunity development approach to helping* (10th ed.). Belmont, CA: Brooks/Cole.

Ivey, A. E., Ivey, M. B., & Zalaquett, C. P. (2016). *Essentials of intentional interviewing: Counseling in a multicultural world* (3rd ed.). Boston, MA: Cengage Learning.

Myers, D. G. (2010). Chapter 12: Helping. In D. G. Myers (Ed.), *Social psychology* (10th ed., pp. 440–480). New York: McGraw-Hill.

National Association of School Psychologists. (NASP, 2018). About school psychology. *National Association of School Psychologists*. Retrieved from www.nasponline.org/about-school-psychology

National Center for O*NET Development. (O*NET, 2018). *O*NET online*. Retrieved from www.onetonline.org

Sayette, M. A., & Norcross, J. C. (2018). *Insider's guide to graduate programs in clinical and counseling psychology* (2018/2019 ed.). New York: Guilford Press.

Texas Department of State Health Services. (2018). Texas state board of examiners of professional counselors. *Texas Health and Human Services*. Retrieved from www.dshs.texas.gov/counselor/

Index

For Product Safety Concerns and Information please contact our EU representative GPSR@taylorandfrancis.com Taylor & Francis Verlag GmbH, Kaufingerstraße 24, 80331 München, Germany

Batch number: 10731051

Printed by Printforce, the Netherlands